Oxford Revision Guides

AS & A Level
GOVERNMENT & POLITICS
Through Diagrams

Paul Fairclough

OXFORD
UNIVERSITY PRESS

Great Clarendon Street, Oxford OX2 6DP

Oxford University Press is a department of the
University of Oxford. It furthers the University's objective
of excellence in research, scholarship, and education by
publishing worldwide in

Oxford New York

Auckland Cape Town Dar es Salaam Hong Kong Karachi
Kuala Lumpur Madrid Melbourne Mexico City Nairobi
New Delhi Shanghai Taipei Toronto

With offices in

Argentina Austria Brazil Chile Czech Republic France Greece
Guatemala Hungary Italy Japan Poland Portugal Singapore
South Korea Switzerland Thailand Turkey Ukraine Vietnam

Oxford is a registered trade mark of Oxford University Press
in the UK and in certain other countries

British Library Cataloguing in Publication Data

Data available

ISBN: 9780199180882

10 9 8 7 6 5 4 3 2 1

Printed in Great Britain by Bell and Bain Ltd, Glasgow

Paper used in the production of this book is a natural, recyclable product
made from wood grown in sustainable forests. The manufacturing process
conforms to the environmental regulations of the country of origin.

Acknowledgements

P50 (top), Press Association; P50 (M), Associated Press; P50 (L), Associated Press;
P51 Press Association; P53 BBC Picture Archives; P84 (T) Museum of City of New York/Corbis;
P84 (L) Bettman/Corbis; P98 (L) Wally McNamme/Corbis; P98 R Nailah Feanny Hicks/Corbis

Artwork by Angela Lumley and PDQ Digital Media Solutions

Contents

How Government and Politics is assessed and examined 5
AS/A2 specification match 6

Section A   An introduction to Politics

1   Politics and democracy
 1.1   What is Politics? 8
 1.2   What is democracy? 9
 1.3   Political culture 10

2   Political ideologies
 2.1   Conservatism 11
 2.2   Liberalism 12
 2.3   Socialism 13
 2.4   Environmentalism 14

3   British political history
 3.1   A post-war survey, 1945–1979 15
 3.2   Thatcherism and Majorism,
       1979–1997 16
 3.3   Blairism, 1997–2007 17

**Section B   People, politics and participation
             in the UK**

4   Elections and referendums
 4.1   The electoral system 18
 4.2   The case for and against electoral
       reform 19
 4.3   Referendums 20

5   Voting behaviour
 5.1   The electorate 21
 5.2   Political participation and abstention 22
 5.3   An introduction to voting behaviour 23
 5.4   Models of voting behaviour 24
 5.5   The media 25
 5.6   Opinion polls 26
 5.7   Recent general elections 27

6   Parties
 6.1   The origins and development of the
       British party system 28
 6.2   The Conservative Party 29
 6.3   The Labour Party 30
 6.4   The Liberal Democrats 31
 6.5   Party policies 32
 6.6   Minor parties 33
 6.7   Internal party democracy 34

7   Pressure groups and protest movements
 7.1   Definitions and classification 35
 7.2   Methods 36
 7.3   The European dimension 37
 7.4   Factors affecting pressure group
       success 38

Section C   Governing the UK

8   The Constitution
 8.1   Sources 39
 8.2   Doctrines and principles 40
 8.3   The Constitution in transition? 41
 8.4   Constitutional reform since 1997 42

9   Parliament
 9.1   The composition of parliament 43
 9.2   The passage of legislation 44
 9.3   Scrutiny of the executive 45
 9.4   The role of an MP 46
 9.5   Parliamentary reform 47

10   Prime Minister and Cabinet
 10.1   The core executive 48
 10.2   The Prime Minister 49
 10.3   The Cabinet 50
 10.4   Special advisors, spin and control 51

11   The Civil Service
 11.1   The role of the Civil Service 52
 11.2   Departments, ministers and
        'their' civil servants 53
 11.3   Quangos 54

12   Sub-national government
 12.1   Unitary and federal systems 55
 12.2   Local government 56
 12.3   Devolution: the Scottish Parliament
        and the Welsh Assembly 57
 12.4   Northern Ireland 58

13   The European context
 13.1   The origins and organisation of the
        European Union 59
 13.2   The EU since Maastricht 60

14   Citizenship and redress of grievances
 14.1   Rights 61
 14.2   Redress of grievances 62
 14.3   The UK judiciary 63
 14.4   The Human Rights Act (1998) 64
 14.5   How effectively are rights protected
        in the UK? 65
 14.6   How democratic is the UK system
        of government? 66

**Section D   People, politics and participation
             in the USA**

15   Elections
 15.1   The electorate 67
 15.2   How elections work 68
 15.3   Direct democracy in the USA 69
 15.4   Some key issues and debates 70

16   Voting behaviour
 16.1   Influences on voting behaviour
        (part 1) 71
 16.2   Influences on voting behaviour
        (part 2) 72
 16.3   Influences on voting behaviour
        (part 3): the media 73
 16.4   Voter turnout (1986–2006) 74
 16.5   The 2000 and 2004 Presidential
        Elections 75

17   Political parties
 17.1   Political parties (outline) 76
 17.2   Democrats and Republicans 77
 17.3   The two-party system and third
        party candidacy 78

18   Pressure groups
 18.1   Definitions and classification 79
 18.2   Methods 80
 18.3   Political Action Committees 81
 18.4   Special interests in Congress 82
 18.5   Are pressure groups 'good' or 'bad'
        for US democracy? 83

Section E   Governing the USA

19   The Constitution
 19.1   Before Philadelphia 84
 19.2   Framing the Constitution 85
 19.3   Principles 86

Contents (cont.)

	19.4 Checks and balances	87
	19.5 The Bill of Rights	88
	19.6 The living Constitution	89
20	**Congress**	
	20.1 Congress	90
	20.2 The passage of legislation	91
	20.3 Pressures acting upon members of Congress	92
	20.4 Congressional committees	93
21	**The President**	
	21.1 An outline of the role and power of the presidency	94
	21.2 The Domestic Policy President	95
	21.3 The Foreign Policy President	96
	21.4 Presidential persuasion	97
	21.5 Recent presidencies	98
	21.6 Presidential power in the wake of 9/11	99

22	**Presidential supports**	
	22.1 The Vice-President and Cabinet	100
	22.2 The Executive Office of the President (EXOP)	101
23	**The federal bureaucracy**	
	23.1 The federal bureaucracy	102
24	**The Supreme Court**	
	24.1 The structure of the US courts system	103
	24.2 Composition and power	104
	24.3 Control and questions of democracy	105
	24.4 The Court in action, 1954–2005	106
25	**Beyond Washington DC**	
	25.1 State and local government	107
Glossary		**108**
Index		**111**

How Government and Politics is assessed and examined

Specifications in outline (as at June 2008)

AQA www.aqa.org.uk/   Edexcel www.edexcel.org.uk/   OCR www.ocr.org.uk

AS

		AQA	Edexcel	OCR
Unit 1	Title	People, Participation and Politics	People and Politics	Contemporary Politics of the UK
	Exam	50% of AS (25% of A Level) 1½ hours	50% of AS (25% of A Level) 1 hour 20 minutes	50% of AS (25% of A Level) 1½ hours
Unit 2	Title	Governing Modern Britain	Governing the UK	Contemporary Government of the UK
	Exam	50% of AS (25% of A Level) 1½ hours	50% of AS (25% of A Level) 1 hour 20 minutes	50% of AS (25% of A Level) 1½ hours

A2

		AQA	Edexcel	OCR
Unit 3	Options	Either: (A) The Politics of the USA; or (B) Ideologies; or (C) Politics and Power	Either: (A) UK Political Issues; or (B) Introducing Political Ideologies; or (C) Representative Processes in the USA; or (D) Structures of Global Politics	Either: (A) Contemporary US Government and Politics; or (B) Political Ideas and Concepts
	Exam	50% of A2 (25% of A-Level) 1½ hours	50% of A2 (25% of A-Level) 1½ hours	50% of A2 (25% of A-Level) 2 hours
Unit 4	Options	Either: (A) The Government of the USA; or (B) Political Issues: Ideologies in Action; or (C) Perspectives on Modern Politics	Either: (A) EU Political Issues; or (B) Other Ideological Traditions; or (C) Governing the USA; or (D) Global Political Issues	Either: (A) US Government and Politics; or (B) Political Ideas and Concepts in Practice
	Exam	50% of A2 (25% of A-Level) 1½ hours	50% of A2 (25% of A-Level) 1½ hours	50% of A2 (25% of A-Level) 2 hours

NB: | Free choice: any Unit 3 plus any Unit 4 | Free choice: any Unit 3 plus any Unit 4 | Must follow **route** A or B |

Units covered in this Oxford Revision Guide

This revision guide covers the **AS** specifications offered by all three main UK examination boards; AQA, Edexcel and OCR.

It is simply not possible, however, to offer coverage of all of the options available at **A2** in a single book.

As a result, this title focuses on the US Government & Politics route at A2; providing only limited coverage of the other Unit 4 and Unit 5 options:

Unit	AQA	Edexcel	OCR
1	●	●	●
2	●	●	●
3a	◉	◉	●
3b	◉	◉	◉
3c		●	
3d		○	
4a	●	◉	●
4b	○	○	
4c	◉	●	◉
4d		○	

● covered
◉ limited coverage
○ minimal coverage

Assessment Objectives and AS/GCE weightings (%)

	Descriptor	AQA		Edexcel		OCR	
		AS	GCE	AS	GCE	AS	GCE
AO1	Demonstrate knowledge and understanding of relevant institutions, processes, political concepts, theories and debates.	50	45	50	40	50	45
AO2	Analyse and evaluate political information, arguments and explanations, and identify parallels, connections, similarities and differences between aspects of the political systems studied.	30	35	30	40	35	39.5
AO3	Construct and communicate coherent arguments making use of a range of appropriate political vocabulary.	20	20	20	20	15	15.5

Stretch and challenge

Politics examinations look to stretch and challenge candidates:

1. by requiring **extended** written responses; and
2. by employing a range of **command words** e.g. assess, evaluate, discuss etc.

In order to secure higher level marks candidates must address the **precise** demands of the questions posed, combining **political theory** with supporting **examples** drawn from 'own knowledge'. In addition, the **synoptic** nature of assessment at A2 demands that candidates are able to identify **links** between different aspects of their studies.

AS/A2 specification match

AQA

AQA Unit and topic headings	Chapter references	
AS Unit 1 [GOVP1]: People, Politics and Participation		
Participation and Voting Behaviour	Ch 1, Ch 5, Ch 14.6	pp 8–10, 21–27, 66
Electoral Systems	Ch 4, Ch 12.3, Ch 12.4	pp 18–20, 57, 58
Political Parties	Ch 6	pp 28–34
Pressure Groups and Protest Movements	Ch 7	pp 35–38
AS Unit 2 [GOVP2]: Governing Modern Britain		
The British Constitution	Ch 8, Ch 12.1, Ch 14	pp 39–42, 55, 61–66
Parliament	Ch 9	pp 43–47
The Core Executive	Ch 10, Ch 11	pp 48–54
Multi-level Governance	Ch 12, Ch 13	pp 55–60
A2 Unit 3A [GOV3A]: The Politics of the USA		
The Electoral Process and Direct Democracy	Ch 15	pp 67–70
Political Parties	Ch 17	pp 76–78
Voting Behaviour	Ch 16	pp 71–75
Pressure Groups	Ch 18	pp 79–83
A2 Unit 4A [GOV4A]: The Government of the USA		
The Constitutional Framework of US Government	Ch 19, Ch 25	pp 84–89, 107
The Legislative Branch of Government: US Congress	Ch 20	pp 90–93
The Executive Branch of Government	Ch 21, Ch 22, Ch 23	pp 94–102
The Judicial Branch of Government: The Supreme Court	Ch 19.5, Ch 19.6, Ch 24	pp 88, 89, 103–106

Edexcel

Edexcel Unit and topic headings	Chapter references	
AS Unit 1 [6GP01]: People and Politics		
Democracy and Political Participation	Ch 1, Ch 14.6	pp 8–10, 66
Party policies and ideas	Ch 6	pp 28–34
Elections	Ch 4, Ch 12.3, Ch 12.4	pp 18–20, 57, 58
Pressure groups	Ch 7	pp 35–38
AS Unit 2 [6GP02]: Governing the UK		
The Constitution	Ch 8, Ch 12, Ch 13	pp 39–42, 55–58, 59–60
Parliament	Ch 9	pp 43–47
The Prime Minister and Cabinet	Ch 10	pp 48–51
Judges and Civil Liberties	Ch 14	pp 61–66
A2 Unit 3c [6GP03]: Representative Processes in the USA		
Elections and Voting	Ch 15, Ch 16	pp 67–75
Political Parties	Ch 17	pp 76–78
Pressure Groups	Ch 18	pp 79–83
Racial and Ethnic Politics	Useful material in Ch 15.1, Ch 16.1, Ch 20.1 and Ch 24.4	pp 67, 71, 90, 106
A2 Unit 4c [6GP04]: Governing the USA		
The Constitution	Ch 19, Ch 25	pp 84–89, 107
Congress	Ch 20	pp 90–93
Presidency	Ch 21, Ch 22, Ch 23	pp 94–102
Supreme Court	Ch 19.5, Ch 19.6, Ch 24	pp 88, 89, 103–106

OCR

OCR Unit and topic headings	Chapter references	
AS Unit 1 [Unit F851]: Contemporary Politics of the UK		
Political parties (mandatory)	Ch 6	pp 28–34
Pressure groups (mandatory)	Ch 7	pp 35–38
Electoral systems and referenda	Ch 4, Ch 12.3, Ch 12.4	pp 18–20, 57, 58
UK parliamentary elections	Ch 4, Ch 5.5, Ch 5.6, Ch 5.7	pp 18–20, 25, 26, 27
Voting behaviour in the UK	Ch 5	pp 21–27
AS Unit 2 [Unit F852]: Contemporary Government of the UK		
The constitution	Ch 8, Ch 9.5, Ch 12.1, Ch 12.3, Ch 12.4, Ch 14.3, Ch 14.4	pp 39–42, 47, 55, 57, 58, 63, 64
The executive (mandatory)	Ch 10, Ch 11	pp 48–54
The legislature (mandatory)	Ch 9	pp 43–47
The Judiciary	Ch 14	pp 61–66
The European Union	Ch 13	pp 59–60
A2 Unit 3 [US Route Unit F853]: Contemporary US Government and Politics		
Elections, presidential and congressional	Ch 15, Ch 16	pp 67–75
Political parties	Ch 17	pp 76–78
Pressure groups	Ch 18	pp 79–83
The constitution	Ch 19	pp 84–89
Congress	Ch 20	pp 90–93
The presidency	Ch 21, Ch 22, Ch 23	pp 94–102
The supreme court	Ch 24	pp 103–106
Civil rights and liberties	Ch 19 (esp. Ch 19.5 and Ch 19.6) and Ch 24 (esp. Ch 24.4)	pp 84–89 (esp. 88–89), 103–106 (esp. 106)
A2 Unit 4 [US Route Unit F855]: US Government and Politics*		
Elections	Ch 4, Ch 5, Ch 12.3, Ch 12.4, Ch 15, Ch 16	pp 18–27, 57, 58, 67–75
Political parties and pressure groups	Ch 6, Ch 7, Ch 17, Ch 18	pp 28–38, 76–83
Civil rights and liberties	Ch 14, Ch 19.5, Ch 19.6, Ch 24	pp 61–66, 88, 89, 103–106
Constitutions	Ch 8, Ch 12, Ch 13, Ch 19, Ch 25	pp 39–42, 55–60, 84–89, 107
Legislatures	Ch 9, Ch 13, Ch 20	pp 43–47, 59–60, 90–93
Executives	Ch 10, Ch 11, Ch 13, Ch 21, Ch 22, Ch 23	pp 48–54, 59–60, 94–102
Judiciaries	Ch 13, Ch 14.3, Ch 14.5, Ch 24	pp 59–60, 63, 65, 103–106

*NB: this is essentially a comparative USA/UK Government & Politics Unit

1.1 What is Politics?

Introduction

Within any society there will be conflicts of interests: situations in which individuals within the group might want to 'pull in different directions'. These conflicts might result from:

Scarcity
When there is a shortage of certain goods, conflict will result over the distribution of available resources.

Ideological differences
Individuals might take a radically different view of the way in which society should be organised.

Differences in approach
Individuals might share an ideology but have a different approach in achieving their common goals.

Divisions of labour and power
Individuals might be unhappy about their own position within society. Conflict might result from their desire to challenge the status quo.

The political process is the process by which these conflicts are resolved. Politics is, therefore, a study of conflict resolution. Part of this study must involve the way in which power is divided up between individuals, between individuals and the state, and between the different institutions that make up the state (Parliament, Cabinet, Prime Minister, police etc.) This is Politics on a 'macro' level, but even on a 'micro' level (family, school, friendship groups etc.) political activity is going on because power relationships exist at all of those levels.

In essence, therefore, Politics is about conflict resolution and the distribution of power.

Key terms

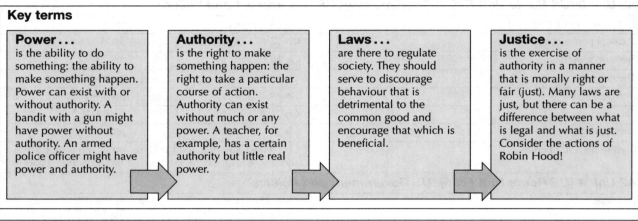

Power...
is the ability to do something: the ability to make something happen. Power can exist with or without authority. A bandit with a gun might have power without authority. An armed police officer might have power and authority.

Authority...
is the right to make something happen: the right to take a particular course of action. Authority can exist without much or any power. A teacher, for example, has a certain authority but little real power.

Laws...
are there to regulate society. They should serve to discourage behaviour that is detrimental to the common good and encourage that which is beneficial.

Justice...
is the exercise of authority in a manner that is morally right or fair (just). Many laws are just, but there can be a difference between what is legal and what is just. Consider the actions of Robin Hood!

What kind of activity is political?

Many different kinds of activity can be considered political. For example:

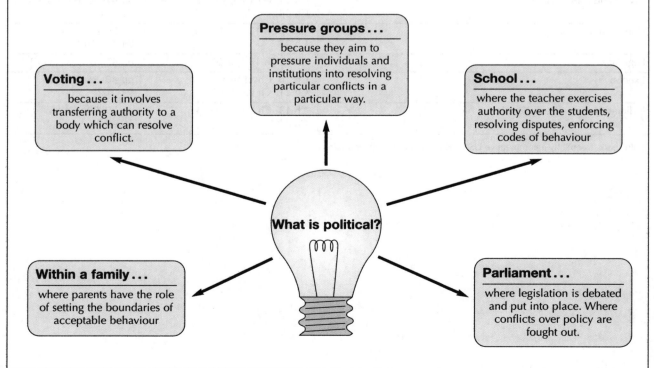

Pressure groups... because they aim to pressure individuals and institutions into resolving particular conflicts in a particular way.

Voting... because it involves transferring authority to a body which can resolve conflict.

School... where the teacher exercises authority over the students, resolving disputes, enforcing codes of behaviour

What is political?

Within a family... where parents have the role of setting the boundaries of acceptable behaviour

Parliament... where legislation is debated and put into place. Where conflicts over policy are fought out.

1.2 What is democracy?

Introduction

The term democracy comes from the Greek – *demos* (meaning 'the people') and *kratos* (meaning 'power'). Literally, therefore, democracy is 'rule by the people' or 'people power'. Some argue, however, that the word *demos* could just as easily be defined as 'the mob'. This would leave democracy as 'mob rule'. John Kingdom sees a natural progression from the 'pure form' of democracy to the corrupt form of mob rule, in the same way that monarchy can descend into tyranny and aristocracy into oligarchy.

As a term, democracy – like 'justice' and 'freedom' – has become so widely misused as to become almost meaningless in itself. More commonly, it is qualified.

Different strands

Many writers draw a distinction between what they call 'representative democracy' and what is known as 'direct democracy'.

What is representative democracy?

Edmund Burke, in a speech to his Bristol constituents in 1774, summed up what many see as the essence of representative democracy in Britain.

'Your representative owes you not his industry only,' Burke noted, 'but his judgement; and he betrays you if he sacrifices it to your opinion.'

The Burkeian view is, therefore, that we elect individuals to represent us in Parliament and other assemblies. They then represent our interests to the best of their ability but they are not delegates sent with specific instructions or orders to follow. As a result, our elected representatives might make decisions which are contrary to our wishes.

What is direct democracy?

Direct democracy is said to have its origins in Athens around 500BC, where the 40 000 free men of the city had the right to attend forum meetings at which certain policies could be approved or rejected. The classic modern tool of direct democracy is the **referendum**. In a referendum voters are asked to voice their view on a particular issue. The result of this vote may be binding or advisory, depending on the nature of the referendum, but the question is normally framed by the government of the day. In some countries **initiatives** operate alongside referendums. Through an initiative a predetermined number of registered voters can initiate legislation.

Does direct democracy get in the way of representative democracy?

Some argue that referendums and other forms of direct democracy undermine our system of representative democracy. If we elect representatives to act in our best interests, it is argued, they should not have to come back to us on a regular basis to ask us what we want. Indeed, it is bad for them to do so because...

- *in doing so it could be argued that they are abdicating their responsibility to govern.*
- *we have elected them as individuals who we believe are capable of judging the issues on our behalf, and they need the space in which they can do this.*
- *our representatives will often have access to a far better body of information on which to make their judgements and a lot more time in which to do it.*
- *people are likely to make decisions which they see as being in their immediate interest, whereas politicians may be able to make decisions which are unpopular but which are in our long-term interests.*

Others argue that such tools of direct democracy actually help strengthen our representative democracy by...
- *helping to focus the mandate on particular issues.*
- *refreshing the mandate several years into a Parliament when circumstances might have changed.*
- *legitimising major constitutional changes that might appear to bind future Parliaments and governments and should not, therefore, be made without explicit public approval.*

What is liberal democracy?

The essence of liberal democracy is limited government. In a liberal democracy the state stands back from the free market and imposes only minimal regulation. It does, however, preserve basic civil rights (expression, assembly, association, movement etc.) and allow people to vote in regular free and fair elections. The term 'liberal democracy' is applied to many western democracies.

1.3 Political culture

What is Political Culture?
According to Lynton Robins, political culture consists of 'the opinions, attitudes and beliefs which shape political behaviour. A country's political culture consists of the whole citizenry's collective attitudes to the political system and their role in it.'

Problems with Definitions: The most fundamental problem with the concept of political culture is that it appears to offer the possibility that we can generalise about the way in which things are likely to operate politically within a country – that we can predict how people might act. In reality, however, there is limited use in talking about the political culture of an entire nation because regional differences make any such generalisations fairly meaningless.

Political Culture in Britain

HOMOGENITY
The view that people within a country share certain key political values and a sense of togetherness that outweigh any things that divide them.

It is often said that Britain of the 1950s demonstrated a high degree of homogeneity. At that time, it was said, the vast majority of UK citizens were white and the majority were said to be practising Christians. Since the expansion of immigration since the 1960s and the rise of Scottish and Welsh nationalism, however, such generalisations have become somewhat flawed. The decline of the Church of England (in terms of those attending services at least) and the rise of other religious groupings within Britain has also created a situation in which the term homogeneity has increasingly been contrasted with the rise of multiculturalism.

CONSENSUS
Where those within a country accept the basic 'rules of the game'. These rules include the need for peaceful negotiation and compromise. There is a distaste for political extremes.

Consensus was, once again, a term often applied to the period following the Second World War – where all of the major UK political parties and a large proportion of the population appeared to share a broad view of where the country was heading and the appropriate manner in which to get there. Since that time, the rise of direct action campaigns across the UK, the increased incidence of rioting and violent protest, the rise of nationalist parties in Scotland and Wales and the BNP in the North West have served to undermine any sense of consensus. Politicians such as Margaret Thatcher have also gone out of their way to distance themselves from a politics driven by consensus and compromise.

DEFERENCE
That people defer to an elite that is seen as 'born to rule'. A natural willingness to accept an ingrained class-based inequality; a hierarchy.

The power of the ruling elite was often perpetuated by the veil of secrecy and mystery that surrounded it. The Monarchy, for example, was almost seen as something that was somehow 'other-worldly' – beyond our grasp. Senior political figures and others (the top levels of the Civil Service, for example) were similarly remote and mysterious. In recent times the development of a modern, less deferential media has done much to demystify such individuals and institutions. Unthinking deference to such elite figures has, as a result, declined significantly.

US Political Culture
The terms **homogeneity, consensus** and **deference** are in many respects alien to the American experience. US political culture is said to reflect the nation's revolutionary history as well as its pluralist nature; being based upon ideas such as Liberty, limited government, individualism, a *laissez faire* approach, and a belief in the American Dream.

Liberty and Limited Government
The USA is rooted in the rejection of colonial rule and the assertion of God-given rights that are 'universal' and 'inalienable'. This makes liberty, and the belief in a government that is limited to only that which is necessary, key elements of US political culture; as reflected in the entrenched nature of the US Bill of Rights.

Individualism
The history of conquest, settlement and later successive waves of immigration have placed an emphasis on the individual's ability to look after him/herself. There is belief in the importance of 'self-reliance' and 'self-improvement' and a rejection of the 'nanny state'. According to Lipset, only 40% of Americans favoured government provision of healthcare in 1997, as compared to 85% of those in the UK.

Laissez-faire
This focus on self-reliance and the rejection of an over-bearing state has manifested itself in a belief in *laissez faire* ('let it be') economics. There is a trust in the market and a belief that the state has no right to interfere in issues of property or contract between individuals.

'The American Dream'
This is the notion that any American can make it in the USA as long as they are prepared to work hard and make sacrifices. It holds that though no-one owes anyone anything, few barriers are put in the way of an hard-working, able citizen who is willing to have a go and take the chances that present themselves.

2.1 Conservatism

Introduction

If an ideology is 'a system of ideas at the basis of an economic or political theory' (*Concise Oxford Dictionary*), it could be argued that conservatism is barely an ideology at all, based as it is in a reaction to the changes put forward by other ideologies. Conservatism is based firmly upon pragmatism and the belief in gradual improvements founded on experience and existing institutions, rather than a priori reasoning and radical change.

Approach

As a result of this, conservatives often take a different approach to solving problems than those coming from a more traditionally ideological perspective.

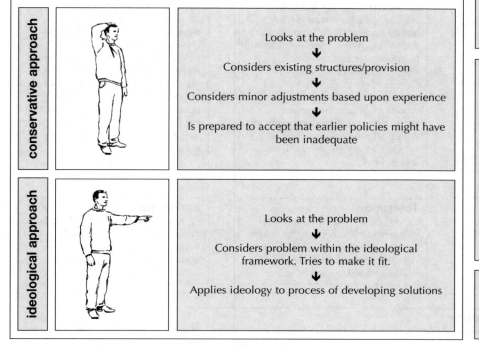

conservative approach

Looks at the problem
↓
Considers existing structures/provision
↓
Considers minor adjustments based upon experience
↓
Is prepared to accept that earlier policies might have been inadequate

ideological approach

Looks at the problem
↓
Considers problem within the ideological framework. Tries to make it fit.
↓
Applies ideology to process of developing solutions

Confusing terms

'conservative'
We often use this term to describe people who are unwilling to change or out of date.

'conservative ideology'
See left: this is a supposedly more coherent approach to directing government policy.

'Conservative'
The capital letter usually denotes a reference to the Conservative Party or its policies/position.

Human nature

This is a phrase used when referring to the natural human state; that is to say, what people are like in their pure state when one removes the influence of the societies in which they live. Some people have a positive view of human nature and believe that society can corrupt individuals. Those with a more pessimistic view would see people as flawed and society as a necessary regulating force.

Paternalism

Where authority is centralised but the state is benevolent; caring for the most needy.

Origins

Modern conservatism dates from the opposition to the popular radicalism prevalent around the time of the French Revolution in the 1790s. It was a reaction first to this radical change and later to liberalism and socialism. Writers such as Edmund Burke in his *Reflections on the Revolution in France* (1790) highlighted the dangers of radical change and the need for societies to evolve in order to avoid the emergence of such destructive radicalism.

Conservatism today

Modern conservatism can be divided into two clear strands:

Liberal/libertarian conservatism
For example, the 'New Right' in the UK and US in the 1980s/1990s. In Britain, the advent of Thatcherism and 'neo-liberal' economic policy.

Collectivist/paternalist conservatism
Describing much of the post-war Conservative history in Britain. 'One-nation Tories'. Often marginalised under Thatcher as 'the wets'.

Free market economics ... deregulation ... privatisation ... restrictions on the power of the unions	Mixed economy (Keynesianism)
Limited state intervention ... 'rolling back the frontiers of the state'	More significant state intervention
Quick and radical change	Slow gradual change ... evolution not revolution
Maintaining national sovereignty	Increasing integration in Europe
Quite individualistic	Collectivistic ... pluralistic
Limited welfare provision ... low 'safety net' only	Support for universal welfare state ... paternalism (see above)

2.2   Liberalism

Introduction
Whereas conservatives traditionally emphasise the role of society in shaping individuals, liberals place a greater emphasis on the importance of the individual. Liberal society is to be formed of free individuals, autonomous and equally valuable. Government intervention in relations between individuals should be considered only when existing practices threaten individual autonomy or freedom. Therefore, legitimate government action centres on protecting the individual. Over time, this liberal view of deregulated 'small government', where people interact freely, has been tempered by a realisation that, without some regulation, abuses can occur. In practice, therefore, traditional ('classical') liberalism has become moderated by the need to protect people from a form of capitalism that appears to restrict freedom.

Main facets of liberalism

Rationality
John Locke believed in rational thought over dogmatism. He believed that differences of opinion were inevitable and that free and rational individuals should – as far as possible – be allowed to resolve problems without the need for oppressive state intervention. There would in effect be . . .

Government by consent
Jean Jacques Rousseau in *The Social Contract* (1762) put forward the idea that men gave up natural freedom in return for social freedom. They could not, therefore, do all that they could in their natural state, but they would gain from the greater protection afforded in a society in which all men gave up their freedom to certain things. This would lead to a . . .

Limited government
. . . where there might be a separation of powers – along the lines advocated by writers such as Montesquieu – between executive, legislative and judicial branches. There might then be a system of checks and balances between branches, which would protect the people from any one branch becoming dominant and infringing those . . .

Toleration
. . . would become the norm and different traditions could be valued and respected. There could be an equality of opportunity, regardless of background.

Inalienable rights
. . . considered vital for individual fulfilment: equality before the law, freedom of expression etc. In so doing, liberals would create a society in which . . .

A liberal view of human nature
Liberals have a generally positive view of human nature. Some early liberals saw men as self-seeking and egotistical, but later writers believed that humans are rational and compassionate, if corruptible. Liberals place the emphasis on guidance (encouragement for individuals to develop in the right direction); they believe that individuals, given choices, can be helped to make the decisions that benefit them and society at large.

Different forms of liberalism

Classical liberalism
Particularly common in the nineteenth century, classical liberalism saw minimal state intervention as being the ideal. There was an emphasis on freedom, toleration and equality. Individuals were rational and had choices to make. Classical liberalism emphasised the desirability of self-help and self-improvement.

New/progressive liberalism
The social impact of industrialisation – particularly its more exploitative face – made many liberals realise that greater regulation might be needed. The market could not be allowed to go unchecked. Self-help would not be enough. There was a need for state provision of schools and hospitals. Pensions and unemployment benefit could be provided. Such ideas were put forward by writers such as T. H. Green and, later, L. T. Hobhouse. John Maynard Keynes and William Beveridge provided the basis for the mixed economy and welfare statism of the years following the Second World War.

Neo-liberalism
Often associated with the 'New Right', neo-liberalism involved 'rolling back the frontiers of the state'; ending or at least minimising state provision/intervention. It was a return to classical liberal ideas of self-help and equality of opportunity rather than outcome. Neo-liberals once again emphasised the centrality of the market in providing for the needs of individuals.

2.3 Socialism

Introduction
Socialists traditionally place a greater emphasis on the importance of society as a whole rather that the specific needs of individuals. For socialists, individuals are social creatures who thrive in close proximity to others. As long as the society in which they live is supportive, they can live successfully and harmoniously, acting selflessly in the interests of all.

Socialists see capitalism and classical liberalism as damaging because they encourage individualism, selfishness and egoism. They create 'wants' and greed, while institutionalising inequality and the (sometimes even artificially perpetuated) scarcity of desired or necessary goods.

The impact of capitalism from a socialist perspective

Human cost
Capitalism is exploitative. Workers are not rewarded for the full value of their labour and are often exposed to unacceptable levels of harm.

Human spirit
Capitalism encourages greed, jealousy and an unhealthy form of competition. It acts against co-operation and altruism.

Democracy
Democracy is illusory. It appears to offer real hope of change but merely acts to preserve the capitalist order through minor concessions and incentives.

Inequality
Capitalism entrenches inequality. Its main motivation is the accumulation of wealth and – given limited wealth – this ensures that there will always be losers as well as winners.

Resources
Capitalism is wasteful of resources. Products are designed to fail or be superseded at a certain points (fail-rates and inbuilt redundancy). The desire for ever-cheaper raw materials and ever-cheaper energy sources encourages the destruction of natural environments. Capitalism acts against long-term environmental planning in favour of short-term profits.

A socialist agenda
Socialists, therefore, have the desire to remould society rather than allowing it to evolve through interaction. Socialists favour: the redistribution of resources resulting in greater equality of outcome, an emphasis on co-operation and common goals rather than competition and individualism, state provision of education and welfare, and collective control of the means of production.

Different strands of socialism

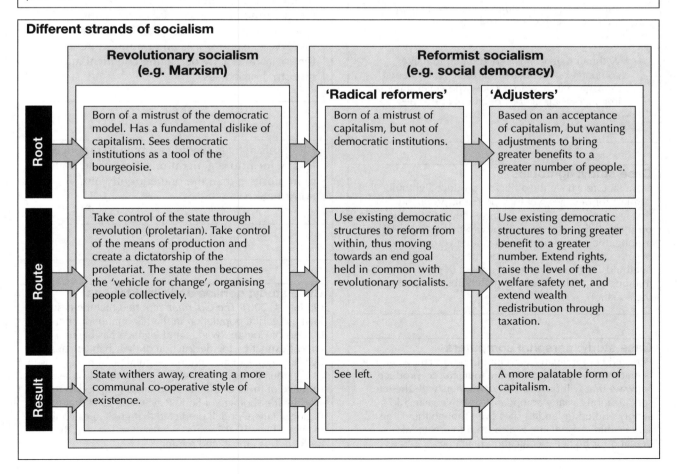

	Revolutionary socialism (e.g. Marxism)	Reformist socialism (e.g. social democracy)	
		'Radical reformers'	'Adjusters'
Root	Born of a mistrust of the democratic model. Has a fundamental dislike of capitalism. Sees democratic institutions as a tool of the bourgeoisie.	Born of a mistrust of capitalism, but not of democratic institutions.	Based on an acceptance of capitalism, but wanting adjustments to bring greater benefits to a greater number of people.
Route	Take control of the state through revolution (proletarian). Take control of the means of production and create a dictatorship of the proletariat. The state then becomes the 'vehicle for change', organising people collectively.	Use existing democratic structures to reform from within, thus moving towards an end goal held in common with revolutionary socialists.	Use existing democratic structures to bring greater benefit to a greater number. Extend rights, raise the level of the welfare safety net, and extend wealth redistribution through taxation.
Result	State withers away, creating a more communal co-operative style of existence.	See left.	A more palatable form of capitalism.

2.4 Environmentalism

Introduction
Environmentalism shares with socialism many of its criticisms of capitalism. However, whereas socialism and other ideologies tend to focus on the distribution of power and of resources between individuals within a society, and the relationship between individuals and the state, environmentalism takes as its starting point the central importance of the relationship between mankind as a whole and the environment. This provides a wholly different perspective on the state.

Environmentalist criticisms of capitalism

1. Capitalism is based upon the exploitation of people and other natural resources. Capitalism sees nature as something to be exploited.

2. Capitalism creates and nurtures false desires and demands through advertising. This leads to the production of unnecessary goods that waste finite resources. This waste, coupled to unnecessary advertising and packaging, is unjustifiable.

3. Manufacturers ensure that their products have deliberately high fail-rates in order to make sure that they have a constant demand for their products. They also ensure that their products have inbuilt redundancy. That is to say, even if they still work (i.e. have not failed), goods will in time become redundant because the manufacturers have a limited interest in maintaining old products compared to their interest in selling new products.

4. Within a market it is very difficult to make companies accountable for the environmental damage that they do because the environmental impact of their actions often only becomes apparent years later.

What does environmentalism involve?

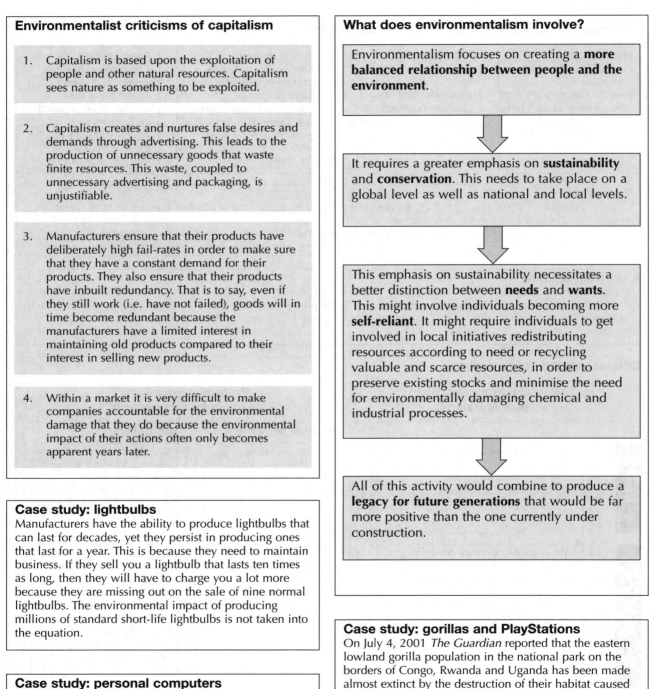

Environmentalism focuses on creating a **more balanced relationship between people and the environment**.

It requires a greater emphasis on **sustainability** and **conservation**. This needs to take place on a global level as well as national and local levels.

This emphasis on sustainability necessitates a better distinction between **needs** and **wants**. This might involve individuals becoming more **self-reliant**. It might require individuals to get involved in local initiatives redistributing resources according to need or recycling valuable and scarce resources, in order to preserve existing stocks and minimise the need for environmentally damaging chemical and industrial processes.

All of this activity would combine to produce a **legacy for future generations** that would be far more positive than the one currently under construction.

Case study: lightbulbs
Manufacturers have the ability to produce lightbulbs that can last for decades, yet they persist in producing ones that last for a year. This is because they need to maintain business. If they sell you a lightbulb that lasts ten times as long, then they will have to charge you a lot more because they are missing out on the sale of nine normal lightbulbs. The environmental impact of producing millions of standard short-life lightbulbs is not taken into the equation.

Case study: personal computers
Personal computers have an inbuilt redundancy and this is made more apparent when manufacturers produce software that will only run on computers with the latest specifications. Many computers over five years old simply end up in landfill sites even though they are still serviceable. Advertising is also used to create false demand for higher specification machines.

Case study: gorillas and PlayStations
On July 4, 2001 *The Guardian* reported that the eastern lowland gorilla population in the national park on the borders of Congo, Rwanda and Uganda has been made almost extinct by the destruction of their habitat caused by mining for Coltan (columbite tantalite), a mineral used as a hardening agent for metals in hi-tech industries. A shortage of this material in 2000 apparently led to the world-wide shortage of Sony PlayStation 2s at that time. Biologist Jane Goodall predicted that great apes could be extinct within 10–15 years as a result of logging, the trade in 'bush-meat' and mining.

3.1 A post-war survey, 1945–1979

Introduction
A lot of what was done in 1945 was based on the 'new liberalism' of men such as William Beveridge and John Maynard Keynes. By 1945 it was clear that classical liberalism and its emphasis on the individual through laissez faire policies (the free market) had failed because it had not offered sufficient protection to the individual. There was, therefore, a need for greater government intervention than might have been considered necessary by liberals in the nineteenth century.

John Maynard Keynes
Keynes believed that limited state intervention in the economy was necessary in order to avoid a spiral of recession. Keynes favoured intervention: a cash boost that might kick-start the economy. He did not believe, however, that the aim should be state-engineered equality. The inequalities of capitalism were a necessary incentive to hard work. This mixed economy would retain the benefits of the free market, while removing its worst tendencies.

William Beveridge and the Beveridge Report (1942)
Beveridge, a liberal civil servant, was commissioned by Churchill to produce a report on welfare provision and make suggestions for change. The Beveridge Report that followed in 1942 identified 'Five Giants' that needed to be defeated: want, disease, ignorance, squalor and idleness.

Beveridge recognised that these 'Giants' were linked, and that a concerted and co-ordinated effort would be required if they were to be conquered. Attlee's Labour Government, elected in 1945 with 393 seats – against the Conservatives' 213 – had the electoral mandate necessary to push ahead with such radical change.

The post-war consensus
Following the Second World War there was a broad agreement on the basis of future policy. In the social sphere, for example, there was an acceptance that:
- *full employment should be the goal;*
- *unions should be consulted over economic/ industrial policy;*
- *there should be public ownership of key industries;*
- *there should be public provision of welfare – covering health care, education, unemployment etc.*

This 'post-war consensus' clearly had its origins – in part – in the national coalition government in office during the war years.

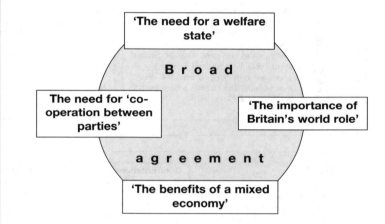

'The need for a welfare state'

Broad

The need for 'co-operation between parties'

'The importance of Britain's world role'

agreement

'The benefits of a mixed economy'

Attacking the 'Five Giants'
The post-war years saw a mass of legislation aimed at defeating the 'Five Giants' identified by Beveridge. The National Insurance Act of 1946 provided for the unemployed, the sick, dependants of the dead and those in maternity. The Butler Education Act of 1944 provided free secondary education, compulsory up to the age of 15. The 1946 National Health Act provided for the creation of the National Health Service.

Post-war Prime Ministers

1945–1951	Attlee
1951–1955	Churchill
1955–1957	Eden
1957–1963	Macmillan
1963–1964	Home
1964–1970	Wilson
1970–1974	Heath
1974–1976	Wilson
1976–1979	Callaghan
1979–1990	Thatcher
1990–1997	Major
1997–2007	Blair
2007–	Brown

The breakdown of the post-war consensus
By the 1970s it was clear that not all was well. Wilson had been forced to devalue the pound, and although unemployment had not risen above 1 000 000 between 1945 and 1974, it hit 1 500 000 in 1979. The co-operation between business, politicians and unions – the **tripartism** or **corporatism** of the earlier decades – was under real pressure as wage demands spiralled out of control and inflation became a real problem. Though the Winter of Discontent of 1978–79 brought the Labour Government crashing down, the problems had been there for some time.

3.2 Thatcherism and Majorism, 1979–1997

Introduction
By 1979 the post-war consensus was already dead. The 1978–79 Winter of Discontent had signalled the end of Callaghan's Labour Administration, and the new government under Margaret Thatcher from 1979 followed a clear neo-liberal, 'New Right' agenda, offering more dogmatism and confrontation than pragmatism and co-operation. Thatcher had emerged from the Conservative Party leadership contest in 1975 following the failure of the former leader Edward Heath in the elections of 1974. A 'dark horse' in the first ballot, she had swept to victory upon the votes of those waiting for the entry of other candidates in the second ballot. Her election as leader in 1975 put an end to any lingering ideas of co-operation between parties.

Key elements of Thatcherism

Domestic policy

Economic
* **Monetarism** rather than Keynesianism
* Full employment not seen as possible or – necessarily – desirable
* An end to 'tripartism'. The reduction of union power
* Aims of controlling public expenditure and improving productivity; low inflation (2.5% by 1986) and low direct taxation

Social
* NHS spending was increased by one-third between 1979 and 1990 but did not keep pace with demand caused by changing demographics.
* A lower benefits safety net
* The sale of council houses to established tenants ('right to buy legislation')
* A focus on law and order
* The **Community Charge** ('**Poll Tax**')

Political
* Talk of 'rolling back the frontiers of the state' (small government) but increasing centralisation
* Civil service reform – increasing 'agencification'
* Major local government reform. Abolition of Greater London Council – seen as a blatant attack on the left

Foreign policy

The 'special relationship'
Thatcher emphasised the importance of the 'special relationship' between the UK and the US. More than any Prime Minister and President since the Second World War, Thatcher and Reagan appeared to be 'singing from the same hymn-sheet'. The UK was a base for US air attacks on Libya.

Europe
Thatcher suspected the motives of other EEC states and forced rebates to compensate the UK for its net contribution to the Community. However, she still signed the 1986 Single European Act and, reluctantly, approved entry into the ERM in October 1990.

Defence policy
An important plank in the Thatcherite programme. Thatcher allowed the siting of US Cruise and Pershing missiles in the UK and upgraded the UK's missiles from Polaris to Trident. In 1986 defence spending was 5% of GDP, and had increased by 27% since 1978. 'Fortress Falklands' was established following the war in 1982.

Style

Image conscious
Thatcher received voice coaching, became famous for her power-dressing, and relied heavily upon speech writers and her Press Secretary, Bernard Ingham.

Confrontational
Thatcher's style was based on confronting opposition inside her party, in the country as a whole, and abroad. She described the miners as the 'enemy within' at the time of the Miners' Strike (1984–85).

Dogmatic
Thatcher was not often prepared to back down. Though she eventually accepted entry to the ERM in October 1990, her support for and defence of the 'Poll Tax' was more typical of her belief in her chosen course.

Domineering
Thatcher became famous for the way in which she controlled and sometime belittled Cabinet colleagues, culminating in high-profile resignations such as those by Heseltine, Lawson and Geoffrey Howe.

Majorism

Context
Major's rise was meteoric. Although only elected to Parliament in 1979, he became Minister for Social Security in 1983, Chief Secretary to the Treasury in 1987, Foreign Secretary in June 1989, Chancellor in October 1989, and Conservative leader and Prime Minister in November 1990. Michael Heseltine, the man who had initially challenged Thatcher for the leadership, was passed over in favour of a man who could unify the Party after the divisions and infighting of the later Thatcher years. Thatcher's legacy demanded a different style – a more consensual approach – as well as some policy changes.

Continuity
Privatisation was continued, as were civil service reforms (the Next Steps Programme). There remained a focus on low inflation and cuts in direct taxation, though the Party's reputation for economic competence was damaged by Black Wednesday and the UK's subsequent withdrawal from the European Exchange Rate Mechanism. As the Major premiership came to its close, it became apparent that many of the key elements of the Thatcherite agenda had – in fact – been realised and that there was a need for new direction. The Party, it was said, needed a spell on the back benches to refocus itself.

Change
There was a marked change in style and tone; a more consensual style as opposed to a confrontational one. This was partly due to the context of the administration and partly due to the fact that the Major Government was having to operate with an ever-shrinking Parliamentary majority. There were key policy changes. The 'Poll Tax' was shelved in favour of the property-based Council Tax. A slightly more sympathetic stance was taken on Europe, approving Maastricht while securing opt-outs on the Social Chapter and the Single Currency. Major was accused of a lack of vision but did have his 'big idea': the Citizen's Charter.

3.3 Blairism, 1997–2007

Introduction
In the same way that Majorism must be seen in the context of Thatcherism, and Thatcherism was itself a result of the failures of Heath and the apparent redundancy of the post-war consensus, Blairism must be seen as a reaction to the failure of the Labour Party in the 1980s – especially in the 1983 general election, where its hard-left manifesto was described as the 'longest suicide note in History'.

Ideology or pragmatism?
It has become fashionable in recent years to refer to the 'end of ideology'. Political parties have moved to the centre. Pragmatic populist policies, rather than ideological dogma, have become the norm. Some writers have hailed the emergence of a 'new consensus' around the centre–right. They cite Labour's jettisoning of Clause 4 (indeed the Party's reluctance to talk about socialism at all – see Ch. 6.5) and Tony Blair's pitch for 'middle England'. This, coupled to Iain Duncan Smith's appeal for the Conservatives to become a more inclusive party in the wake of a second humiliating general election defeat, had, for many, signalled the end of adversarial party politics as we knew it.

Is there now more of a focus on style and presentation than on doctrine and dogma? Is it all about 'spin'?

Catch phrases
Part of the new emphasis on presentation has been an increased awareness on the importance of catch phrases. This is by no means totally new, but some argue that it has become particularly apparent in recent years. The Blair administration employed a large number of these phrases, for example:

'a stake-holder society'; 'welfare to work'; 'joined-up government'; 'economic prudence'; 'a third way'.

Such phrases are, by their very nature, difficult to pin down and define even when leading figures attempt to do so. Tony Blair, for example, tried to outline the 'third way' in a speech to the French National Assembly in March 1998. 'When I talk of a third way, I mean neither laissez faire nor state control and rigidity' he asserted. Yet explaining what the third way *is* has proved more difficult than asserting *what it is not*.

Tangible changes (?)

Policy
Social – Increased spending on public services: health, education and welfare. Extensive programmes unveiled before the 2001 general election, including greater support for single working mothers and partial nursery funding for pre-school children. A ban on fox hunting was not forced through until 2005.

Political/constitutional – The Human Rights Act, the Freedom of Information Act, partial reform of the Lords and devolution, including the use of new electoral systems in the Scottish Parliament and Welsh Assembly. Lots of unfinished projects and half-way houses. A coherent programme?

Economic – In 1997 Gordon Brown accepted Conservative spending plans for the first two years and has placed an emphasis on 'economic prudence' since. Low direct taxation and low inflation have been maintained (control over interest rates was given to the Bank of England with a 2.5% inflation target upon taking power). Controlled public expenditure, with a realisation that full employment is hard to achieve.

Foreign policy – New Labour promised a 'moral foreign policy' and achieved a number of early successes (e.g. Sierra Leone). It was the interventions in Afghanistan and Iraq that blighted Blair's premiership.

The Blair project

Power
The years 1997 to 2005 saw a centralisation of power around Downing Street. Blair reduced the number of full Cabinet meetings held each week, preferring instead to use 'bilaterals', meetings between himself and another minister. He attended the Commons less frequently than most other post-war Prime Ministers and reduced Prime Minister's Questions from two to one (albeit longer) session on Wednesdays. Blair took personal control of certain key issues (for example, 'foot and mouth') and became reliant on an ever-increasing band of policy advisors. The overall effect was a much more central role for the Prime Minister above and beyond Cabinet.

Style/presentation
A lot has been made of the importance of presentation and spin. At the centre of much of the criticism was Alastair Campbell, as Press Secretary and later Director of Communications, through whom so much political information was filtered during Blair's first term. The activities of the Press Office – for example, the use of pagers to brief Labour MPs in the Commons during debates – gave the impression of an extremely controlling administration. Some spoke of Blair's 'control freak' tendencies, and their fears were reinforced by briefings against Ken Livingstone as the Party first tried to force its preferred candidate for London Mayor onto the ballot paper as the official Labour candidate, and then tried to discredit Ken Livingstone's independent candidacy.

4.1 The electoral system

General Elections (The First Past the Post System)

In 2005, the UK was divided into 646 Parliamentary Constituencies. Each Constituency elects a single MP to represent them in the House of Commons. In a General Election, voters cast a single vote for the Candidate that they would like to represent their Constituency. At the end of the voting process, the votes are totalled and the candidate with the largest number of votes wins. The winning candidate needs only one vote more than their nearest rival to secure victory; hence 'first past the post' (FPTP). Where a vacancy arises (through death or resignation for example), a by-election takes place in the affected constituency using the same rules. Local elections also operate under FPTP in England, Scotland and Wales.

Quirky Results

1935 was the last year in which the winning party in a General Election secured more than 50% of the votes cast.

In the General Elections of 1950, 1951 and February 1974 the winning party gained fewer votes nationally than the party that ended up forming the official opposition.

In 1983 the Labour Party gained 27.6% of the votes nationally and won 209 seats. The Liberal/SDP Alliance, in contrast, gained 25.4% of the votes but only won 23 seats.

The Majority of 2 votes achieved by the LibDems in Winchester in 1997 was the lowest constituency majority in any seat for 50 years.

The voter turnout in the 2001 General Election – 59% – was the lowest since 1918.

Labour's victory in 2005 was achieved with only 35.2% of the popular vote – the lowest ever. This equates to 21.6% of the electorate.

European Elections (A Closed Regional List System)

European Parliament Elections in Northern Ireland have operated under Proportional Representation (PR) since 1979. 1999 saw the first European Parliament (EP) Elections in Britain to be conducted under a system of PR. Under the d'Hondt or Closed Party List system voters in each British region voted for their preferred party. The 84 British EP seats were then divided up within regions according to votes cast. This led to a result which was more proportional than FPTP, for the main parties at least:

Party	% Votes 1999	No. Seats 1999	% Seats 1999
Labour	28	29	34.5
Conservative	35.8	36	42.9
LibDem	12.7	10	11.9
UKIP	7	3	3.6
Green	6.3	2	2.4

Scottish Parliament and Welsh Assembly Elections (First Past the Post Top Up)

2007 saw the third set of elections to the new Scottish Parliament and Welsh Assembly, conducted under the First Past the Post Top Up system (FPTP-TU). This system gives a top up number of seats to parties that lose out through the First Past the Post system. It does this by awarding top-up seats in proportion to the votes cast for each party. Each voter casts two votes, one for their chosen candidate in their constituency and one for their chosen party. The second 'party' votes are then totalled within each region and the regional top-up seats are awarded proportionally; whilst taking into consideration the constituency seats that the party has already won under FPTP. Top-up seats are then filled from lists of candidates drawn up before the election by each party. For example, if a party wins two top-up seats then the first two candidates on their list are duly elected. In Scotland there are 129 MSPs in total (73 FPTP and 56 TU). In Wales there are 60 MWAs (40 FPTP and 20 TU).

2007 Elections	Scottish Parliament			Welsh Assembly		
Party	FPTP	TU	Total	FPTP	TU	Total
Labour	37	9	46	24	2	26
Conservative	4	13	17	5	7	12
LibDem	11	5	16	3	3	6
SNP	21	26	47			
Plaid Cymru				7	8	15
Others	0	3	3	1	0	1

In Focus – 2005 Election

(a) Largest Majority: Bootle (Lab. Hold)
47.7% turnout
Conservative 1 680 (6.2%)
Labour 19 345 (75.5%)
LibDem 2 968 (11.7%)
Other 1 709 (6.7%)

A Labour majority of 16 357 votes (63.8%)

In Focus – 2005 Election

(b) Smallest Majority: Crawley (Lab. Hold)
58.2% turnout
Conservative 16 374 (39%)
Labour 16 411 (39.1%)
LibDem 6 503 (15.5%)
Other 2 685 (6.4%)

A Labour majority of 37 votes (0.1%)

4.2 The case for and against electoral reform

What is an electoral system?

In the British context, an electoral system is a set of rules by which popular votes are translated into seats in a legislature. Electoral systems can be broadly divided into those which are *majoritarian* (i.e. require the winner to secure a majority), those which are *proportional* (i.e. attempting to distribute seats in proportion to votes cast), and those which are a combination of the two – *hybrid systems*.

What should an electoral system seek to offer?

According to Lord Jenkins' Independent Commission on Electoral Reform, an effective electoral system should seek to address four main objectives. These scores (out of five) are only for purposes of discussion and are adapted from the report:

Objective	FPTP	AV	STV	List	AMS
Proportionality	1	2	4	5	5
Stable government	4	3	2	2	2
Voter choice	1	3	5	2	3
The MP-constituency link	5	5	3	1	3
Total	**11**	**13**	**14**	**10**	**13**

First past the post: arguments for/arguments against

Arguments for:

- The system is a part of our traditions.
- The system is cheap and easy to operate.
- The system is easily understood, which helps voters and contributes to the result.
- The single-member constituency allows for a close MP-constituency link.
- The system normally produces strong, majority governments, making coalitions less likely.

Arguments against:

- The system distorts the popular vote to an unacceptable degree.
- It leads to large numbers of wasted votes.
- It disadvantages small parties.
- It provides too little voter choice.
- It leads to artificially polarised adversarial politics. Coalition government would be more constructive in the long term.
- It perpetuates the current geographical strongholds of some parties.

Electoral reform in favour of what?

Alternative Vote and AV+

AV is a *majoritarian* system whereas AV+ is a *hybrid* system. AV retains the single-member constituencies present in FPTP but requires the winning candidate in each constituency to gain 50%+ of the votes cast. Instead of putting a cross in a single box, voters have the opportunity to rank candidates in order of preference (1,2,3 etc.). Any candidate achieving 50%+ of the votes when the first preferences are counted is elected. If no candidate wins on first preferences, the bottom candidate is eliminated and their votes are transferred to the second preferences indicated on each ballot paper. This continues until a candidate crosses the 50%+ winning line. AV+ operates in the same way as FPTP-TU (with the voter voting once for candidates and once – the '+' bit – for their preferred party) but the FPTP element is replaced with the AV system above. Supplementary vote (SV) works in a similar way except all but the top two candidates are eliminated after first preferences are counted.

AV used in Australia.
AV+ recommended by the Jenkins Commission.
SV used for London Mayor.

Single Transferable Vote

STV is a *proportional* system. STV is probably the most complicated system. Its aim of achieving clear proportionality and eliminating wasted votes requires a fairly complex system of counting and vote transference. STV replaces single-member constituencies with larger multi-member constituencies. Voters indicate their preferences for a number of candidates in order (1,2,3 etc.). In order to be elected, a candidate must achieve a quota. Once this quota is achieved, any surplus votes for that candidate are transferred in accordance with second preferences. If no candidate is elected on first preferences, then the lowest-polling candidate is eliminated and their votes are redistributed in the same way. This process continues until enough candidates have achieved the quota for all of the seats in the multi-member constituency to be filled.

STV used in: Northern Ireland Assembly elections, Irish Republic, Scottish local elections.

Party list (regional or national)

PL is a *proportional* system. Under PL voters cast their vote for a party, either on a regional (RL) or a national basis (NL). Each party draws up a list of candidates in the order (top down) that the party would want to see them elected. Each party will often include as many candidates on their lists as there are seats available. An 'open list system' allows voters to express preferences between candidates standing for the same party, whereas a 'closed list system' only gives the voter the chance to vote for their own party of choice. After the voting process, the votes are totalled and the seats are then distributed in proportion to votes cast. In a closed list system, a party achieving a 20% share of the vote would achieve 40 seats in a 200-seat parliament. The top 40 names from that party's list would, therefore, be elected.

Used in: Israel (NL), European elections in UK (RL).

Additional members system

AMS is a *hybrid* system. Under AMS a proportion of seats are contested using the FPTP system and the remainder are used to reward parties in proportion to the number of votes that they achieve. This second, proportional, element can be organised on a national or a regional basis. In Germany, for example, 50% of seats are elected under FPTP with the remaining 50% being distributed proportionally. In the Scottish Parliament and Welsh Assembly elections another variant of AMS, FPTP top-up, was used (see Ch 10.1). In Germany there is a threshold of 5% which parties must cross before they are entitled to any of the additional/top-up seats.

Used in: Germany, Scottish Parliament and Welsh Assembly, Greater London Assembly.

Conclusions: Prior to the 1997 general election, the Labour Party offered an independent report on electoral reform, to be followed by a referendum on any resulting proposals. Lord Jenkins duly led the investigation, which selected AV+ as the most appropriate system. Had this system been operating in 1997, it is estimated that the actual Labour majority of 179 would have been reduced to 60. The Labour Government has not implemented the Jenkins Report but it has brought in a variety of new systems for elections to, amongst others, the European Parliament, the Scottish Parliament, the Welsh Assembly and the London Assembly. Under many of these systems, Labour has fared worse than it did under FPTP in 1997. Some have argued that this has dampened the Party's enthusiasm towards the introduction of PR for parliamentary elections. Many more feel that the introduction of so many different systems in such a short space of time has been counterproductive.

What is a referendum?

A referendum is a popular vote in which the electorate decides an issue by answering 'yes' or 'no' to a question. In the UK context, the questions are set by the government. In some countries, however, there are mechanisms which allow citizens to initiate referendums on their own questions. Referendums can be either 'advisory' (i.e. only for the purpose of giving the government a clear view of the public mood) or 'binding' (committing the government to legislate in line with the referendum's outcome).

Referendums are often held when a major constitutional change is on the cards but many countries use these mechanisms far more frequently (see bottom right).

Arguments for	Arguments against
• Referendums offer a greater degree of 'direct democracy'. Citizens can have a real input into key decisions.	• Referendums are inconsistent with our system of parliamentary government and they undermine the principles of a representative democracy.
• They encourage political participation. People are more likely to participate when they care about the issues involved and the choices are black and white.	• Far from encouraging participation, regular use of referendums could lead to apathy and low turnouts that might distort the results.
• They provide a way for governments to 'test the water' before making certain changes.	• They undermine collective responsibility in Cabinet.
• They allow government to focus on other issues, rather than getting bogged down in long-running squabbles.	• Governments can use referendums to duck their responsibility to make decisions – to 'govern'.
• They can be used to provide a clear and final answer.	• Most issues are too complicated to be condensed into a simple yes/no question.
• They can prevent dangerous divisions within political parties over controversial issues. This prevents governments from collapsing and, therefore, provides greater continuity in government.	• Funding differences between the 'yes' and 'no' camps might mean that the referendum is not played out on a level playing field.
• They provide a way of focusing or renewing the mandate on a particular issue.	• The questions might be biased; phrased in such a way as to encourage a certain response.
• They provide a method for resolving tricky moral questions.	• Governments can time referendums to make a favourable result more likely.
• They provide a way of legitimising major constitutional changes.	• Decisions are not always considered final. Governments sometimes go back again and again until they get the result that they want.
	• Referendums create a tyranny of the majority.

UK referendums to date

All of the referendums in the UK thus far have been concerned with the distribution of power between the various tiers of government: supra-national, national and sub-national.

Summary

	Date	Who voted	Questions	Turnout (%)	Yes (%)	No (%)
1.	1973, March	N Ireland	Should NI stay in the UK?	58.1	98.9	1.1
2.	1975, June	UK	Should UK stay in the EEC?	63.2	67.2	32.8
3.	1979, March	Scotland	Should there be a Scottish Parliament?	63.8	51.6	48.4
4.	1979, March	Wales	Should there be a Welsh Parliament?	58.3	20.3	79.7
5.	1997, Sept.	Scotland	Should there be a Scottish Parliament? With tax-varying powers?	60.4	74.3 / 63.5	25.7 / 36.5
6.	1997, Sept.	Wales	Should there be a Welsh Assembly?	50.1	50.3	49.7
7.	1998, May	London	A London Mayor and London Assembly?	34	72	28
8.	1998, May	N Ireland	Approval for the Good Friday Agreement.	81	71.1	28.9
9.	2004, Nov.	North East	A Regional Assembly for the North East?	48	22	78

Future UK referendums?

The government is committed to a referendum before entry into the European Currency (euro). In the past there has been a commitment to a referendum before any change to the electoral system used in general elections. Referendums could also be employed to decide other key constitutional changes concerning institutions such as the monarchy. In 1998 Lord Neill's Committee on Standards in Public Life recommended that future referendums in the UK should be state-funded, that the 'yes' and 'no' campaigns should share a £1.2 million pot and that the precise wording of any future referendum would have to be independently approved. Such recommendations were addressed in the PPER Act (2000).

The experience in other countries

Referendums are widely used in other countries. For example:

• In the **United States** many states operate a system of initiatives (propositions). Citizens often have the opportunity to raise questions for public vote if they can gain the support of a specified proportion of the state's population. Though not all of these propositions are passed, many have been significant. For example, Proposition 184 in California created a mandatory 25-year sentence for those convicted of a serious felony for the third time (the so-called 'three strikes and you're out' rule).

• In **Ireland** a 1995 referendum legalised divorce (by a margin of only 9124 votes). The 1998 referendum authorised constitutional changes in line with the Good Friday Agreement. The Irish referendum of 2001 rejected the Treaty of Nice. In March 2002 the Irish rejected a further tightening of their strict anti-abortion laws by 629 041 votes to 618 485.

• In **Switzerland** a referendum on a law can take place if 50 000 voters sign a petition and 100 000 voters can initiate a referendum on a constitutional amendment. Since referendums started in Switzerland 135 years ago there have been over 450. The current rate is four per year. In December 2001, for example, the Swiss rejected a proposal to abolish their armed forces. A similar proposal had been rejected three years earlier. In March 2002 the Swiss voted to join the UN by 55% to 45%. In 1986 they had rejected a similar proposal 3:1.

• In **Italy** 500 000 of the country's electors can initiate a referendum.

• In **New Zealand** the 1993 Citizen's Initiated Referenda Act requires support of 10% of the electorate to initiate a non-binding referendum.

5.1 The electorate

Introduction

Before studying voting behaviour, it is helpful to have some understanding of the composition of the electorate in socio-economic and demographic terms. This page considers areas such as gender, class, age and ethnicity as well as highlighting changes in occupational structure

The extension of the franchise (right to vote)

In 1831 only 5% of adults (over 18) or 450 000 individuals out of a population of around 25 million were able to vote. The 1832 Great Reform Act only increased the electorate to around 700 000, but many see it as important because it opened the door to later reforms. Around a million voters were added in 1867 as the property qualification for voting was lowered in boroughs. The Act of 1884 extended this to counties and added 2.5 million more voters. The 1918 Act enfranchised all adult men (over 21), and women over 30. The 1928 Act enfranchised all other women over 21. In 1969 the voting age was lowered from 21 to 18. By 1969, 99% of adults (over 18) or around 40 million individuals out of a population of 58 million had the vote.

Key changes

1832	Great Reform Act
1867	Second Reform Act
1884	Franchise Act
1918	Representation of the People Act
1928	Equal Franchise Act
1969	Representation of the People Act

Socio-economic trends and issues

The North–South Divide?

During the 1980s political scientists focused on the growing divide between the prosperous South and the declining Northern parts of the country. During the 1980s many Northern-based primary (e.g. mining) and manufacturing (e.g. textiles) industries were in decline, whereas the 'service sector' and financial sectors (often based in the Home Counties) were booming. Sociologists also noted marked health and life expectancy differences between North and South.

In 1994 the average income per head in the North was only 89% of the average for the UK as a whole (the South-Eastern average income was 117% of the UK figure). Northern unemployment was 10.8 % compared to the UK figure of 8.6%. Though the phrase is still used, some argue that differences such as those identified are now less pronounced.

Gender

The traditional gender stereotypes have been broken down somewhat over the last few decades. Many more women now work (they made up 38% of the workforce in 1971, and 44% in 1996), though they are still more likely than men to be working in part-time employment, and 26% of women workers are still employed in clerical and secretarial occupations (compared to only 8% of men). Women also, therefore, have a lower median wage e.g. 2007; women £394, men £498.

Changing patterns of occupation

The 1980s and 1990s saw a decline in traditional heavy and manufacturing industries (36% of GDP in 1951; 27% in 1980; 22% in 1995) and a rise in the service sector (51% in 1951; 55.3% in 1980; 71% in 1995). The numbers of workers involved changed accordingly. Between 1955 and 1996 employment in the service sector increased from 36% to almost 76%, while manufacturing employment fell from 43% to 18%. By 1996 only 0.9% worked in heavy industry compared even to the 1991 figure of 1.7%.

At the same time, many nationalised industries (e.g. steel, gas, water, BT etc.) were transferred to the private sector. Individual share ownership jumped from 7% of adult population in 1979 to 22% in 1997. More women came into the workforce and there was an increase in part-time work (20% of jobs by 1996). The number of people who were self-employed increased by 75% between 1979 and 1990, hitting 3 million by 2001.

Home ownership

The Housing Act of 1980 gave long-term council house tenants the 'right to buy' their homes at discounts of between 50% and 70% of market value. After 1988 most of the remaining housing stock was transferred to Housing Associations or Housing Action Trusts. As a result, the rate of home ownership increased from 49% to 69% (1971–2002) and the number of people living in rented council accommodation decreased from 31% to 14% during the same period.

Ethnicity

In 2001 the ethnic minority population of Great Britain numbered 4.6 million (7.9% of the population). Of these:

Indian = 23%; Pakistani and Bangladeshi = 22%; Black = 25%; Chinese = 5.3%; mixed race = 15%

Members of ethnic minorities are still subject to considerable discrimination, and are more likely to be victimised, achieve less in school, be unemployed or in low-paid employment. A survey reported in *The Guardian* in 1997, for example, showed that 32% of white people still said that they would mind if one of their close relatives were to marry an Afro-Caribbean (as did 13% of Jews and 29% of Asians). There have also been numerous studies showing unequal treatment in the justice system.

Age

Britain has an ageing population. There has been a marked decrease in the birth-rate since the early part of the century but people are, on average, living longer. Women tend to live around three years longer than men do and for both sexes the average life expectancy is well over 75. This has already had and will increasingly have a massive impact on the health and welfare systems.

Social class

A social class is best defined as a group of people sharing a similar social position. Market researchers tend to divide people up into six socio-economic classes, though AB and DE are normally grouped together:

Class band:	% 2006
A Professional/senior managerial	4.0
B Middle managers/executives	21.9
C1 Junior managers/non-manual	29.0
C2 Skilled manual	20.7
D Semi-skilled/unskilled manual	24.3
E Residual and casual workers.	
Those on benefits.	

5.2 Political participation and abstention

Different kinds of participation

Studies of political participation often – rightly – focus on levels of voter turnout. It is, though, important to remember that there are other forms of political participation; not least, involvement in political parties and pressure group activity. This page, however, focuses largely on voter turnout, factors that affect it and the implications of low turnout in elections.

Levels of political activism

The fact that fewer people are voting and that the membership of most political parties is significantly lower than it was in the 1950s does not necessarily mean that people are not politically active. As Noreena Hertz remarked in *The Independent* (June 2001), 'it's not about apathy … while voting is waning, other forms of political expression are on the rise'.

The membership of mainstream pressure groups such as Greenpeace has risen as the membership of the major political parties has fallen. Greenpeace's membership rose from 30 000 in 1981 to over 400 000 in 1992, whereas the Conservative Party's membership fell from 2.8 million in the 1950s to 780 000 in 1992 and 335 000 by the end of 2000. There has also been a marked increase in direct action.

Voter turnout

One of the most obvious ways in which an individual can participate within a political system is to vote. Levels of turnout are, therefore, one important measure of political participation. There was widespread concern at the low voter turnout figure in the 2001 general election, but we should remember two things. Firstly, the overall figure masks massive regional variation. In Wyre Forrest, for example, the independent Dr Richard Taylor won on a 68% turnout. Secondly, turnout in other forms of elections is often far lower than in general elections.

European elections

Turnout at European elections is notoriously low. In some voting districts in Sunderland in 1999, for example, turnout was as low as 1.5%. In 1999 the overall national turnout for UK elections to the European Parliament was only 24%. This was the lowest for any EU member state, though it improved to 38% in 2004.

Local elections

In the 2000 local government elections turnout was 29% nationally and in 2002 it was 35%. This slight improvement was brought about by experiments with postal voting, text voting, and e-mail voting that improved turnout in some wards to over 50%. In the 2008 local elections, turnout was around 35%.

Scottish Parliament, Welsh Assembly elections and Greater London Assembly elections

The turnout for the first elections for all these bodies was considered poor (though perhaps not now in light of the general election turnout). In Scotland 59% of voters turned out in 1999. In Wales only 40% voted. In 2007 it was 52% and 43.5% respectively. In London the turnout in the 2004 mayoral contest was only 36%, though the race between Boris Johnson and Ken Livingstone saw this figure rise to 45% in 2008.

By-election turnout

It is hard to generalise on the subject of by-elections because of the variations caused by so many factors: the cause of the by-election, the nature of media coverage, and topical local issues – to name three. What we can say is that turnout in by-elections has often been around the 40–50% mark.

In the 2001 by-election in Ipswich there was serious media coverage concerning the effect that the scheduling (on the same night) of the home leg of the UEFA Cup tie between Ipswich Town and Inter Milan might have on voter turnout, given the fact that the match had a sell-out crowd of over 20 000. In the event, turnout was not far off what it had been in the general election.

Voter turnout in general elections 1945–2005			
Year	%	Year	%
1945	73	1974 (Feb)	79
1950	84	1974 (Oct)	73
1951	83	1979	76
1955	77	1983	73
1959	79	1987	75
1964	77	1992	78
1966	76	1997	71
1970	72	2001	59
		2005	61.5

NB: Figures rounded.

Why is turnout so low?

Intelligent voters

Voters are more likely to turn out to vote when they can see that the resulting institutions are important. They are also aware of other contextual factors. Voters didn't vote in 2001 because Labour was 'bound to win', whereas they had voted in 1997, 'when it mattered'.

Apathetic voters

Voters can't be bothered to vote. There is, some argue, a need for compulsory Citizenship lessons.

Disaffected voters

Increasing numbers of voters are coming to the conclusion that elections don't matter. All parties are the same and it is more profitable to spend one's time engaged in direct action on single issues.

Media-driven voters.

Only vote when the media brings the elections to their attention and makes them want to vote. Do not vote in low-profile elections.

Does it really matter?

Legitimacy – a government elected on the votes of a small proportion of the electorate might not have the same degree of legitimacy as one elected on a high turnout.

Mandate – it could be argued that a government elected on a low turnout does not, therefore, have as strong a mandate for its policies as a government elected on a high turnout.

5.3 An introduction to voting behaviour

Introduction

Psephologists have always tried to explain voting behaviour by constructing theoretical 'models'. Different writers favour different models but most of the models share some common elements – they simply have a different emphasis. The easiest way to explain voting behaviour is to think about **long-term** and **short-term** factors, where the long-term factors might include issues such as the social background of the individual voter and the short-term factors might include issues such as which party leader they may prefer at a particular time, or particular events which are linked to a particular time. Most political scientists however, take the analysis of voting behaviour a little further.

The primacy and recency approaches

The primacy model:

The primacy model suggests that factors such as age, gender, ethnicity and class (i.e. social divisions) can determine electoral outcomes. Such an analysis of voting behaviour would lead one to believe that stability is a major feature of voting behaviour, because such social factors only change very slowly. People who support this model would argue that although short-term factors are important, they do not really do enough to prevent the underlying social forces from shaping an individual's political outlook.

The recency model:

Other writers believe that voting patterns are in fact more volatile and that developments such as partisan dealignment and embourgeoisement have reduced many individuals' loyalty to a particular political party. As a result, they argue, short-term factors (issues, events, leaders, competence etc.) are much more important. They argue that the fact that the same numbers of voters tend to vote for the same parties does not mean that the same voters vote for the same party. There is a certain amount of 'churn' and many voters don't make up their minds until the last minute. In 1997 for example, 8.5 million voters changed their minds in the three-week period prior to the election, but the overall levels of support stayed the same.

Stability v. volatility

If you believe that long-term factors are more important in determining voting behaviour, then you will tend to feel that there is a certain amount of stability in voting behaviour because such factors do not change quickly. If, however, you believe that short-term factors are more significant in the present day, then it is inevitable that voting patterns will be more volatile because short-term events are less predictable. Some have argued that trends such as partisan dealignment (the weakening of the bonds between voter and party) have led to a greater number of floating voters and that this has increased volatility. Others have pointed to the similarity between the 1997 and 2001 general election results and emphasised the stability in the system. The latter judgement is, however, dangerous. Though the results in terms of seats won might be similar in each election, this does not mean that the voters voted in the same way or indeed voted at all in each election. Many voters might have voted differently with only the net result in terms of votes or seats remaining unchanged. This is known as **churn**.

Voting behaviour in by-elections

Voting behaviour in by-elections – as noted above – can be extremely volatile. This is a partly a result of the greater tendency towards protest voting and tactical voting in such elections, but also a result of the media focus often afforded such events. Though the 'swing' in by-elections is, therefore, often impressive, many seats are recaptured by their original holders at the next general election, when the context is different and the stakes are often considered higher.

Key terms

Tactical voting

Tactical voting is where an individual chooses to vote for a candidate that is not his or her preferred candidate in order to prevent his/her least favourite candidate being elected. It occurs most often where Labour voters vote LibDem in seats where the LibDems stand the best chance of defeating the Conservative candidate or where LibDems vote Labour in Labour/Conservative marginals.

Tactical voting was particularly prevalent in the 1997 and 2001 and 2005 general elections, often encouraged by newspapers. *The Independent* (in its 'Rough Guide to the Election') produced two lists of 33 Conservative-held seats. The first 33 were seats in which LibDems should vote Labour if they wanted to unseat the Conservative MP. The second list of 33 seats were those in which Labour supporters should vote LibDem to achieve the same end.

A number of vote-swapping websites also appeared during the 2001 and 2005 general elections. On these sites people could agree to vote for a party other than their natural choice in their own constituency in return for someone voting in a similar fashion in their constituency. Thus, Labour voters in Labour no-go areas could see their vote – effectively – transferred into a constituency where it might matter.

Protest voting

In some cases voters choose to vote for a candidate or party other than their normal choice in order to send a message – often to their 'natural' party or to the government of the day. Protest voting often takes place in elections where the outcome is less crucial to the voter. Thus, the LibDems achieved spectacularly impressive by-election results in supposedly safe Conservative seats towards the end of the Tories' 18-year spell in office. In the same way, the Conservatives secured impressive results in the 1999 European elections, despite having lost the general election so comprehensively only two years before. This was at least partly attributable to protest voting.

Swing

Swing is the movement of votes from one party to another expressed as a percentage. It is normally measured against the last general election. If swing were uniform across the country then a 1% swing from one party to another would see all of the seats with less than a 1% majority change hands. In reality we see differential swing, with different constituencies behaving differently. This, coupled to the fact that there are third and minor parties involved, is why the 'swingometer' often used in election broadcasts is a flawed device.

5.4 Models of voting behaviour

Introduction

Numerous models have been advanced to explain the dynamics of voting behaviour. While all have their merits, it is important to remember that they are not necessarily mutually exclusive. It might be possible, for example, to argue that 'social structures' position an individual politically, but that the 'context' or issues that are unique to a particular election might moderate their behaviour and make them more likely to vote against their 'natural party'.

Do we need voting models?

Voting models attempt to make a science out of human behaviour and are therefore bound to be flawed to a greater or lesser extent. What such models do offer us is a way of approaching what is a complex topic in a relatively structured way. If nothing else, they provide something to argue against.

Social structures model

This model emphasises the importance of certain social structures in shaping individuals' voting habits. Factors such as social class, ethnicity, occupation, education, geographical location and gender are, it is argued, important in this process. For example . . .

Gender

Commentators once spoke of a gender gap: women being more likely to vote Conservative, perhaps due to traditional female roles. This gender gap appears to have closed. Why might this be?

% voting Conservative		
1987	Men 44%	Women 44%
1992	Men 38%	Women 44%
1997	Men 31%	Women 32%
2001	Men 32%	Women 33%
2005	Men 34%	Women 32%

Ethnicity

Thirteen of the 15 ethnic minority MPs elected in 2005 represented the Labour Party. Around 70% of Asian voters and 80% of black voters have supported Labour historically. Many would therefore argue that ethnicity is a major determinant of voting behaviour.

Party identification model

Strong party identification or 'partisan alignment' was often said to go hand in hand with class alignment. People identified with a particular party and stuck with it. In the 1950s over 90% of voters voted for either the Labour Party or the Conservatives. In 1997 this figure was down to 74%, and up to 11 million voters changed their minds. Up to 10% of the electorate were said to have voted tactically rather than for any party they identified with. An ICM/BBC poll in 1997 showed that 50% of those 'likely' to vote felt that it didn't matter which party got into power because things would end up much the same. Amongst 'unlikely voters' the proportion agreeing with this view was 70%.

Rational choice model

In the rational choice or judgmental model, voters make rational and considered judgements taking on board factors such as current issues, party leaders and perceived competence. The latter might be a judgement on past performance (retrospective) or a perception of how the party might do if given the chance (prospective). In the 1992 general election Neil Kinnock was regarded as an electoral liability and was criticised following the triumphalist Sheffield Rally. In 1997 the Conservatives were suffering from the fact that they had lost their reputation for economic competence in the wake of Black Wednesday in 1992.

Dominant ideology model

This model takes the view that there is a dominant ideology amongst the elite that controls key institutions such as business, the media and political parties. This elite uses its influence to orchestrate elections in order to serve its own interests.

Voting context model

This model raises the possibility that voting behaviour is affected by factors such as by the nature of the election being contested, the importance of the resulting institution and the workings of the electoral system employed in the election. Thus, voters might be more likely to vote in general elections than local elections if they have a low opinion of local government. They might choose to vote tactically or cast a protest vote if such a vote suits the situation. In a European election under a PR system, a LibDem voter might vote LibDem, whereas under the first past the post system they might vote tactically or not vote at all. **Why?**

Class and voting

The 1950s and 1960s were decades of high class alignment – that is to say that the party one voted for was most often the party of one's class. Pulzer, in the 1960s, went as far as to suggest that 'class is the basis of British party politics; all else is embellishment and detail'. Put simply, the working class was expected to vote Labour and the middle classes were supposed to vote Conservative.

Class dealignment

Since those days, many commentators have charted what they have described as a process of class dealignment. For some, this is a result of **embourgeoisement** – working class people feeling more middle class (due to material possessions and changes in occupational structure, for example) and therefore voting for the party of the middle classes – the Conservatives. Others have written of **deferential voters** who, despite being working class, vote for the Conservatives because they see them as the natural party of government, a party of leaders. Ivor Crewe has put forward the idea that we are now faced with a **new working class** (occupied in new industries – particularly the service sector) who do not act politically in the same way as the **old working class** (who were heavily unionised). For David Denver, the 1997 election, with its 10% swing, underlined the validity of the dealignment thesis. The Alford Index (calculated by subtracting the percentage of non-manual voters voting Labour from the percentage of manual voters voting Labour) went down from 42% in 1964 to only 22% in 1997. The figures below show voting by class in the 1997, 2001 and 2005 General Elections. What conclusions can we draw from these figures? How can we account for the changes since 1997?

Class and Voting 1997–2005

Class	Conservative			Labour			LibDem		
	2005	2001	1997	2005	2001	1997	2005	2001	1997
AB	37	40	43	28	33	30	29	21	21
C^1	36	33	35	32	40	37	23	21	19
C^2	33	29	28	40	47	52	19	17	13
DE	25	28	21	48	49	58	18	17	15

5.5 The media

Introduction

Studies of elections and voting behaviour often see the media as having a significant influence on both the course of elections and, in a broader sense, the formation of the political agenda. This page considers a number of different theories concerning the operation of the media, and attempts to assess the extent of media influence in the political sphere.

Daily newspaper circulation, April 2008

Sun 3 131 919	Mirror 1 478 036	Star 730 244
Mail 2 324 428	Express 727 180	Telegraph 871 598
Times 618 160	FT 448 241	Guardian 351 031
Independent 243 398		

Media theory

Manipulative theory

The mass media is controlled by an elite that uses it with the sole purpose of preserving the status quo and, therefore, its own position. It submerges a radical agenda in meaningless trivia. As Billy Bragg wrote in his song 'It says here':

'...If this does not reflect your view you should understand that those who own the papers also own this land and they'd rather you believe in Coronation Street capers in the war for circulation, it sells newspapers. Could it be an infringement of the freedom of the press to print pictures of women in states of undress.'

Under this theory, New Labour's re-branding under Blair might have had the effect of making it more acceptable to the dominant elite and, therefore, worthy of support in the face of a divided and unstable Conservative Party.

Hegemonic theory

The people who edit and write in newspapers and those involved in broadcast journalism have a particular view due to their education, age, social class etc. They write, therefore, from a particular perspective – however unconscious their bias might be.

Pluralist theory

There is a range of media output, and individuals choose what to read and what to watch based upon their own outlook and interests. The media, therefore, reflects opinion rather than shaping it. At best the media probably only reinforces views that the reader already has.

Media bias?

The press

Newspapers are not legally required to be impartial and most, if not all, take up clear party positions during election campaigns. *The Sun* was particularly vocal in support of the Conservatives in the 1992 general election, coming up with such memorable headlines as 'Will the last person to leave Britain please turn out the lights?' when a Labour victory appeared likely. Both Neil Kinnock (the then Labour leader) and Norman Tebbit (a former leading Conservative) believed that the tabloid press had been crucial in achieving the surprise Conservative victory in that year. The paper's owner, Rupert Murdoch, was courted by New Labour in the run-up to the 1997 general election and *The Sun* eventually backed Labour. Paul Whiteley has estimated that this switch in support cost the Conservatives around 500 000 votes in the election and this might well have made the difference in key marginals.

Broadcasting

The BBC and the ITC (Independent Television Commission) control broadcasting. The former controls public channels (for example, BBC1, BBC2, and Radio 1, 2, 3 and 4) the latter controls private stations. Under the terms of the BBC's Royal Charter and the Television and Broadcasting Acts, the BBC and ITC are supposed to remain politically impartial. This partly reflects the influence credited to broadcast material as opposed material published in the press. What this impartiality means in practice is that the various channels have to ensure that they are giving fair coverage. They should give the major parties a right to reply when running stories or interviewing ministers and should not give one party or another a disproportionate share of the air-time. Channels are also required to broadcast quality news coverage and provide slots for party political broadcasts. These are demands not made of the press. Despite all of this there are almost constant allegations of bias in the media from one party or another. BBC Radio 4's Today Programme, for example, is often criticised for the vehemence of its presenters' attacks on government ministers. It is also important to remember that while legislation might outlaw bias against a party, it does not account for the perhaps unconscious bias towards a particular class or region.

Press ownership

Despite the strengthening of anti-monopoly legislation in the 1990s, media moguls such as Rupert Murdoch still have massive concentrations of media power. Murdoch himself for example controls *The Sun*, the *News of the World* and *The Times*, as well as the BSkyB network.

How influential is the media?

Writers such as the American psychologist Festinger (in the 1950s) and David Denver (in the 1980s) argued that media influence was limited by three processes:

Selective exposure

Individuals generally choose to expose themselves to newspapers and television programmes that reflect rather than challenge their outlook.

Selective perception

Individuals mentally edit the media that they are exposed to, filtering out content that doesn't fit in with their own ideas.

Selective retention

People tend to forget programme and newspaper content that challenges the views that they hold, while retaining material that can be used to justify their position.

'Filters'

Individuals, it is argued, view media output through filters – different filters being applied to different types of material. Some argue that television is so powerful because people believe what they see – their filters are effectively down when watching television. When reading newspapers, however, they are expecting bias and their filters are up.

5.6 Opinion polls

What are opinion polls?

Opinion polls are surveys of public opinion on specific issues. They are most visible at election times when the major polling companies (Gallup, Harris, ICM, MORI and NOP) question the voting intentions of sample groups. These sample groups are selected with the aim of creating a cross-section of the electorate in a sample of perhaps 1000 individuals. The sampling methods used are critical because errors in sampling can greatly reduce the accuracy of the poll. Even with a reasonable sample of 1000, pollsters normally allow a margin of error of plus or minus 3%. In 1997 ten out of 15 final polls were within the margin of error and in 2001 some of the companies produced extremely accurate results. According to Duncan Watts, ICM (for *The Guardian*) had an average error of only 0.55%. Polls were similarly impressive in 2005. Errors **up to** 1992 are shown below – poor polling accuracy **in** 1992 is explained to the right.

Polling error in elections 1979–1992			
1979	1983	1987	1992
2.4%	3.6%	4%	8.9%

'Bandwagons' and 'boomerangs'

In some countries (France, for example) opinion polls are banned in the days leading up to elections for fear that they might influence voting intentions. Some believe that voters are more likely to vote for parties that are doing well in the polls (the so-called 'bandwagon effect'); others argue that there is in fact a 'boomerang effect'. This is where people vote for parties that are doing badly in the polls because they see them as the underdogs or, more likely, don't turn out to vote because the polls show their party well ahead.

Party polls and focus groups

Part of the remodelling of Labour under Blair was the opening of the new campaign and media centre at Millbank Tower. Millbank became synonymous with all that was spin and control during the first term of the Labour Administration. A lot of the work of those working in and around Millbank was informed by findings from the organised polls. Millbank organised specialised task forces to bring together the polling data upon which decisions and presentational approaches could be based. Focus groups were also central to the new strategy. Focus groups consist of a small number of individuals brought together to consider particular issues. Sometimes these groups are asked to respond to certain policies. In the US such groups are used extensively in pre-screenings of party election broadcasts and this is now becoming more common practice in Britain.

Exit polls

Exit polls are different from the ordinary polls conducted during the election campaigns. Rather than asking people how they intend to vote, exit polls ask people how they have voted. In theory, this should make them more accurate and this accuracy should be augmented by the fact that exit polls often use a far larger sample and, therefore, have a far smaller margin of error. This said, it is not necessarily the case that voters are prepared to tell the truth in such circumstances. In 2005, the BBC's exit poll came within a couple of seats of predicting the actual Labour majority of 65.

Tactical voting

Many have argued that opinion poll findings can cause an increase in tactical voting. Where polls, for example, show the Liberal Democrats a distant third and the Labour candidate in with a reasonable chance of unseating a Conservative MP, a LibDem voter might be more inclined to vote Labour tactically. Michael Portillo believed that his loss in Enfield in 1997 was partly the result of poll findings.

Opinion polls and the 1992 general election

The 1992 general election was a low point for most of the polling companies. For whatever reason, they got it very wrong indeed. The average predicted lead for Labour of 1.3% was not even close to the eventual 7.6% Conservative lead. Given the cost of commissioning such opinion polls (Harris claimed £200 000 from ITN alone during the 1992 campaign), such inaccuracy was a major disappointment and brought into question the very worth of such polls.

What went wrong?

Respondents not registered

Part of the problem in 1992 was that some of those being asked the questions (the 'respondents') were not registered to vote. This was made worse by the fact that such non-registration might have been more prevalent amongst potential Labour voters. Some Labour supporters had not registered to vote for fear of being tracked down and forced to pay the 'Poll Tax'.

Respondents lying

For whatever reason, some respondents were clearly not telling the truth. When asked which policies were the priorities, the majority offered health care. When asked which party would deal most effectively with problems in health care, the majority said Labour – yet the majority did not vote Labour. It has been suggested that people were too embarrassed to admit publicly that they were going to vote Conservative.

Respondents unrepresentative

Sampling errors, and samples that were too small or inappropriate, meant that some surveys were doomed from the start.

Respondents 'floating'

There was clearly a 'late swing' to the Conservatives. Was this perhaps due to a large number of floating/undecided voters?

5.7 Recent general elections

Introduction

Some have argued that the similarity in the general election results of 1997, 2001 and even 2005 (where only 62 seats changed hands) demonstrates the underlying stability in voting behaviour. The headline figures, given below, would certainly appear to support such a view. Others, however, maintain that both class and party dealignment remain the norm and that the similarity in the headline results masks enormous volatility amongst the electorate with millions of voters switching their allegiances and many more simply staying at home in 2001 and 2005.

The 2001 General Election

Context

Having won a landslide victory in 1997, the 2001 general election offered the promise, failing a massive swing to the Conservatives, of a second consecutive term in office for Labour. The Government had faced problems in the run up to the election – with the fuel protests and the foot and mouth crisis – but the Conservative Party was still well behind in the polls by the time of the election. Though those on the left criticised the Labour Government for failing to deliver a radical agenda, it was difficult to see where else their votes could be cast to good effect.

Voting behaviour

There was some movement in terms of class support (see below and left) and the high levels of tactical voting seen in 1997 were repeated. Indeed, some MPs who were only just elected in 1997 were returned with far larger majorities in 2001 as a result of the campaign to 'keep the Tories out'. A key feature of the election was the low turnout – the lowest since 1918.

Class	Con	Lab	LibDem
AB	40 (−2)	33 (+2)	21 (0)
C1	33 (+7)	40 (−7)	21 (+2)
C2	29 (+4)	47 (−7)	17 (+3)
DE	28 (+7)	49 (−12)	17 (+4)

Issues and events

As a whole, the 2001 campaign was lacklustre. The Conservatives characterised the vote as the 'last chance to save the pound' and were widely adjudged to have overestimated the electorate's interest in the issue – particularly in light of the referendum on the currency promised by all major parties prior to any UK entry into the euro-zone. The enduring images of the campaign were of Tony Blair being confronted outside a hospital by the angry partner of a patient and of the scuffle between the Deputy Prime Minister and a farm worker that led to *The Sun* updating John Prescott's nickname from 'two Jags' to 'two Jabs'.

Media coverage

The Sun stuck with Labour, having switched its support from the Tories in 1997. Many newspapers, including *The Independent*, offered advice on how and where to vote tactically. New media, in the form of vote-swapping websites, also made an impression, though more as a discussion point than in terms of seats won or lost.

Results

Party	% UK votes	Seats won
Conservative	31.7	166
Labour	40.7	413
Liberal Democrat	18.3	52
Plaid Cymru and SNP	9.3%	9
Others*		19
Turnout (UK) 59.4% (−11.8%)		

*Northern Ireland Parties + Independents

The 2005 General Election

Campaigns

Compared to 1997 and 2001, Labour's campaign was rather **negative**: reminding voters of Michael Howard's past ('cut services', Poll Tax, Clause 28). In the last week of the campaign Labour warned of how voting for the LibDems might let the Conservatives back in. The Conservative Party's 2005 Campaign, orchestrated by Australian consultant **Lynton Crosby** (the Party's General Election Campaign Director) was far slicker than in 2001. The LibDems made a good deal of the benefits that LibLab coalition government had brought to Scotland.

Issues

Crosby succeeded in shifting the whole campaigning period onto core issues such as **immigration** and **law and order**. The Party avoided the mistake of focusing entirely on Europe; as Hague had in 2001 over the Euro. Both Labour and the Conservatives argued that they could provide better services and tax less. LibDems played on issues such as public services, local taxation and Iraq.

Voting behaviour

The 2005 General Election saw both Labour and the Conservatives losing support amongst AB voters to the Liberal Democrats. The Election also saw the Conservatives gain support amongst the C2s who had backed the Party in the 1980s (**working class Tories**). Women favoured Labour (38%:32%), but the male vote split evenly (34%:34%).

% VOTES BY CLASS 2005 (2001)				
PARTY	**AB**	**C1**	**C2**	**DE**
Labour	28 (−5)	32 (−8)	40 (−7)	48 (−1)
Conservative	37 (−3)	36 (+3)	33 (+4)	25 (−3)
Lib Dem	29 (+8)	23 (+2)	19 (+2)	18 (+1)

Results

Party	% votes	MPs
Conservative	32.3%	192
Labour	35.2%	355
Liberal Democrat	22.1%	62
Plaid Cymru and SNP	10.4%	9
Others (NI and Indep.)		22
Turnout (UK) 61.5% (+2.1%)		

'Labour polled 9.5 million votes. That is equivalent to 35.2% of the total, the lowest share of the vote ever recorded for a winning party at a UK General Election and 5.5% points lower than in 2001. It is equivalent to 21.6% of the electorate, again a record low for a winning party.'
House of Commons Research Paper 05/33

6.1 The origins and development of the British party system

Introduction

Political parties have a long history in Britain, but modern mass political parties have their origins in the waves of electoral reform, starting in 1832, that extended the franchise (right to vote). Before the 1830s the two parties – the Whigs and the Tories – existed not as mass political parties with formal institutions outside Parliament and a mass membership, but merely as groups of like-minded individuals within Parliament, bound together by ideas, friendship or family ties. With electoral reform, however, came a need to organise – to mobilise the (however slowly) expanding electorate in support of one's party. Certainly, by the time the Labour Party was formed at the start of the twentieth century, political parties were organisations that would be more familiar to anyone studying their modern counterparts.

Different types of party systems

It is often said that Britain operates as a two-party system. The truth or otherwise of this statement will be discussed below, but the statement itself does beg the question 'what other kinds of party systems exist?'

The two-party system	The single-party system	The dominant-party system	The multi-party system
Where a two-party system operates, two fairly equally matched parties compete for power. Smaller parties might also be involved in elections but they will have no realistic prospect of breaking the monopoly held by the big two.	In some countries a single party is able to monopolise government, ban other political parties and exercise total control over all candidates, where elections occur at all.	This system exists where many parties may exist but only one ever gets elected, or at least forms the senior member in a coalition government.	In a multi-party system many parties compete for power and the government will often pass between coalitions formed by different combinations of parties.
Britain is often cited as a two-party system (see debate below). The US would be another good example.	This type of system operated in the USSR and in many Eastern European states after the Second World War and in Nazi Germany.	In Japan the Liberal Democratic Party remained in power for 38 years following its formation in 1955.	Prior to electoral reform in 1993, Italy was often seen as a classic multi-party system. Israel is another good example.

Is Britain a two-party system?

YES

The Labour and Conservative Parties are the only parties that have a realistic chance of forming a government in the near future or being the senior partner in a coalition.

Even in the 2005 general election the Labour and Conservative Parties secured 67.5% of the popular vote and around 86% of the seats in Parliament.

Despite making progress, the third party (the Liberal Democrats) is still a long way behind the second party (the Conservatives), even when the latter is at one of its lowest ebbs.

There is a good deal of stability. The swing from Labour to Conservative was only 1.8% between 1997 and 2001 and the numbers of seats for each party hardly changed. Fewer than 30 seats changed hands. Even in 2005 only 62 seats changed hands.

NO

The Labour Party won 246 seats more than the Conservative Party in 2001, whereas the Conservative Party only won 114 seats more than the LibDems. Do we really have two parties capable of winning power?

32.5% of voters backed a party other than the big two in 2005, and the 86% share of seats gained by Labour and the Conservatives remains artificially exaggerated by the electoral system.

The rise of the Liberal Democrats as a third party ignores the fact that they are often second to Labour in the North and West and the Conservatives in the South and East.

Although there appears to be a good deal of stability in the system, the raw figures mask a lot of localised swing (differential swing) as well as a massive fall in turnout since 1997. A party that could mobilise the 41% of the population who chose not to vote in 2001 could clearly break the two-party system.

Could Britain become a multi-party system?

Many of the countries said to have multi-party systems have electoral systems more geared towards creating multi-party outcomes. It is no coincidence that countries that abandon PR systems (Italy, for example) often see a decline in minor party support. The introduction of PR in Britain could, therefore, bring about a multi-party system where coalition government would become the norm – though even in countries such as Ireland (using STV) they could not be said to have a true multi-party system. It could also be argued that we already have a three-party system or (more accurately) three two-party systems in different constituencies: Labour v. Conservative, Labour v. LibDem, and Conservative v. LibDem. In other areas we see genuine three-way races and in some Scottish constituencies four-way races, where the Conservatives are the outside bet.

6.2 The Conservative Party

The origins of the party

The Conservative Party emerged from the Tory Party in the 1830s. Many date its birth to Robert Peel's Tamworth Manifesto in 1834. In the twentieth century, the Party was in office (either alone or in coalition) for 67 years and enjoyed two extended periods in office: 1951–64 under Churchill, Eden, Macmillan and Home, and 1979–97 under Thatcher and then Major. During the latter period, in particular, the Conservative administrations brought massive changes to government, the economy and society as a whole. This period also saw the Party move away from its consensual post-war 'one-nation Tory' position to a more neo-liberal 'New Right' approach.

The policy-making process

The party leader has the major role in policy-making within the Party, though the leader is expected to take some notice of the views of backbenchers (represented by the 1922 Committee), party elders, members of the front bench and the broader membership. The 'Fresh Future' initiative launched by William Hague following the 1997 general election defeat was supposed to make policy-making more inclusive. Two new bodies – the National Conservative Convention and the Conservative Political Forum – were formed, but both remained merely advisory. Hague did make use of ballots of the members to endorse his policies but – as is the case with referendums generally – these votes were all on issues and at times chosen by Hague, where he could feel confident of success.

Conservative landmarks

1830 Conservative Party emerges
1867 National Union established
1870 Central Office established
1923 The 1922 Committee formally established to co-ordinate and articulate views of backbench Conservative MPs
1951–64 Conservatives in office
1975 Margaret Thatcher defeats Edward Heath in leadership election
1979–97 Conservatives in office
1990 Thatcher fails to secure sufficient votes in first ballot of leadership election over Heseltine. Resigns. John Major becomes leader/PM
1992 Election victory
1995 Major survives John Redwood's leadership challenge
1997 Worst election defeat for 165 years. Major resigns and is replaced by William Hague
1999 Party wins European elections
2001 General election defeat. Hague resigns. Iain Duncan Smith elected as new leader.
2003 Michael Howard's 'coronation' as Conservative leader following Iain Duncan Smith's resignation.
2005 General Election defeat. Howard announces his intention to stand down and initiates a debate over possible changes to the system under which party leaders are chosen. Howard's proposals for changes to the system are rejected. The contest to replace him takes place under the system in place since 2001 (see left).
2005 (December) David Cameron defeats David Davis in the ballot to become the new party leader.

Choosing the party leader and parliamentary candidates (2001–2005)

Choosing the party leader

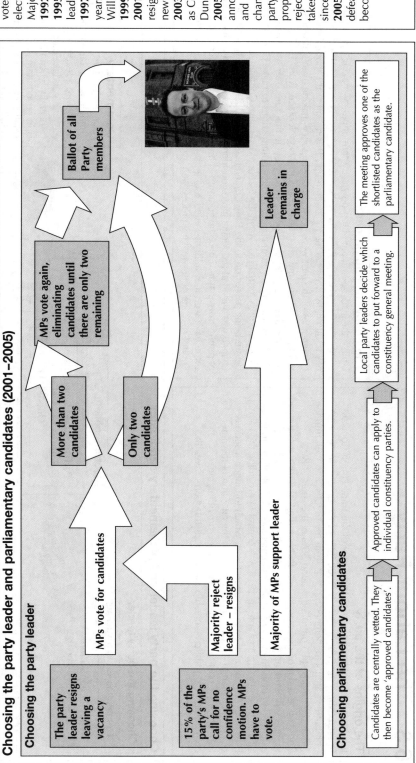

The party leader resigns leaving a vacancy

15% of the party's MPs call for no confidence motion. MPs have to vote.

MPs vote for candidates

Majority reject leader – resigns

Majority of MPs support leader

More than two candidates

Only two candidates

MPs vote again, eliminating candidates until there are only two remaining

Ballot of all Party members

Leader remains in charge

Choosing parliamentary candidates

Candidates are centrally vetted. They then become 'approved candidates'.

Approved candidates can apply to individual constituency parties.

Local party leaders decide which candidates to put forward to a constituency general meeting.

The meeting approves one of the shortlisted candidates as the parliamentary candidate.

6.3 The Labour Party

The origins of the party

It is important not to underestimate the role of the Trade Union Congress in establishing the Labour Party. In 1900 94% of the Labour Representation Committee's affiliated membership was from the unions, and well into the 1990s the unions still controlled around 80% of the votes at Party Conference and provided over 80% of Party funding. The Party was formed to represent working people at a time when the franchise was being extended to include many of its potential members. The decision to give all adult men the right to vote in 1918 was central in providing the Labour Party with the potential base of support from which to launch a serious electoral challenge. This also coincided with the adoption of the new Labour Party Constitution with its Clause Four, providing clear commitments to public ownership and the redistribution of wealth.

The policy-making process

Unlike the leader-dominated ('top-down') system of policy-making operating within the Conservative Party, the policy-making process in the Labour Party has traditionally been decidedly 'bottom-up'. This meant that Labour Party Conferences of the past were often genuinely policy-making events at which serious discussions and often heated arguments took place. From 1997, however, the Party adopted a policy-making cycle that runs over two years. The National Policy Forum appoints policy commissions to make proposals which are then formalised within the National Executive Committee (NEC) before being passed on to the Party Conference for final approval. Though this change was aimed at producing more considered policy and avoiding the kind of public rows that had become common at the Annual Party Conferences, some have seen it as a thinly-veiled attempt by the leadership to gain a greater control over the policy-making process and avoid nasty surprises.

Labour landmarks

1900 The Labour Representative Committee is formed.

1906 LRC becomes the Labour Party

1918 New Constitution including Clause Four

1945 Landslide election victory sees Clement Attlee elected as head of first Labour majority government

1975 Holds (to date) only national referendum on continued EEC membership

1979 Callaghan loses election to Thatcher. Foot eventually replaces Callaghan as leader

1981 Gang of Four leave to form the SDP

1983 Kinnock replaces Foot as leader

1992 Election loss. Smith replaces Kinnock

1993 OMOV established

1994 Smith dies, Blair becomes leader.

1995 Clause Four abolished

1997 and 2001 General election victories.

2001 (December), Labour MP Paul Marsdon defected to LibDems.

2003 (September), Brent East by-election. Labour lose seat to LibDems.

2005 General Election victory.

2007 Blair steps down as leader and is replaced by Gordon Brown, unopposed.

Choosing the party leader and parliamentary candidates

Choosing the party leader

Nomination to fill a vacancy

While in opposition
12.5% of Parliamentary Party (PLP)

While in government
20% of PLP

To challenge an incumbent

While in opposition
20% of PLP

While in government
20% of PLP
+ two-thirds Annual Conference.

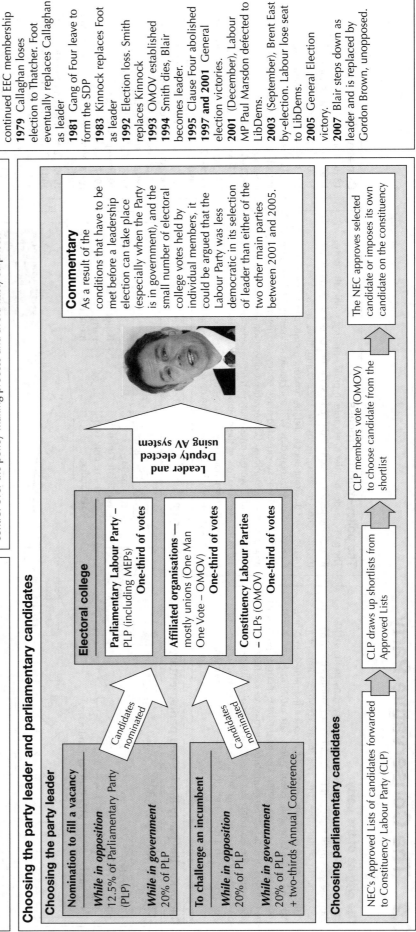

Electoral college

Parliamentary Labour Party – PLP (including MEPs)
One-third of votes

Candidates nominated

Affiliated organisations — mostly unions (One Man One Vote – OMOV)
One-third of votes

Candidates nominated

Constituency Labour Parties – CLPs (OMOV)
One-third of votes

Leader and Deputy elected using AV system

Commentary

As a result of the conditions that have to be met before a leadership election can take place (especially when the Party is in government), and the small number of electoral college votes held by individual members, it could be argued that the Labour Party was less democratic in its selection of leader than either of the two other main parties between 2001 and 2005.

Choosing parliamentary candidates

NEC's Approved Lists of candidates forwarded to Constituency Labour Party (CLP)

CLP draws up shortlists from Approved Lists

CLP members vote (OMOV) to choose candidate from the shortlist

The NEC approves selected candidate or imposes its own candidate on the constituency

6.4 The Liberal Democrats

The origins of the party

The Liberal Party had been the main party of government in the early twentieth century but was, by some distance, the third party by the middle of the century – rarely polling more than 10% of the vote. The SDP, in contrast, was formed as a result of the decision of leading Labour politicians to leave the Party in 1981. Roy Jenkins, David Owen, Bill Rogers and Shirley Williams (collectively known as the Gang of Four) launched the SDP with their Limehouse Declaration of that year. With the Labour Party in disarray, the SDP formed an electoral alliance with the Liberals (the SDP–Liberal Alliance) in 1983 and rode high in the polls. They secured 25.4% of the popular vote yet only gained 23 seats in Parliament. Following a similarly disappointing return for the Alliance in 1987, the parties merged in 1988 to form the Social and Liberal Democrats with Paddy Ashdown elected as leader. The following year the party renamed itself the Liberal Democrats. Charles Kennedy became leader in 1999.

The policy-making process

The Party is federal in structure comprising English, Scottish and Welsh State Parties. The State Parties are further subdivided into tiers (England has four, Scotland and Wales three each). Policies that only affect the area covered by one level of the Party would be dealt with at the appropriate level. Thus, a policy only affecting Scotland would be dealt with at a conference organised by the Scottish State Party. The English State Party has delegated its policy-making power to the Party's Federal Conference. The Federal Conference (meeting twice a year) is the supreme policy-making body in the Party but limits itself to dealing with policies that affect the UK as a whole (or England alone). The Conference deals with policy proposals from the Federal Policy Committee, State, regional and local parties. Once accepted, proposals become Party policy. The Party leadership has a good deal of control over the Federal Policy Committee and, therefore, policy.

LibDem landmarks

1922 Liberals out of government. Labour becomes main opposition party

1977–78 LibLab pact

1981 The Social Democratic Party (SDP) formed by Labour dissidents (see left)

1983 Liberal/SDP Alliance wins 25.4% of votes in General election but only secure 23 seats

1987 Alliance secures 23% of votes but only 22 seats

1988 Alliance parties merge to form Social and Liberal Democrats

1989 Renamed Liberal Democrats

1992 18% votes, 20 seats

1997 17% votes, 46 seats

1999 Kennedy succeeds Ashdown. LibLab coalition in Scotland

2000 LibLab coalition in Wales

2001 Party secures 52 seats in general election (18% votes)

2005 62 seats (22% votes) in General Election.

2006 Charles Kennedy steps down amid allegations of excessive drinking. Menzies Campbell becomes leader.

2007 Nick Clegg elected leader following Campbell's resignation.

Choosing the party leader and parliamentary candidates

Choosing the party leader

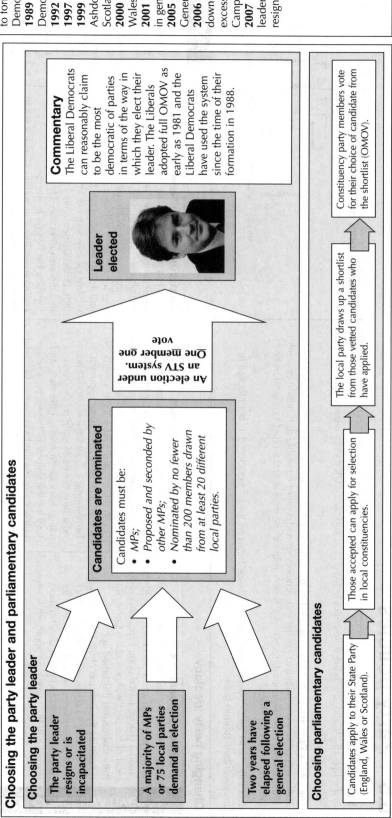

The party leader resigns or is incapacitated

A majority of MPs or 75 local parties demand an election

Two years have elapsed following a general election

Candidates are nominated

Candidates must be:
- MPs;
- *Proposed and seconded by other MPs;*
- *Nominated by no fewer than 200 members drawn from at least 20 different local parties.*

An election under an STV system.
One member one vote

Leader elected

Commentary

The Liberal Democrats can reasonably claim to be the most democratic of parties in terms of the way in which they elect their leader. The Liberals adopted full OMOV as early as 1981 and the Liberal Democrats have used the system since the time of their formation in 1988.

Choosing parliamentary candidates

Candidates apply to their State Party (England, Wales or Scotland).

Those accepted can apply for selection in local constituencies.

The local party draws up a shortlist from those vetted candidates who have applied.

Constituency party members vote for their choice of candidate from the shortlist (OMOV).

6.5 Party policies

Introduction

In the late 1970s and 1980s the differences between the two major UK parties were relatively plain to see (see right).

The Labour Party, which had been founded by the unions and socialist societies at the start of the 20th century, was committed to greater state ownership and a more equitable distribution of wealth. The Conservatives, in contrast, favoured a greater role for the market and tended to appeal more to those on higher incomes.

From the mid-1990s onwards, however, the divide between the parties closed as both looked to broaden their support base.

The traditional political spectrum

left wing — communist — Green? — 'old' Labour? — LibDems? — Conservative? — BNP? — fascist — right wing

centre

Changing party ideology

CONSERVATIVES

Traditional positions

UK Conservatism was traditionally associated with pragmatism and a belief in the worth of gradual change based upon experience. For most of the post-war period the Conservative Party maintained this broad approach, supporting the creation of the Welfare State under Attlee's Labour administration. Such 'One Nation Tories' accepted the need for cooperation between politicians, business leaders and the unions; an approach known as 'corporatism' or 'tripartism'.

The rise of Thatcherism

Under Margaret Thatcher's leadership, the Conservative Party moved away from its pragmatic position towards an approach that was rather more ideological. Thatcher accepted most of the New Right agenda. She adopted a broadly neo-liberal approach, championing a monetarist economic policy and a programme of rapid privatisation; 'rolling back the frontiers of the state' and attacking the unions as 'the enemies within'. Thatcher also pursued a conservative agenda in social policy.

Cameron and the New Tories

The Thatcher years left the Party divided between the 'Iron Lady's' acolytes – the Thatcherites – and those who looked more towards the 'One Nation Tory' model. The four leaders who followed Thatcher were all individuals who accepted her ideas or had worked closely with her in government. The fifth, David Cameron, looked to take the Party in a different direction. He sought to make the Party the natural home for environmentalists – as well as reaching out to those on lower incomes.

LABOUR

Traditional positions

The Labour Party was founded along socialist lines. Clause 4 of its 1918 Constitution committed the Party to working towards a more equitable distribution of wealth based upon need. Attlee's Labour administration, which took office in 1945, established the idea of a Welfare State that would provide care 'from the cradle to the grave', that would be open to all, and would be free at the point of delivery. Such positions reflected and perpetuated Labour's core support amongst the working classes.

Labour in the early 1980s

Labour's defeat in the 1979 General Election brought internal party divisions to the fore. Those on the left believed that the reason for Labour's ejection from office – following the Winter of Discontent and a lost vote of confidence – was that it had lost touch with its roots. Those on the right, in contrast, felt that the Party needed to modernise. Left wingers were able to install Michael Foot as leader and the Party went into the 1983 election on a manifesto widely described as 'the longest suicide note in history'. Many of those on the right had by then left to form the SDP.

The emergence of New Labour

By the time that Tony Blair was elected as Labour leader, following the death of John Smith, the Party had faced four consecutive general election defeats. Blair had a clear mandate to modernise the Party. He took Labour away from its socialist roots, abolishing the old Clause 4 in 1995, and tried to appeal to middle-class voters by accepting the principle of capitalism and the role of the market. The Party also promised to accept Conservative spending plans, if elected, thus distancing themselves from the tax-and-spend approach of earlier Labour administrations.

The end of ideology?

The extent to which the two main UK parties were coalescing around the centre ground by 2008 led to renewed speculation that the UK was entering a post-ideological age. The fact that both parties were increasingly similar in their core policies was apparent even in the 2005 General Election.

Conservative pledges in 2005
- Lower Taxes
- Improve School Discipline
- Clean up Hospitals
- Put more Police on the Streets
- Control Immigration

Labour pledges in 2005
- Your Family Better Off
- Your Family Treated Better and Faster
- Your Child Achieving More
- Your Country's Borders Safer
- Your Community Safer
- Your Children with the Best Start

With Blair (ultimately Brown) and Cameron in charge in 2007, the difference between the two was smaller still; at least in terms of core economic and social policy.

6.6 Minor parties

Introduction

Mainstream political parties generally have the belief that they might eventually secure enough votes to win the seats necessary to carry them into government. Even the Liberal Democrats – who won only 62 seats in the 2005 general election – can imagine a time when they have built up enough of a parliamentary party to allow them to form an administration or, at least, become the minor party in a coalition government following an inconclusive election. There are, however, a great number of political parties who have no real hope of becoming part of a government or even returning a single MP. Such parties may use elections as a way of applying pressure to mainstream political parties or providing media exposure for what will inevitably be less mainstream ideas. There are also those nationalist parties who only stand in their respective areas and, therefore, have no ambition to secure control of Parliament.

Nationalist parties

Some of the largest minor parties are not, in fact, minor in the areas in which they operate. In Scotland, Wales and Northern Ireland parties unique to each area operate with considerable success.

The Scottish National Party (SNP)

Introduction

The Party was formed in 1934 and has the central aim of achieving an independent Scotland. It campaigned for a 'yes, yes' vote in the 1997 Referendum – supporting the creation of a devolved parliament with tax varying powers.

The Party was kept out of government by the LibLab coalition in place between 1999 and 2007. However, the SNP formed a minority administration in 2007.

General election performance

Year	% votes [1]	MPs (659)
1992	21.5	3
1997	22.1	6
2001	20.1	5
2005	17.7	6

Scottish Parliament election

Year	MSPs (129)
1999	35
2003	27
2007	47

(1) NB % of votes in Scotland

Plaid Cymru

Introduction

The Party was formed in 1925 and has the central aim of achieving an independent Wales as well as encouraging Welsh culture and, in particular, the use of the Welsh Language.

The Party supported the 'yes' campaign in the 1997 Referendum but has been excluded from the administration by the Labour and LibLab administration in power between 1999 and 2007. In 2007 Plaid entered a coalition with Labour.

General election performance

Year	% votes [2]	MPs (659)
1992	8.9	4
1997	9.9	4
2001	14.3	4
2005	12.6	3

Welsh Assembly election

Year	MWA (60)
1999	17
2003	12
2007	15

(2) NB % of votes in Wales

The Green Party

The Green Party is often remembered for its impressive showing in the 1989 European elections – securing 15% of the votes, though winning no seats. In the 1999 European elections, under a more proportional electoral system, the Party secured 6.3% of the votes and returned two MEPs, a result they repeated in 2004. Some argue that the group is more pressure group than party.

Fascist parties

The National Front (NF) was founded in 1967 and was claiming the support of about 20 000 members within 10 years. The British National Party (BNP) was born out of the NF split in the 1980s and has continued to campaign vigorously in elections – particularly in urban areas with significant ethnic minority populations. In the 2001 general election the BNP gained significant numbers of votes in a number of North-Western constituencies. In Oldham West, for example, BNP leader Nick Griffin gained 16.4% of the vote, claiming third place ahead of the Liberal Democrats. In Oldham East the BNP secured 11% of the vote. In 2005, their support increased in other areas, achieving 0.7% of the vote nationally and 16.9% of the vote in Barking. The Party has also achieved success in local elections. In 1993 their candidate Derek Beackon won a local council by-election in Tower Hamlets. In the 2002 local elections the Party won three council seats in Burnley. This success in local elections, particularly in the North West, continued through to 2005. In 2008 BNP candidate Richard Barnbrook won a seat on the Greater London Assembly and the Party secured 5.3% of the vote in the Mayoral contest.

Other minor parties

There are numerous other minor party candidatures. The UK Independence Party (UKIP), for example, won 16.1% of the votes in the 2004 European elections, enough to win them 12 seats under the regional list system. They also gave creditable performances in the 1997, 2001 and 2005 general elections. James Goldsmith's Referendum Party averaged 3.1% of the vote in each of the 547 seats where it stood in the 1997 general election. The anti-abortion ProLife Alliance (formed by Bruno Quintsvalle) put up 53 candidates in 1997 (securing 18 545 votes nationally) and 37 candidates in 2001 (9453 votes nationally). All 90 candidates lost their deposits. The Party did not put up candidates in 2005.

	CONSERVATIVES	LABOUR	LIBDEMS
POLICY MAKING	As in the case with the Labour Party, recent years have witnessed the emergence of a number of policy forums and other bodies which give the impression of a greater role for individual members. The reforms, introduced by William Hague in 1998, appear to be in stark contrast with what went before; where Party policy was largely decided by the leader of the day in consultation with senior colleagues and advisors. In reality, however, little has changed. Though the Party's 2001 Manifesto appeared to have been the product of greater consultation, the Policy Forum was downgraded under Iain Duncan-Smith and the 2005 Manifesto was largely decided by Michael Howard.	The Party Conference traditionally had the responsibility for making policy. From 1997, however, the Party adopted a two-year rolling policy cycle which in theory gave members the right to set up local policy forums. In reality, however, the introduction of the new process was seen more as a way of avoiding the nasty surprises and public shows of disunity common at earlier Conferences. Critics have argued that the reforms have seen the Conference transformed from being the sovereign policy-making body, to little more than a rubber stamp for policies agreed elsewhere.	The Party operates under a federal structure. What this means in practice is that policy that will only affect Scotland, for example, will be developed by the Scottish State Party and confirmed at the Conference of that Party. Policies affecting England and the whole of the UK are dealt with at the main national conference – the Federal Conference – which meets twice-yearly. This Conference is the supreme policy-making body of the Party but it spends most of its time considering proposals from the Federal Policy Committee. As a result, senior figures in the Party have a good deal of control over what is discussed at the Federal Conference.
CANDIDATE SELECTION	Those wishing to become prospective parliamentary candidates for the Party must first get their names onto an approved list by attending a formal interview. They can then apply to Constituency Associations. If shortlisted, their fate is then decided at a Constituency General Meeting. Before 1997, Conservative Central Office rarely got involved in the process by which local Constituency Associations selected their parliamentary candidates. However, under William Hague the Party's new Ethics and Integrity Committee was given a role in vetting candidates selected by local Associations.	Those wishing to become prospective parliamentary candidates for the Party must first get their names onto the National Executive Committee's (NEC) approved list. This list is forwarded to Constituency Labour Parties (CLPs) who draw up a shortlist from those approved candidates who have applied. Constituency Party members then select their preferred candidate under one-member-one-vote (OMOV). The NEC can impose its own choice of candidate, even where the CLP has already made a selection. The choice of members has also been limited by the introduction of all-women shortlists in many safer seats.	Those wishing to become prospective parliamentary candidates for the Party must first apply to their State Party (England, Scotland or Wales). Those who pass this vetting procedure and become approved candidates can then apply to individual constituencies for selection. Those candidates shortlisted by the Constituency Party go forward to a ballot of all party members in the constituency in question.
CHOOSING LEADERS	The current system for electing Conservative leaders was introduced under William Hague's leadership, with his successor Iain Duncan-Smith the first Party Leader elected under the new system in 2001. Under the system, Conservative MPs hold a series of ballots, eliminating the lowest placed candidate at each stage, until there are only two candidates remaining. Individual members are then invited to choose between these two candidates in a secret ballot. Though this system appears democratic, critics argue that those in Parliament can all too easily manipulate the choice presented to members.	The Party leader was once chosen by the Parliamentary Labour Party (PLP) alone, but since the 1980s it has operated under an electoral college system where 1/3 of the votes are cast by the PLP and MEPs, 1/3 by trade unions and the final 1/3 by ordinary members. Since 1993, with the reform of the union block vote, such contests have operated under OMOV. Though this system is obviously far more democratic than that which went before it, individual members still have a fairly limited influence.	The method by which the Liberal Democrats elect their leader gives individuals a far greater say than under those systems used by either Labour or the Conservatives. Candidates are nominated either by fellow MPs or by no fewer than 200 individual members drawn from at least 20 different local parties. Those nominated are the subject to a ballot by all members, conducted under a preferential, single transferable vote system.

Party finance

The Conservative Party traditionally relied upon donations from business. The Labour Party, in contrast, relied heavily on the trade union movement for its funding, with 96% of the Party's income coming from unions in 1983. However, the removal of the union block vote in the 1990s was accompanied by a reduction in union funding. As a result of this, and falling revenues from individual membership, Labour became more reliant on donations from businesses and wealthy individuals such as Formula 1 chief Bernie Ecclestone. The LibDems have traditionally relied far more on individual membership fees than either the Conservatives or Labour – though they have attracted more substantial donations from wealthy individuals in recent years. Some argue that party finance has a bearing on how democratic a party is – on the basis that 'he who pays the piper calls the tune'.

7.1   Definitions and classification

What are pressure groups?

Pressure groups are groups of like-minded individuals who campaign for their own interests and/or to achieve goals or pursue common causes. Pressure groups are significantly more numerous than political parties because they often fragment opinion whereas political parties tend to aggregate and accommodate with a view to being elected. Pressure groups do not generally seek election, but some groups do so as a way of raising public awareness, even though they have little realistic chance of being elected. In recent years such groups have included the Referendum Party and the ProLife Alliance. One exception to this rule is, perhaps, the election of a single-issue candidate in each of the last two general elections – Martin Bell as an anti-corruption candidate in Tatton in 1997, and Dr Richard Taylor as the Kidderminster Hospital and Health Concern candidate in Wyre Forrest in 2001.

Classifying pressure groups

Classification by aims

Sectional and cause groups

Early attempts to classify groups focused on who or what causes they represented.

Sectional groups...

represent the interests of a particular section of society. They are, therefore, sometimes referred to as sectoral, interest or protectionist groups. Membership of such groups is normally restricted to the groups whose interests they serve – for example, a teachers' union such as the NASUWT or the NUT will represent the interests of its members who will, for the most part, be practising teachers. The BMA, another good example of a sectional group, promotes the interest of the medical profession.

Cause groups...

campaign for a particular cause or objective. They are sometimes referred to as promotional groups. Unlike most sectional groups they seek a broader membership and do not necessarily stand to benefit individually from their campaigns.

Sectional cause groups...

protect a section of society. Shelter, for example, works on behalf of the homeless but its members are not all homeless.

Attitude cause groups...

aim to change people's attitudes on a particular issue. Greenpeace, for example, seeks to change attitudes on the environment.

Political cause groups...

aim to achieve certain political goals. The Chartists, for example, put forward their People's Charter in the nineteenth century.

Classification by strategy or status

Insider and outsider groups

Writers such as Wyn Grant have suggested that it is more helpful to classify groups according to their status in relation to the government.

Insider groups

Core insiders...

are those who have close two-way relationships with policy-makers over a broad range of issues (e.g. BMA, NFU).

Specialist insiders...

are more focused but have a large input within their area of expertise. They are trusted by government and provide reliable and authoritative expertise (e.g. WWF).

Peripheral insiders...

have insider status but have little real influence, due to the nature of their interest/cause. They are only rarely needed by government (e.g. the Canine Defence League).

Outsider groups

Potential insiders...

are groups that would ultimately like to attain insider status but have not achieved it due to, for example, the nature of their cause (e.g. Charter 88 before 1997) or inexperience.

Outsiders by necessity...

include single-issue and local groups who do not seek insider status, and those not afforded insider status; therefore outsider by necessity (e.g. CND).

Ideological outsiders...

do not want to become part of 'the system' because their objectives require outside status and with it full independence and freedom of action (e.g. anti-globalisation groups).

Problems with classifications

Both types of classification carry with them their problems. In attempting to distinguish between those that campaign for their own interests and those that campaign for a cause, the first model ignores the fact that many pressure groups do both. The teaching unions, for example, aim not only to serve their members' interests but also to support developments in education policy. The model also fails to consider the scale or status of groups. The insider/outsider model addresses some of these weaknesses but ignores the fact that many groups can operate both as insiders and outsiders to some extent, and that groups can move very quickly from outside to inside and vice versa, for example following elections. Charter 88 was clearly outside the political loop before the 1997 general election but has assumed more influence since Labour's victory. Wyn Grant suggests that the NFU's insider status is under threat.

7.2 Methods

'Traditional methods' (?)

There was a time when discussion of pressure group activity focused on letter-writing campaigns, petitions and marches. Such activities are clearly still worthy of note. The anti-abortion LIFE organisation, for example, compiled a petition of more than 2 000 000 names in the mid-1980s, organised a 'Mail MPs a Mountain' campaign in 1987 and employed postcard campaigns in 1989 and 1990 against the Human Fertilisation and Embryology Act. Marches against the 'Poll Tax' in the early 1990s and in support of the Countryside Alliance in recent years have also been influential. Clearly, however, we need to move beyond the anecdotal and impose some kind of structure on the discussion.

Pressure group tactics

Most major modern pressure groups adopt a variety of strategies in pursuit of their aims. There are, however, a number of obvious approaches.

Influencing the legislative process directly

Some groups have regular contact with government over a broad range of related issues. These 'core insider groups' have the ability to influence the formation of policy at an early stage through meetings with ministers, civil servants and government-appointed bodies working on legislative proposals. Beyond these core insiders are other groups who might be called in to give specialist information on a particular issue. This will normally take place where the group has a relevant expertise and information not readily available elsewhere and/or where the group represents a particular viewpoint or section of society likely to be directly affected by the measure. Consultation might take the form of informal discussions, or be more structured around a Green Paper. Many larger groups employ lobbyists to pursue their legislative goals and the richest groups maintain permanent offices close to Westminster.

Influencing political parties

Pressure groups can cultivate links with political parties with a view to influencing the formation of policy (see pages on individual parties for detail on policy formulation). When a party is in government this is likely to be harder to achieve because the government is likely to be subject to far greater demands on its time, and policy formation is likely to be more 'top-down'. The easiest time for pressure groups to gain a foothold within parties is when they are in opposition. At such a time the party will normally be looking to ground itself, take on board a variety of ideas, build up a broader base of support and formulate new policy. During Labour's lengthy period in opposition, groups such as Charter 88 and the Electoral Reform Society cultivated links with the Party. Such links have been important since the Labour victory in 1997.

Embarking on legal action

British courts do not have the same powers of judicial review open to the US Supreme Court. Legal action can still, however, be an effective pressure group tactic – if an expensive one. Such action can work on two levels. Firstly, where the court finds that the government has acted in a manner beyond the authority granted it, the court could find against that government. Secondly, such action raises public awareness of a particular issue and may, therefore, have positive outcomes for the group even where it/they loses the case. Bruno Quintsvalle's ProLife Alliance, for example, has taken legal action on a number of occasions recently; for example, using the Human Rights Act to try and prevent the separation of the conjoined twins Jodie and Mary, when it was clear that one of them (Mary) would die as a result of the procedure, and using legal action to highlight loopholes in the Human Fertilisation and Embryology Act that could allow reproductive human cloning. In both cases the group gained considerable press coverage.

Mobilising public pressure

Media manipulation

The media can often be used to good effect. Groups can employ **paid media**, taking out whole-page adverts in the national press, by using direct mail or by producing and airing adverts. During the 1997 general election the Referendum Party used newspaper advertisements to good effect and also produced a video, which it sent free of charge to millions of households. Established 'caring' charities have also made use of such tactics. Barnardo's has recently run a series of controversial magazine adverts depicting the fate of children that they might not be able to help. The NSPCC has used television advertising in its 'Full Stop' campaign against violence aimed at children. All of this said, there are even greater opportunities in **unpaid media**. By placing stories in the news (see Brent Spa) groups can get free air time and newspaper coverage. Organising stunts, marches or employing direct action techniques (see right) can attract such coverage.

Direct action

Direct action is an increasingly popular form of pressure group action. It starts from the premise that conventional methods of influencing policy are flawed and that more visible and direct protests – often involving illegal methods or violence – offer the best opportunity of success because they make the politicians take notice and can broaden public support. The anti-roads protests of recent years, the campaign against live animal exports, the campaigns against fox hunting and vivisection, and the fuel protest have all been seen to have some effect on policy or opinion.

Effectiveness

The effectiveness of pressure group activity is hard to gauge because if – as most people accept – insider groups have more influence than outsider groups, such groups are not likely to publicise the extent of their influence for fear of alienating the government and losing it. Equally, high-profile protests and stunts might appear impressive but only rarely succeed in changing policy. Even at the time of the fuel protests the Government chose to speak more to the Road Hauliers' Association than to those organising the protest.

7.3 The European dimension

Introduction

Many pressure groups, faced with national governments that are unsympathetic to their causes or interests, turn to the European arena. Under the European Communities Act that came into force in the UK in 1973, European law and regulations take precedence over national laws where the two are in conflict. In theory, therefore, pressure groups can force change on their national governments by effectively going over their heads. This route has proven particularly effective for groups whose causes or interests are heavily regulated by or affected by the European Union. In the broad areas of economic environmental policy, for example, the proliferation of Europe-wide regulation provides an opportunity for real influence not often afforded pressure groups at a national level. As the EU becomes more involved in aspects of common social policy and foreign and security policy, a greater range of UK pressure groups are likely to turn to Europe, when their resources allow it.

Qualified majority voting

QMV was brought in under the terms of the Single European Act (1986). Under QMV a single country is no longer able to veto (block) most measures alone. Before QMV, pressure groups were able to focus their attentions entirely on the domestic front in the knowledge that, if they convinced their national government, they would be able to block any European measures that affected the group's interests. Under QMV, however, it is necessary to build up a broader European support in order to block or indeed pass any measure. Under the Treaty of Nice (2001) QMV was extended into new areas.

Though QMV makes life more complicated, it does bring with it some real advantages. A group can, for example, now campaign for a measure affecting the UK in the knowledge that the UK government alone cannot prevent it from happening.

Environmental pressure groups and Europe

Environmental pressure groups have two good reasons to focus their attentions on Europe rather than solely on their national governments

- Environmental issues by definition do not respect national boundaries. It therefore makes more sense to deal with environmental issues at a European or international level than simply at a national level.

- The EU is already committed to environmental action and is therefore more sympathetic to the aims and objectives of many environmental pressure groups than are national governments.

On issues such as the improvement of water quality, environmental groups have made great progress. Many beaches in England, previously categorised as unfit for bathing due to sewage pollution, have been improved under pressure from the EU. The policy of awarding blue flags for clean beaches has also raised the public profile of the EU.

Environmental groups do, however, face major problems in getting to the root of the problem. Though environmental groups often come together as a **Eurogroup** (see right) to increase their 'punch', business interests remain better funded and better equipped to put their case than most environmentalists.

The practicalities of lobbying in Europe

Though lobbying in Europe provides clear benefits, it is not an avenue open to all groups. The scale of the EU means that there are many points of leverage where pressure can be applied. The most successful groups will, therefore, need the resources to make the most of these opportunities. A permanent EU office is the ideal, but not all groups can afford a permanent office in Brussels.

Eurogroups

The European Union consists of 27 member states, and Turkey, Croatia and Macedonia have been accepted as candidates. If pressure groups in each of these countries were to conduct their efforts in the European sphere independently, their voices might well be lost. As a result, like-minded pressure groups often aggregate their efforts, forming Eurogroups possessing sufficient resources and representing a large enough 'constituency' for their views to be heard. Having said this, the efforts of such Eurogroups are often hampered by internal divisions and difficulty in obtaining and deploying sufficient resources.

COPA-COGECA

The National Farmers Union (NFU) is a member of the Eurogroup COPA-COGECA. COPA is the umbrella organisation representing the main agricultural organisations in the EU. COGECA is the equivalent organisation for agricultural co-operatives. In 2005, COPA-COGECA had 69 member organisations, representing around 11 million farmers across the 25 EU member states.

Eurogroups and the European Commission

As we have already seen, the Commission has a role initiating legislation, making proposals upon which the other EU institutions can act. As a result, the Commission has a massive appetite for information and recognises Eurogroups as a legitimate source of information.

7.4 Factors affecting pressure group success

AIMS

Practical achievability?

The extent to which a group's aims are achievable, in a practical sense, will clearly have a bearing on whether or not it will ultimately be successful.

Groups which have a clearly defined and limited goal are far more likely to achieve measurable success that those whose aims are unrealistic or open ended, e.g. a group campaigning for improvements to a local children's play area will have more chance of success than one campaigning against globalisation.

Public receptivity?

The extent to which the broader public is receptive to a group's stated aims will obviously have a major bearing on whether or not that group's aims will be achievable.

E.g. The Snowdrop Campaign was able to secure its goal of a ban on all handguns in the wake of the deaths of 16 children and their teacher in the Dunblane Massacre (1996). In contrast, the Howard League for Penal Reform has found it more difficult to gain broad-based public support for their campaign to improve conditions in prisons.

RESOURCES

Human?

A group's chances of achieving its goals are greatly enhanced where its members possess the skills necessary to prepare and execute an effective campaign. Groups who have amongst their members web-designers, individuals with legal expertise, or experience in the world of public relations are particularly well placed to put their case.

E.g. Fathers 4 Justice was led by Matt O'Connor, an articulate and telegenic former marketing executive.

Material?

Money is obviously the most important material resource which a group can have at its disposal. This is because it affords a group the opportunity to buy in the skills and services which it cannot provide from within its own membership.

Even without large quantities of money, groups that possess other material resources (e.g. an office address, photocopying facilities, a domain name and an e-mail address) are obviously better placed to campaign than those that do not.

STATUS

Insider/outsider?

The way in which the government of the day views an individual group will obviously have a bearing on its chances of success. Under the insider/outsider typology developed by Wyn Grant and others, those groups which are granted a privileged insider status by government are far more likely to achieve their goals than those which are forced to operate outside of the policy-making loop. To a degree, the government's willingness to grant access may reflect the public mood (see above) but this is not always the case.

Specialism/authority?

Groups which emerge as a respected authority within their chosen field are more likely to gain access to government (see left) and therefore more likely to get a sympathetic hearing. This is because their specialism within a given area will make them an invaluable source of information for government; as well as a useful sounding-board when proposals are still at an embryonic stage, e.g. groups such as the RSPCA and RoSPA are in regular consultation with government as a result of their specialist knowledge.

METHODS

Traditional?

The ability to mobilise large numbers of members and supporters in more conventional forms of pressure group activity will clearly enhance a group's chances of persuading the government to act. This is because a government is more likely to respond to a group which appears to represent a significant proportion of the electorate. Traditional tactics such as marching have helped to bring about changes in the law (e.g. the replacement of the 'Poll Tax' in 1993), though mass protests do not always move the government (e.g. the Stop the War Coalition's march in February 2003).

Direct?

It is often argued that those groups using more direct tactics are far less likely to achieve their goals; for the simple reason that their decision to use such tactics often comes as a result of their failure to win the argument using more conventional means. In recent years, however, many groups have adopted more direct tactics at the outset, with some success, e.g. hunt saboteurs helped to pave the way for the Hunting Act (2004) and the fuel protests (2000) resulted in a short-term delay to the increase in fuel duty.

8.1 Sources

What is a constitution?

A constitution is a body of rules that defines the manner in which a state or society is organised. It sets out the way in which sovereign power is distributed between the government and the people, and between the government's constituent parts. In so doing, a constitution provides a framework upon which more complex rules, structures and processes can be built.

Codified and uncodified constitutions

Within the broad definition given above, it is possible to discern two styles of constitutions: those which consist of a full and authoritative set of rules written down in a single place (*codified* – for example, the US Constitution) and those which are less tangible, often having evolved over time and having become as much reliant on traditions and customs as any written documents (*uncodified* – for example, the UK Constitution). The fact that the UK Constitution is uncodified does not mean, however, that it is 'un-written'; some of its sources are indeed in written form. What then are the main sources of the UK Constitution?

Statute law

Acts of Parliament are referred to as statutes. Some of these statutes play a significant role in outlining the extent and distribution of government powers; the Parliament Acts of 1911 and 1949, for example, limit the power of the House of Lords. Other statutes outline our rights within a democracy; in the various Representation of the People Acts, for example, rules governing elections and the franchise are set out.

Statute law is generally regarded as taking precedence over all other constitutional sources and this is linked to the idea of parliamentary sovereignty.

Some argue that our membership of the EU limits the importance of statute law (and parliamentary sovereignty) but others maintain that this is untrue, as long as Parliament retains the power to withdraw from the EU by repealing the 1972 European Communities Act.

Treaties and EU law

The increasing globalisation of politics and UK involvement in supra-national organisations have led some to question the extent to which statute law is still the overriding source of our constitution.

Our membership of the EU is particularly significant. In passing the 1972 European Communities Act, European law and regulations were given precedence over our own national laws. Thus, it is argued, statute law no longer conquers all and Parliament is no longer sovereign.

Some argue that power has only been delegated to the EU and that Parliament still has the power to repeal the 1972 Act, thereby removing us from the Union. In this sense, Parliament is still theoretically sovereign and statute law is still theoretically pre-eminent. Such a withdrawal would, however, be extremely difficult to execute.

Conventions

Conventions are traditions or customs that have evolved over time and have, through deference to precedent, become accepted rules of behaviour. Unlike common law, however, conventions will not stand up in a court of law.

Important conventions include the doctrines of individual and collective ministerial responsibility, as well as the rule requiring the royal assent before a bill passed by both Houses of Parliament can pass into law.

Common law

Common law consists of established customs and precedent developed through the actions of judges. This 'precedent' is often referred to as 'case law' or 'judge-made law'. When a case is heard, the court will generally look for previous examples of similar cases and look to follow precedent when arriving at a decision. Where no precedent exists, the decision made will itself set precedent; though in areas such as this, it is common for the case to be passed around through the appeals process before a final judgement is made. A lot of the original law concerning civil liberties and a good deal of consumer protection rests upon common law.

The royal prerogative (including the power to declare war and agree treaties) is also based in common law. When John Major signed the Maastricht Treaty, he was doing so under the prerogative powers exercised by the Prime Minister in the name of the monarch. He could, therefore, have argued that there was no need for Parliament to approve this Treaty.

The Constitution

Works of authority

As Philip Norton has noted, whereas statute law takes precedence over all other sources, works of authority have only a persuasive authority; a role in settling disputes. When politicians want to ascertain correct procedure, they may call into play certain specialist works dealing with the constitution. Over time, therefore, some of these books have themselves become part of the constitutional framework because they codify practices not outlined on paper elsewhere. Such works include:

Fitzherbert's *Abridgement* (1516); Coke's *Institutes of the Law of England* (1624–44); Erskine May's *Parliamentary Practice* (first published in 1844); A V Dicey's *An Introduction to the Study of the Law of the Constitution* (1885).

8.2 Doctrines and principles

Key principles

Parliamentary sovereignty...

is based in the belief that:

1. *Parliament can make or unmake any law in the UK;*
2. *only Parliament can make UK law;*
3. *Parliament cannot bind future Parliaments.*

Parliamentary sovereignty is not rooted in statute law but in common law, following developments since the Glorious Revolution in 1688. More recent developments such as the increased use of referendums and the closer integration of the UK with Europe have, it is argued, diminished parliamentary sovereignty.

The rule of law...

was most famously defined by A V Dicey in 1885. It is based on the principle that:

1. *no-one can be punished without trial;*
2. *no-one is above the law. All are subject to the same justice;*
3. *the general principles of the Constitution (e.g. personal freedoms) result from the decisions of judges (case law), not from acts of statute or executive order.*

As is the case with parliamentary sovereignty, the rule of law is said to be under threat from a number of directions.

Parliamentary government under a constitutional monarch

A parliamentary government is one in which the government operates on the basis of the mandate given to it periodically through free and fair elections. This government is limited and all politicians as well as ministers are ultimately accountable for their actions to the electorate. The government is expected to act in a reasonable manner in furthering the interests of its citizens.

In Britain our Parliament operates alongside a constitutional monarch. The monarch is technically part of Parliament ('the Queen in Parliament') but – unlike past monarchs – is strictly controlled in what they can do, both by statute and convention. As a result, the monarchy in Britain is largely a 'dignified' part of the Constitution, that is to say symbolic or ceremonial. In practice, the Prime Minister exercises most of the 'effective' powers of the monarch. That said, the monarch does, in theory, retain significant powers and it is possible to imagine a situation in which they might have to use them.

The unitary state

Britain is a unitary state as opposed to a federal one. This means that all ultimate power in the UK is held by the central government at Westminster. Any power that local government or regional government appears to have is delegated to it by the central government and can be taken back at any time. Wales was brought into the union by Acts in 1536 and 1542 and saw the appointment of the first Welsh Secretary in 1907. Scotland entered the union through the Act of Union in 1707 and the first Scottish Secretary was recognised in 1885. The situation with regard Northern Ireland is rather more complicated and is dealt with in later chapters.

Some argue that moves devolving some powers, such as the creation of the Scottish Parliament, the Welsh Assembly and the Power Sharing Executive in Northern Ireland, have undermined this key principle of the Constitution.

8.3 The Constitution in transition?

Parliamentary sovereignty

The doctrine of parliamentary sovereignty has, it is argued, been undermined by a number of factors.

1. Increasing European integration has seen significant power delegated to the EU. The European Communities Act of 1972 gave European law precedence over UK law, and the Maastricht Treaty of 1991 broadened and deepened the Community significantly, creating the European Union. While a simple Act of Parliament (probably backed up with a referendum) could remove us from the EU – thus, in theory, meaning that Parliament is still technically sovereign – such a move would be difficult to achieve in practice and extremely expensive.

2. Others argue that Parliament as a whole has become dominated by the Commons, the Commons by the majority party, the majority party by the government, the government by the Cabinet and the Cabinet by the Prime Minister. In reality, therefore, the idea of a sovereign Parliament is questionable and some maintain that our government is effectively an 'elected dictatorship'. Against this argument one could bring in examples of the fate of Prime Ministers and governments who consistently and systematically appeared to repress the power of Parliament, party and government – Margaret Thatcher's downfall is a good case in point.

The rule of law

There are numerous long-standing exceptions to the rule of law and these are documented in all standard textbooks: the favourable treatment of accused foreign diplomats, for example, or the specific limitations placed upon the rights of those accused of acts of terrorism (under the various pieces of anti-terrorism legislation). More recent developments have also brought some key aspects of the rule of law into question: the suggestion that trial by jury could be further limited, for example, or the removal of the 'presumption of innocence' or the 'right to remain silent' without having inferences drawn from one's silence. At the same time, we are seeing the creation of what some have hailed as a 'rights culture' with the Human Rights Act and the Freedom of Information Act being passed. These apparent rights, however, are still not entrenched in a codified constitution and, as such, they can be repealed as easily as any other act. In the case of the HRA in particular, the courts only have the power to highlight inconsistencies between the rights offered in the Act and other legislation. They cannot invalidate laws infringing the protected rights.

The unitary state

Although the UK remains, in theory, a unitary state, some power has been delegated in such a way that it would be very difficult to get it back. This is particularly true of the Scottish Parliament and the Welsh Assembly, though the Northern Ireland Power Sharing Executive has been suspended from time to time as a tactic during the peace process. Opinions differ as to the extent to which these institutions remain an end in themselves or steps on a path to a federal system. The principle of subsidiarity – enshrined in the Maastricht Treaty – states that decisions should be taken at the most appropriate level and this, together with the EU's use of 'regions' for other purposes (such as economic development) and the use of the regional list system in elections to the EU Parliament, has fuelled demands for greater regional government in the UK. Such demands have been further heightened by a sense that England and its regions are now under-represented in relation to Scotland, Northern Ireland and Wales.

Parliamentary government under a constitutional monarch

The nature of Parliament is changing. Reform of the Lords, though incomplete, is likely to lead to a second chamber that is at least partially elected. This would raise questions regarding the division of power between the Commons and the new second elected chamber. Eurosceptics and some others argue that, in any case, parliamentary government is undermined by the increasing delegation of power to the EU. Those who speak of 'elective dictatorship' also question the worth of the term 'parliamentary government'. The increased use of referendums in recent years is also said to undermine the principle of representative government.

The monarch has been said to be under threat in recent years, though approval ratings for the Queen herself remain high. In the wake of the death of Diana, Princess of Wales, the monarchy took a good deal of criticism, but there has been an attempt to rehabilitate leading figures in recent years and there has been no significant move towards republicanism despite the efforts of some newspapers. The abolition of the monarchy or the removal of its residual powers/responsibilities would also create significant knock-on constitutional effects. Who, for example, would give the assent to bills (a president perhaps) or act as a national figurehead?

Conclusion

Although the Constitution has evolved over time, it is now clearly entering a phase of major change. Many of the key elements of the state are being reassessed, as is the relationship between the state and the individual. There does not appear to be a coherent master-plan. Progress is unpredictable and crab-like.

8.4 Constitutional reform since 1997

CONSTITUTIONAL REFORM

Parliamentary Reform

The **House of Lords Act** (1999) delivered on Labour's 1997 Manifesto commitment to remove the right of hereditary peers to sit and vote in the Lords, though under the **Weatherill Amendment** 92 former hereditaries were allowed to remain in the House until the second stage of reform was completed. Despite attempts to complete a second stage of reform by changing the composition of the second chamber more radically, further **White Papers** on Lords reform stalled in both 2003 and 2007. The latter saw the Commons vote for an entirely elected second chamber (337:224), with the Lords preferring one which remained entirely appointed (361:121).

Though Commons reform was also discussed – not least the strengthening of the system of **Departmental Select Committees** – progress was slow. The main changes came in terms of changing working practices in the Commons, with fewer all-night debates, better office accommodation for MPs in **Portcullis House**, and the move to a single 30-minute slot for **Prime Minister's Questions**.

Judicial Reform

The traditional role of the **Lord Chancellor** had long provoked controversy – not least because the office holder sat as head of the judiciary, as a member of Cabinet, and as **Speaker of the House of Lords**.

Labour sought to address this aspect of the UK's system of fused powers with the **Constitutional Reform Act** (2005). Under this Act the role – if not the title – of Lord Chancellor was all but abolished. The Lords elected their own Speaker and most judicial appointments were to be processed by the new **Judicial Appointments Commission** (JAC). A new **Justice Department** was later established by merging what remained of the Department of Constitutional Affairs with some elements of the Home Office.

Another major element of the Constitutional Reform Act (2005) was the creation of a new **UK Supreme Court**, which will open in the renovated Middlesex Guildhall in **October 2009**. This Court, which will initially comprise the 12 serving Law Lords, will further serve to enhance the **separation of powers** by removing the Lords' judicial function.

Rights

The UK was traditionally said to operate under a system of **negative rights**, where the freedoms and liberties were not set out explicitly in a **codified, entrenched** document, but simply existed in the absence of any law restricting them. New Labour sought to make such rights more explicit and more accessible to the public with the **Human Rights Act** (HRA, 1998). This Act **incorporated** most of the provisions of the **European Convention on Human Rights** (ECHR, 1950) into UK law, meaning that for the first time UK citizens could enforce such rights through UK courts rather than having to go to the **European Court of Human Rights in Strasbourg**. As it came from the intergovernmental **Council of Europe** – rather than the supranational EU – the ECHR lacks the force of European law. Courts can merely make a **declaration of incompatibility** where UK statute appears to violate the terms of the HRA (1998). Labour also introduced the **Freedom of Information Act** (FOI, 2000) which came into force in 2005.

Devolution

Though earlier attempts to provide devolved government in Scotland and Wales had failed following **referendums** in both countries in **1979**, Labour came to power in 1997 with a manifesto commitment to revive these plans by establishing a **Scottish Parliament** and a **Welsh Assembly**, alongside new executives in both countries. Elections to the devolved legislatures were held for the first time in **1999**, once the legislation establishing devolved arrangements had been confirmed by the means of referendums held in each country in 1997. The **'yes, yes'** vote secured in the two-question referendum in Scotland saw the establishment of a Parliament with both **primary legislative powers** and **tax-varying powers**. The **secondary legislative** or **administrative** powers granted to the devolved institutions in Wales were less wide-ranging.

The **Good Friday Agreement** resulted in the establishment of a devolved **power sharing executive** in **Northern Ireland** and **London** was also given its own elected **Assembly** and **Elected Mayor**. The devolution programme stalled when voters in the **North East** rejected the opportunity to have their own regional assembly in a referendum held in **2004.**

9.1 The composition of parliament

Introduction

Parliament comprises monarch, the House of Commons and the House of Lords. Though the Commons has changed in size periodically – most recently as a result of the activities of the Boundary Commissions in creating new constituencies – it is the House of Lords which has seen the most dramatic changes in its composition in recent years.

The House of Commons

The Commons consisted of 646 MPs in July 2005. Each MP represents a single-member constituency, being elected using the First Past the Post electoral system – either in the General Election or, where a vacancy has arisen, in a by-election. This total was 13 seats fewer than that prior to the 2005 General Election; a result of the removal of 13 Scottish seats.

The Commons in July 2005:

Labour	355	Plaid Cymru	3
Conservative	198	Respect	1
Liberal Democrat	62	Sinn Fein	5
Ulster Unionists	1	SDLP	3
DUP	9	Independent	2
SNP	6	The Speaker	1
		Total	646

The House of Lords

Up until 1999 the House of Lords consisted of around 750 hereditary peers and 500 life peers. The House of Lords Act (1999) removed the right of most hereditary peers to sit and vote in the Lords. At the same time it allowed them to vote and stand as candidates in parliamentary elections (privileges that had previously been denied them due to their status). The intention had been to remove the voting rights of all hereditary peers but the Weatherill Amendment allowed 92 such peers to stay on in a transitional House prior to the completion of Lords reform: 75 were elected by their fellow hereditary peers, whilst the Earl Marshal, the Lord Great Chamberlain, and 15 deputy speakers remained as of right. Ten other hereditary peers were granted life peerages.

On June 1 2008, the Lords – excluding 12 on leave of absence – consisted of:

615 life peers	92 'hereditary peers'	26 Bishops

At the time that Labour came to power in 1997 the Conservatives had 476 peers to Labour's 120. The removal of the majority of hereditary peers, alongside the appointment of life peers between 1997 and 2008, meant that the Lords of June 2, 2008, comprised:

Conservative 201	Labour 216	LibDem 76	Crossbenchers & others 230

Socio-Economic Background of MPs (2005)

Age

The average age of MPs following the 2005 General Election was 50.6 years. This compares to 49.8 in 2001 and 48.8 in 1997. The youngest MP elected in 2005 was Liberal Democrat Jo Swinson (25) in East Dumbartonshire.

Gender

In 1987 only 6% of MPs (41) were women. This figure increased to 10% (60) in 1992 and 18% (120) in 1997 before falling back to 18% (118) in 2001. In 2005, 127 women (20%) were returned.

Sexual orientation

In 2002, there were nine openly 'gay' MPs; six by their own admission and a further three identified as a result of media attention and the activities of other groups.

By 2005, the figure had risen to 12, though gay rights group *Outrage* claimed that there were over 30 other 'closeted' gay MPs.

Ethnicity

In the 2005 General Election, 15 of the 113 ethnic minority candidates who stood for the three main parties were returned to Parliament. This compared to the 12 out of 57 ethnic minority candidates returned in 2001. There has been an upward trend in ethnic minority candidature since 1979, when only 5 such candidates sought election.

Education

60% of the Conservative MPs elected in 2005 attended public school, compared to 18% of Labour MPs and 39% of LibDem MPs. 25% (163) of those elected in 2005 went to Oxford (100) or Cambridge (63). 58 Labour MPs (16%) went to Oxbridge, as did 86 Conservatives (43%) and 19 LibDems (31%).

Occupation

39.3% of those MPs returned in 2005 were from the professions; 19.2% from business; and 6.2% manual. Within the professions 14.8% of MPs were trained teachers and 5.5% were barristers. 7.0% of MPs were involved in publishing or journalism by trade.

Socio-economic background of local councillors

Average Age:	58
Gender:	71% Male, 29% Female
Ethnicity:	96% white
In full time work:	23%
Retired:	40%

Source: The Improvement and Development Agency for Local Government. Quoted in the *Guardian* (February 9, 2007).

9.2 The passage of legislation

Different Types of Bill

Private Bills
Generally affect a particular area of policy or an organisation as opposed to the population as a whole. Some Private Bills only affect one or two people and these are sometimes referred to as Personal Bills.

Personal Bills
Personal Bills normally deal with regulations affecting one or two people. Sometimes they grant individuals a dispensation from existing law.

Public Bills
Public Bills affect the entire population. The vast majority of Public Bills are government sponsored bills but there is also limited time available for Private members bills sponsored by backbenchers.

Government Bills
Government Bills often seek to fulfil manifesto commitments and are much more likely of success because the government controls the parliamentary timetable. Ministers pilot these Bills through the legislative stages.

Private members Bills
A private members ballot allocates slots for such bills and MPs who have entered the ballot and been successful can then advance their legislation. Private members bills offer a way of legislating on controversial issues (eg the Abortion Act) without dividing parties.

Passage of a Government Bill

Preparation
Before a bill is introduced it will normally go through a consultation stage. This can start with a Consultation (Green) Paper. This may then be turned into a firm proposal (White Paper) before the bill is eventually drafted.

Commons Stages

First reading
Bill introduced. Date set for second reading. bill printed up ready for second reading.

Second reading
Minister outlines proposals and deals with general questions. Principles of bill discussed.

Committee stage
Bill sent to standing committee. Separate committees formed for each bill

Report stage
Amended bill reported out of committee and voted through to…

Third reading
No major amendments at this stage. Look at bill as a whole. Pass or reject.

Lords Stages

Third reading
If the Bills is passed it moves towards the Royal Assent. If it is rejected or significantly amended then it will return to the Commons for consideration

Under the Parliament Act (see Glossary) the Lords can only delay bills

Report stage

Committee stage
As in the Commons, the bill passes into its committee stage following the second reading. In the House of Lords, however, this is normally done in the Chamber as a committee of the whole House.

Second reading

First reading

Royal Assent
Before a bill becomes law it must receive the Royal Assent. By convention the monarch does not refuse. The last monarch to refuse was Queen Anne (1707) over the Scottish Militias Bill.

The Work of Committees
There are two broad types committee in the House of Commons

Standing committees
Standing committees usually have the role of considering legislation (see left) or documents. They are made up of 15–60 members, the numbers from each party reflecting the composition of the House itself. Where formed to consider a piece of legislation, standing committees can last for several months, suggesting minor changes and more serious amendments before reporting out to the House.

Select committees
Select committees are not often as involved in the passage of legislation. Since 1979 departmental select committees have had the role of scrutinising the work of the various government departments. Of the non-departmental select committees, the Public Accounts Committee is one of the most high profile and has the role of ensuring value for money in government. This Committee has developed a fearsome reputation for making departments accountable for their spending.

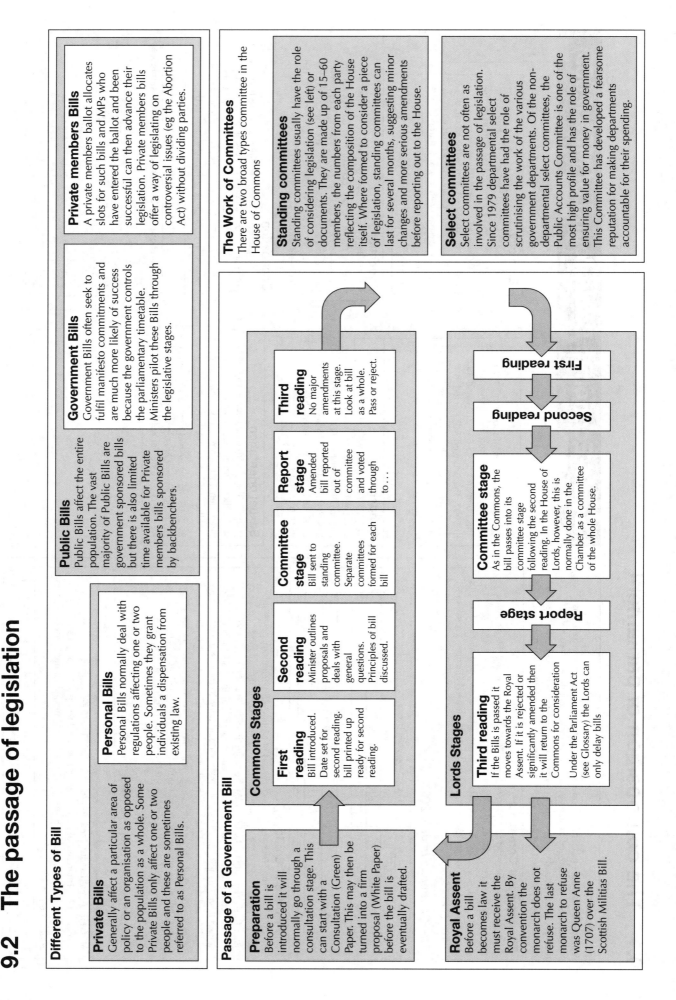

9.3 Scrutiny of the executive

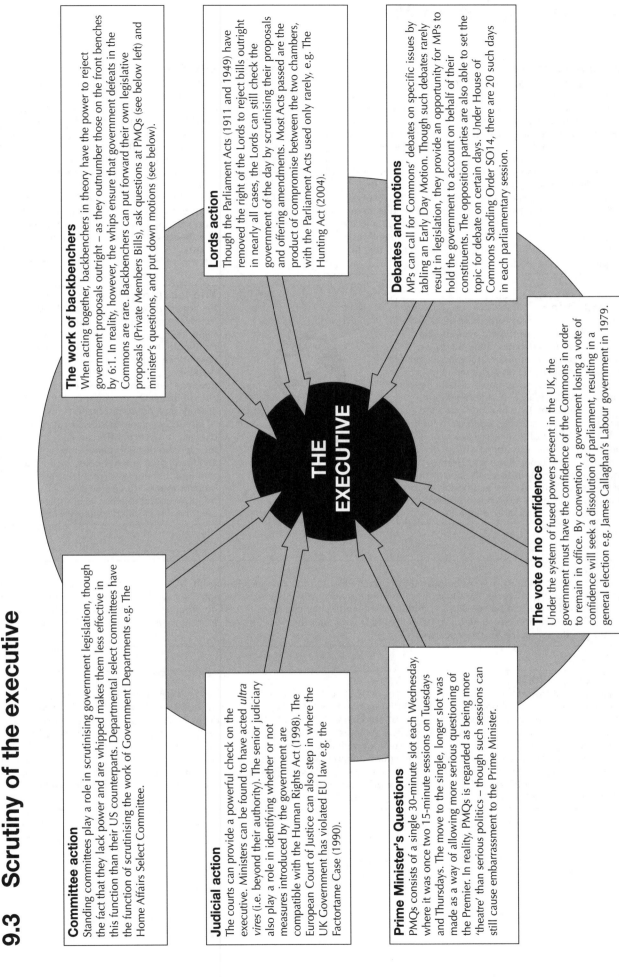

Committee action

Standing committees play a role in scrutinising government legislation, though the fact that they lack power and are whipped makes them less effective in this function than their US counterparts. Departmental select committees have the function of scrutinising the work of Government Departments e.g. The Home Affairs Select Committee.

Judicial action

The courts can provide a powerful check on the executive. Ministers can be found to have acted *ultra vires* (i.e. beyond their authority). The senior judiciary also play a role in identifying whether or not measures introduced by the government are compatible with the Human Rights Act (1998). The European Court of Justice can also step in where the UK Government has violated EU law e.g. the Factortame Case (1990).

Prime Minister's Questions

PMQs consists of a single 30-minute slot each Wednesday, where it was once two 15-minute sessions on Tuesdays and Thursdays. The move to the single, longer slot was made as a way of allowing more serious questioning of the Premier. In reality, PMQs is regarded as being more 'theatre' than serious politics – though such sessions can still cause embarrassment to the Prime Minister.

The work of backbenchers

When acting together, backbenchers in theory have the power to reject government proposals outright – as they outnumber those on the front benches by 6:1. In reality, however, the whips ensure that government defeats in the Commons are rare. Backbenchers can put forward their own legislative proposals (Private Members Bills), ask questions at PMQs (see below left) and minister's questions, and put down motions (see below).

Lords action

Though the Parliament Acts (1911 and 1949) have removed the right of the Lords to reject bills outright in nearly all cases, the Lords can still check the government of the day by scrutinising their proposals and offering amendments. Most Acts passed are the product of compromise between the two chambers, with the Parliament Acts used only rarely, e.g. The Hunting Act (2004).

Debates and motions

MPs can call for Commons' debates on specific issues by tabling an Early Day Motion. Though such debates rarely result in legislation, they provide an opportunity for MPs to hold the government to account on behalf of their constituents. The opposition parties are also able to set the topic for debate on certain days. Under House of Commons Standing Order SO14, there are 20 such days in each parliamentary session.

The vote of no confidence

Under the system of fused powers present in the UK, the government must have the confidence of the Commons in order to remain in office. By convention, a government losing a vote of confidence will seek a dissolution of parliament, resulting in a general election e.g. James Callaghan's Labour government in 1979.

THE EXECUTIVE

9.4   The role of an MP

The representative
MPs are representatives rather than delegates. Most MPs hold regular surgeries in order to deal with constituency issues and gauge opinion. Some MPs (such as the Prime Minister and members of the government) may have difficulty in representing their constituents as effectively, due to the demands on their time. Others (such as the Speaker and Deputy Speakers) might be restricted in what they can say due to the nature of their jobs. Voters can remove MPs through the ballot box, but in reality most MPs owe their positions more to those who selected them as their party's candidate. Few MPs have sufficient personal support to be elected without the party label (Martin Bell in 1997 and Dr Richard Taylor in 2001 and 2005 being recent exceptions) and many can be said to have been elected purely due to their party label.

The loyal party drone
Most MPs are elected by virtue of the party label that they carry during the election. It is logical, therefore, the parties would argue, that MPs should toe the party line once in Parliament. To this end the party whips cajole and punish troublesome MPs. Such MPs might find their chances of promotion limited. Those that persistently ignore the whips might have the whip withdrawn. This effectively throws the MP out of the parliamentary party and leaves them vulnerable to de-selection in their constituency. Some MPs choose to resign the whip or even cross the floor of the House and join another party by taking that party's whip. They can do this without seeking re-election because – in theory – **they** are elected, not the party.

The watchdog
Traditionally, MPs within Parliament have had the role of holding government accountable through the various debates, committees, Prime Minister's and Ministers' Questions and – ultimately – by voting on government bills. This is crucial, but a government usually has a big enough majority to over-ride rebellions and MPs, controlled by whips, are often too fearful to act as a watchdog, particularly in the age of the 'career politician' (see below). Though there have always been MPs who prioritise this role (Tony Benn and Dennis Skinner, for example), individuals such as the Parliamentary Commissioner and bodies such as the Public Accounts Committee probably carry more weight than individual MPs.

Conscience?

The local trouble-shooter
Regardless of whether or not MPs ever follow the views of their constituents rather than the party whips, all MPs play an important role in trouble-shooting within their constituency and representing the interests of constituents facing problems either within the constituency or abroad. In 2002, for example, MPs were at work making representations on behalf of the British plane spotters arrested and charged in Greece. MPs can also intervene in disputes between constituents and local government bodies. Many MPs also find that domestic problems are brought to their surgeries. This troubleshooting role has seen some MPs described as glorified social workers.

The legislator
For a bill to become an act, it must be passed through the House of Commons. As a result, MPs have total power over legislation. In reality, however, the situation is far different. MPs, as we have already noted, are under pressure to conform. Parliamentary debates can be cut short, committees and committee chairmen leaned on. Ironically, as the passage of the recent anti-terrorism legislation has shown, it is often the Lords who offer the more spirited opposition to government policy; a fact particularly true during the Thatcher years.

The future for MPs
Many writers have observed the increasing number of what are called 'career politicians' in the House. Whereas MPs in the 1940s served an average of only five years in Parliament, today's MPs often linger for 15 or 20 years. The job has changed: MPs now often have more comfortable office accommodation in Portcullis House, they receive a reasonable salary (close to £62 000) and over £100 000 in allowable expenses on top of that salary, and the hours of debate have been moderated. The accompanying desire to secure and then retain such a position is likely to lead to greater party loyalty within the Chamber. At the same time, however, many voters are becoming unhappy with the extent to which their representatives represent them and by the continual allegations of sleaze and scandal. The resulting disillusionment has – it is argued – contributed to lower turnout in 2001 and 2005 as well as to the election of non-party parliamentary candidates (for example, Martin Bell and Dr Richard Taylor). This disaffection with MPs will need to be addressed.

9.5 Parliamentary reform

Roles and criticisms of Parliament

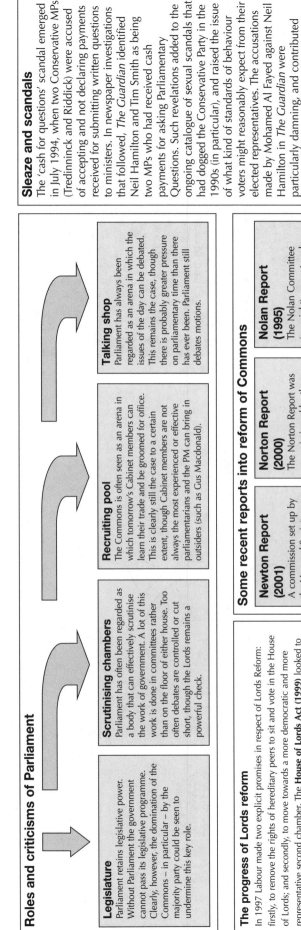

Legislature

Parliament retains legislative power. Without Parliament the government cannot pass its legislative programme. Clearly, however, the domination of the Commons – in particular – by the majority party could be seen to undermine this key role.

Scrutinising chambers

Parliament has often been regarded as a body that can effectively scrutinise the work of government. A lot of this work is done in committees rather than on the floor of either house. Too often debates are controlled or cut short, though the Lords remains a powerful check.

Recruiting pool

The Commons is often seen as an arena in which tomorrow's Cabinet members can learn their trade and be groomed for office. This is clearly still the case to a certain extent, though Cabinet members are not always the most experienced or effective parliamentarians and the PM can bring in outsiders (such as Gus Macdonald).

Talking shop

Parliament has always been regarded as an arena in which the issues of the day can be debated. This remains the case, though there is probably greater pressure on parliamentary time than there has ever been. Parliament still debates motions.

The progress of Lords reform

In 1997 Labour made two explicit promises in respect of Lords Reform: firstly, to remove the rights of hereditary peers to sit and vote in the House of Lords; and secondly, to move towards a more democratic and more representative second chamber. The **House of Lords Act (1999)** looked to deliver on the first of these pledges by removing all but 92 of the hereditary peers. A further White Paper was produced in 2001 but the Commons rejected all eight proposed models – ranging from outright abolition to a wholly elected second chamber – in February 2003. Labour promised 'a predominantly elected second chamber' in 2005 – and a further White Paper followed in 2007 (see below) – but the process stalled again with the Commons voting 337:224 for a fully elected chamber and the Lords favouring one that was entirely appointed (361:121).

2007 White Paper:

- the Commons to **retain its primacy** over legislation;
- an upper chamber split **50:50** between elected and appointed members who would serve a **single, fixed term**, far longer than that enjoyed by those in the Commons;
- elections to be held under a **partially open regional list system** and **staggered in three cohorts**, along the same lines as the US Senate;
- appointments to be made by a new, independent **Statutory Appointments Commission**, with **20% of those chosen being non-political appointees**
- A chamber where **no single party** would be allowed to enjoy an **overall majority**.

Some recent reports into reform of Commons

Newton Report (2001)

A commission set up by the Hansard Society, chaired by Tony Newton (Lord Newton of Braintree), produced the Newton Report.

The Newton Report's focus was on improving government accountability. Like the Norton Report (see right) it concluded that what was needed was the strengthening of the select committee system, as well as a greater willingness to communicate to the broader public in a sincere and comprehensible manner.

Norton Report (2000)

The Norton Report was commissioned by the Leader of the Opposition in 1999 and chaired by Philip Norton (Lord Norton of Louth).

The Report recommended, amongst other things, the strengthening and broadening of the system of select committees. This would allow for greater scrutiny of legislation and might also help to improve financial efficiency. It would make the work of government and Parliament more transparent, allowing for greater public appreciation of Parliament's work.

Nolan Report (1995)

The Nolan Committee (see right) was set up by the Government and chaired by Lord Justice Nolan.

In its first report (1995) it recommended, amongst other things, that there should be a 'code of conduct' for MPs and an Independent Parliamentary Commissioner for Standards. In November 1995 the House introduced a number of key changes. Crucially, it created a Select Committee on Standards and Privileges and appointed a Parliamentary Commissioner for Standards (PCS), Sir Gordon Downey.

Sleaze and scandals

The 'cash for questions' scandal emerged in July 1994, when two Conservative MPs (Tredinnick and Riddick) were accused of accepting and not declaring payments received for submitting written questions to ministers. In newspaper investigations that followed, *The Guardian* identified Neil Hamilton and Tim Smith as being two MPs who had received cash payments for asking Parliamentary Questions. Such revelations added to the ongoing catalogue of sexual scandals that had dogged the Conservative Party in the 1990s (in particular), and raised the issue of what kind of standards of behaviour voters might reasonably expect from their elected representatives. The accusations made by Mohamed Al Fayed against Neil Hamilton in *The Guardian* were particularly damning, and contributed greatly to Hamilton's exit from Parliament at the hands of Martin Bell (the anti-sleaze independent candidate) in 1997. The Nolan Committee on Standards in Public Life was set up to investigate the whole area and produced the Nolan Report.

Elizabeth Filkin ...

replaced Gordon Downey as PCS and gained a reputation for the thoroughness of her investigations into complaints against – amongst others – Peter Mandelson and Keith Vaz. When she was not re-appointed in 2001, she accused some of those who had criticised her style of organising a 'whispering campaign' against her. John Lyon CB took up the post on January 1, 2008.

10.1 The core executive

Definition

Although discussions of executive power in the UK often tend to focus on the ever-changing relationship between the Prime Minister and the Cabinet, recent years have seen some commentators trying to put PM–Cabinet relations into their proper context by considering the part played by other individuals and bodies within the core executive. According to R.A.W. Rhodes, 'the term core executive refers to all those organisations and procedures which coordinate central government policies, and act as final arbiters of conflict between different parts of the government machine'.

The core executive today

The main elements of the core executive

The core executive is an ever-evolving network of **individuals**, **offices** and **processes.** As such it is impossible to identify what it consists of at any one time. The diagram below identifies many of the bodies commonly said to operate within the core executive.

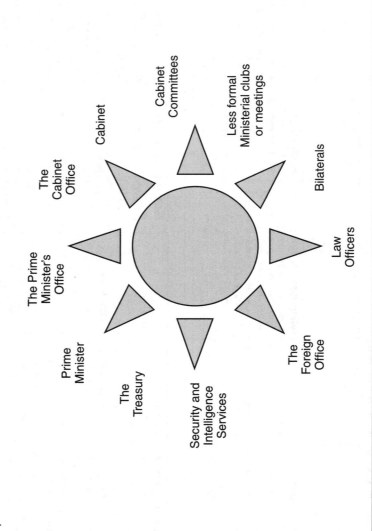

A virtual 'Prime Minister's Department'?

A series of structural changes brought to the Cabinet Office (CO) since Labour were returned to government in 1997, and the increasing overlap between the CO and the Prime Minister's Office (PMO), have led some to argue that we now have a *de facto* Prime Minister's Department.

The Cabinet Office today

The CO was founded in 1916 with the creation of a series of secretariats. It was designed to help the coalition government of the time co-ordinate the work of government departments in response to the challenges brought by the First World War. The modern CO is the key player in co-ordinating the activities of government and has expanded beyond the original secretariats to comprise over 20 separate units e.g. the Performance and Innovation Unit and the Prime Minister's Delivery Unit.

The Prime Minister's Office today

The PMO, often referred to simply as 'Downing Street' or 'No.10', has its origins in the nineteenth century and consists of the bodies that support the Prime Minister in his day to day work. No.10 is staffed by a mixture of civil servants and special advisers and headed by a Chief of Staff. Under Tony Blair this post was held by Jonathan Powell. The PMO is not a physical entity in the sense of the US President's Oval Office. It instead consists of a series of units, some of which are now also part of the formal structure of the CO. As is the case with the CO, the period since 1997 has seen the PMO become a rather more important and more complicated structure than was the case previously.

10.2 The Prime Minister

Origins of the office

The office of Prime Minister is based largely on convention. Once the monarch stopped attending Cabinet meetings (under George I, who reigned 1714–27), the First Lord of the Treasury began chairing Cabinet meetings. This is the formal title still held by Prime Ministers today. Robert Walpole is generally regarded as the first Prime Minister (1721–42), though in reality Robert Peel (1841–46) has a better claim as the first modern Prime Minister. The powers of the Prime Minister have evolved gradually, largely as a result of the assimilation of royal prerogative powers (see right). While the monarch still retains these power in theory, in practice the Prime Minister acts in place of the monarch.

The royal prerogative

These powers, formally held by the monarch but – in practice – exercised by the Prime Minister include the power to:

declare war; make treaties; annex and cede territory; control the armed forces; control patronage; control the workings of the civil service; make use of emergency powers.

The powers of the Prime Minister

Patronage and the control of Cabinet

The Prime Minister has massive powers of patronage over the Church of England (archbishops, bishops etc.), senior judges (e.g. the Lord Chief Justice), Privy Councillors and civil servants. It is in Cabinet and government, however, that the power of patronage becomes crucial. The Prime Minister ultimately decides who gets what at all levels of the government. He or she also controls the timing and agenda of Cabinet meetings as well as 'taking the feeling of the meeting'.

Limitations: the seniority of colleagues might demand their inclusion (e.g. Jack Straw from 1997), as might a need for balance (e.g. John Prescott) or a need to reward those who have supported your rise (e.g. Gordon Brown). If the Prime Minister excludes or forces out key figures they can often become dangerous enemies on the back benches (e.g. Heseltine under Thatcher). There are also the questions of availability for office, ability and experience. Margaret Thatcher was often criticised – particularly in the latter years of her administration – for passing over or forcing out more experienced ministers in favour of 'yes-men'. Some items also demand inclusion on the Cabinet agenda.

Party and Parliament

As the leader of the majority party in the Commons (most often), the Prime Minister has considerable power. They can control the parliamentary timetable and pursue the government's programme. They are the public face of party and government. They control key appointments within their own party as well as within government, and can rely on a certain amount of loyalty from the party simply by virtue of the fact that they are in government. When backs are against the wall, they can even threaten to ask the Queen to dissolve Parliament and call an election (a threat made by John Major in 1992).

Limitations: the party will not always remain loyal (back bench support for Thatcher failed in 1990). Parliament can also – in theory – call errant governments to account (e.g. through Prime Minister's Questions on Wednesdays, or debates and motions). Ultimately the Commons can pass a vote of no confidence, bringing down the government, and, by convention, forcing an election.

What is the core executive?

The term 'core executive' is a collective term usually taken to refer to the key institutions and processes involved in co-ordinating the work of central government: the Prime Minister, Cabinet, Cabinet Committees and Cabinet Office, Treasury and Foreign Office bodies, law, security and intelligence officers, and certain other top civil servants.

Models of executive control

Cabinet government

This places the Cabinet at the centre of decision-making, while accepting that some decisions might need to be made elsewhere. Cabinet is seen as a unified body, operating under the doctrine of collective responsibility. The Cabinet acts as a check against any attempts by the Prime Minister to dominate the process. The Prime Minister is merely 'primus inter pares' – first among equals. John Major's administrations (1990–97) are often offered as examples.

Prime Ministerial cliques/kitchen cabinet

In this model, the Prime Minister works within a reduced (kitchen) cabinet or clique of key advisors. The composition of this clique is fairly fixed, but key additional individuals might be brought into the circle on certain issues. Cabinet is reduced to a rubber stamp, being informed of and then approving those decisions made in the smaller meetings. Some feel that the Blair administrations from 1997 worked in this way, though he preferred 'bilaterals' to cliques.

Prime Ministerial government

Writers such as Richard Crossman in the 1960s and Tony Benn in the 1980s (both former Labour ministers) spoke of the rise of Prime Ministerial power. They saw the increasing dominance of the Prime Minister within Cabinet. This, they argued had been achieved largely as a result of the increasing centralisation of the party machines and the civil service in the hands of the Prime Minister. Since then, the media has further focused attention on the Prime Minister.

Departmentalised/ministerial government

Under this analysis, government departments have control over their respective areas and the ministers in charge can act with a fair degree of autonomy upon the advice of those more junior politicians and civil servants within their departments. The Prime Minister bows to departmental expertise but holds ministers to account for their decisions (an aspect of ministerial responsibility). Cabinet becomes an arena for resolving conflicts between departments.

Differentiated/segmented decisions

This model accepts that the distribution of power within the executive might vary in different policy areas. The Prime Minister might dominate the heights of government – foreign policy, defence, key economic policy decisions – whereas the Cabinet might be given a considerable degree of autonomy in all other areas. The Prime Minister only interferes in these low-priority areas when ministers make mistakes, or when events move the issue further up the agenda (e.g. Blair and the 'foot and mouth' crisis in 2001).

A general model of executive power

In reality, any attempt to provide a simple model explaining the distribution of power within the core executive is likely to be flawed. The interrelationships between the various offices and institutions depend largely upon the characters and approaches of the incumbent politicians/officials as well as circumstances (e.g. the size of the government's majority in the Commons). Administrations do not always fit into a box, much less studies of particular episodes within the term of an administration.

10.3   The Cabinet

Introduction

As is the case with the office of Prime Minister, the Cabinet has evolved over time; from a group of individuals linking the King and Parliament into what Walter Bagehot (1867) saw as an institution central to the decision-making process. The Prime Minister, it was argued, was merely 'primus inter pares' (first among equals). Even in Bagehot's time, however, this argument would have been open to question, and over the last 20 years the apparent expansion of Prime Ministerial power has led some to question how significant a role the Cabinet still retains in the process of government. The modern Cabinet consists of around 23 paid members and fulfils a number of important functions (see below). Traditionally, Cabinet Ministers have been expected to work within the principles of **collective responsibility** and **ministerial responsibility** (see Glossary).

The various roles of the Cabinet

Decision-making

Traditionally, Cabinet has been seen as central to the decision-making process. The Cabinet's role in this area, however, has been undermined by the development of Prime Ministerial power that has come with the increased centralisation of bureaucratic controls and the increased importance of the media.

Co-ordinating departments

Cabinet always had a role in co-ordinating the activities of government departments. While the decision-making role of Cabinet has been diminished somewhat, its position as an arena in which individuals can report on their activities and bring colleagues up-to-date remains significant.

Forward planning

Cabinet retains a role in addressing problems arising from policy and/or events. Cabinet provides a 'talking shop' where the direction of policy can, if necessary, be discussed and where the broad direction of policy can be re-focused. It is also a place where ministers can raise genuine concerns.

Recent Cabinets

The Cabinet under Thatcher

Thatcher's first Cabinet contained a good number of ministers who had served under Heath – the old guard of 'one-nation Tories'. Using the hire-and-fire power ruthlessly, she gradually brought in her own people to a point where many felt there was greater talent on the back benches than on the front. Her confrontational style led to high-profile resignations, such as Heseltine (right), Lawson and Howe in particular. The style of Heseltine's resignation in 1986 (walking out of a Cabinet meeting) and the savage attack on Thatcher made by Geoffrey Howe in his resignation speech contributed to her eventual downfall in 1990.

The Cabinet under Major

Following Thatcher's fall in November 1990, John Major emerged as the compromise candidate. Including his rivals for the leadership (Heseltine and Hurd) in the Cabinet, he sought to develop a more consensual style. After the general election of 1992, Major was working with a small majority and, as it shrank further, infighting became more apparent – particularly over Europe. Describing his opponents in Cabinet as the 'bastards' for briefing the press against him, he invited them to 'put up or shut up' in a leadership election in which he defeated John Redwood (above). This victory did not, however, stop the infighting, and accusations of sleaze further contributed to an appearance of an administration in crisis.

The Cabinet under Blair

Blair's first Cabinet included many heavyweight politicians who had their own power bases within the Party (Cook, Prescott and Brown for example). While all were retained post-2001, only Gordon Brown (right) kept a high-profile office, as Blair moved in more of his own people and promoted other Blairites within Cabinet – as a block, some suggest, against Brown's ambitions. Mo Mowlam spoke of the 'crippling' battle at the top between Blair and Brown. *The Guardian* claimed that the administration had 'a bad case of the TB-GBs' (November 20, 2001). Blair continued to favour bilateral meetings over larger cliques after 2001. He dominated key decisions, though in many less important policy areas ministers were allowed to act fairly independently; though he often took personal control during major crises.

What is the Cabinet Office?

In 2005, the Cabinet Office consisted of around 2000 staff. It is the key player in co-ordinating the activities of government. The Office was strengthened by Labour in 1998. This strengthening involved creating new elements and also bringing together a number of previously independent bodies under the Cabinet Office umbrella. The result was what amounted to a Prime Minister's Department, in all but name; a power base to challenge Gordon Brown's in the Treasury, perhaps. The new Cabinet Office comprised:

a Cabinet Office Minister (the so-called 'Cabinet Enforcer') as well as the Cabinet Secretary (Sir Richard Wilson), four separate Secretariats (Economic and Domestic, Defence and Overseas, European (EU), Constitution), the Performance and Innovation Unit, the Women's Unit, the Centre for Management and Policy Studies, the Head of the Government and Communication Service, and the Chief Scientific Advisor.

There was also a physical centralisation of the Cabinet Office, with the staff from around 17 former Cabinet Office buildings being relocated to new accommodation in Downing Street. *The Guardian* saw these bureaucratic developments as a major threat to Cabinet government.

Cabinet committees

As the pressures on the work of Cabinet increased after the Second World War – both in volume of work and in its complexity – the Cabinet was forced to delegate significant aspects of its work to Cabinet committees and sub-committees. These committees are given authority over specific areas and, as far as possible, decisions are then taken at that level, so as to lighten the burden on full Cabinet meetings. Committees are generally chaired by senior Cabinet members; sometimes the Prime Minister of the day. The rest of the members are drawn from the Cabinet as appropriate. The many committees generally fall into one of three categories: foreign and defence, domestic/home affairs, and economic. Some ministers will attend committees in all three categories (the Leader of the Commons or the Home Secretary, for example), whereas other ministers will only be involved in committees that are more directly linked to their portfolios (the Health Secretary, for example). As a result of the expansion of committee work, the full Cabinet has increasingly become a body for reporting and reviewing decisions taken at committee level rather than making decisions itself. It has also been noted that the full Cabinet only rarely fully debates matters that have already been dealt with at committee level.

10.4 Special advisors, spin and control

Introduction
One of the key features of the first two Blair Administrations was their emphasis on presentation and control; the importance of keeping everyone 'on-message' (i.e. maintaining the appearance of unity in Cabinet, government, parliamentary party and beyond). One aspect of this was the high profile attained by the Prime Minister's Press Secretary (later Director of Communications), Alastair Campbell. Another was the attempt to control the selection of Party candidates for high office often with disastrous results – Alun Michael for First Minister in Wales, Donald Dewar as First Minister in Scotland, and Frank Dobson as Labour's candidate for London Mayor. At the same time, there has been a physical concentration of resources in Downing Street with the strengthening of the Cabinet Office. All of this, and much more, led to claims that Blair had 'control freak tendencies' and that the Government was 'spinning out of control'.

What are special advisors?
There were 5 so-called special advisors in 1990, a figure that increased to around 36 in the last year of John Major's Government, 69 by the end of the first year of the new Labour Government in 1997, and 68 by 2007. Special advisors have two key roles:

- to make the government less reliant on the work of the Civil Service;
- to help the Prime Minister keep up-to-date with government departments that are often far better staffed and resourced.

Blair made extensive use of special advisors. Jonathan Powell was appointed as a 'US-style' Chief of Staff, Alastair Campbell took the role of Director of Communications, and Sally Morgan is the Director of Government Relations. She replaced Anji Hunter following the 2001 general election. Other ministers have also made extensive use of such advisors. Stephen Byers, for example, relied heavily on Jo Moore prior to her resignation.

Task forces
Such groups generally consist of 'outsiders' (in particular, business people), who examine a particular area or policy. The Labour Government was accused of becoming over-reliant on task forces after returning to office in 1997.

Some have suggested that the Government set up task forces and working groups as a way of avoiding actual 'action'. Others suggest that the Government only chooses to act on the recommendations of the task forces when they fit in with the Government's own preconceived agenda. Some task forces, such as the Advisory Group looking into Citizenship Education under Bernard Crick, have seen their recommendations taken up almost word for word. Others, such as Lord Rogers' report on urban renewal, have been rejected or put on the back burner.

The Government had instituted 50 separate task forces by the end of 1997, and 75 by the end of 1998. As early as 1997, Labour had over 500 people working in government-appointed task forces.

The role of government whips
The role of the government whips is to ensure that the government maintains a majority in votes taken in Parliament. The Chief Whip attends Cabinet meetings and has the status of a senior minister. The whips' ultimate sanction, removing the whip from an MP and thus effectively expelling him or her from the party, is used only rarely. In 1994 under John Major, however, eight Conservative MPs (the so-called 'whipless wonders') had the whip removed for disloyalty in matters connected to the Party's policy on Europe.

The Prime Minister's Office
From 1997 the Prime Minister's Office took on a clearer and more substantial structure. The Office comprises a total of around 150 staff divided between a number of different Office groupings. Until 2001 these were:

the Private Office, the Political Unit, the Strategic Communications Unit, the Press Office, and the Policy Unit.

It is the latter two that have probably provoked most discussion.

Alastair Campbell and the Press Office

The Press Office traditionally operates under the control of the Chief Press Officer (a role filled by Alastair Campbell from 1997– 2003). The role of the Office, and the Chief Press Secretary in particular, was to govern the Prime Minister's relations with the media. Prior to Alastair Campbell's appointment, the role of Chief Press Secretary was often associated with Bernard Ingham, who held the post under Margaret Thatcher and who was noted for his combative, no-nonsense style. Under Blair, Campbell became a central figure, as a greater emphasis was placed upon presentation and spin. Campbell, officially the Prime Minister's Director of Communications following the 2001 election, continued to control access to the Prime Minister, and also regulated media access to other Government ministers up to the point of his resignation in 2003. Campbell had a central role in efforts to manage the public perception of the Government's efforts, as his two civil service deputies – Godric Smith and Tom Kelly – took over the responsibility for managing lobby briefings.

The Policy Unit
The Policy Unit originated under Prime Minister Harold Wilson in 1974 and was supposed to be a planning and research body, consisting mainly of outside specialists. The staff of the Policy Unit were politically appointed. Each new Prime Minister had the opportunity to replace the entire Policy Unit Staff. In 1997, Tony Blair appointed David Miliband as the Head of the Policy Unit. After the election victory in 2001, the Policy Unit was merged with the Prime Minister's Private Office, forming the Number 10 Policy Directorate under civil servant Jeremy Heywood.

11.1   The role of the Civil Service

Introduction
The Civil Service is often described as the administrative side of the UK Government (the bureaucracy). In reality, however, top civil servants are increasingly politicised and active in the policy-making process. This has undermined the idea of **neutrality**; one of the three principles which was traditionally said to characterise civil servants. The other two principles – **anonymity** and **permanence** – have also been undermined by recent changes: the former as some civil servants become publicly known and are, in some cases, identified as being responsible for the execution of policy (for example in government agencies such as the Child Support Agency); the latter as incoming governments find it impossible to work with the civil servants appointed by the previous administration (or vice versa) or civil servants are forced to resign over policy failures (most obviously in Government agencies). Sir Richard Mottram, the senior civil servant at the heart of the Jo Moore row, for example, complained that Stephen Byers had compromised his position by forcing him to release a public statement clearing Byers of any wrongdoing (*Guardian*, March 8, 2002).

The Structure of the Civil Service
The Administration Group, which is probably the most significant part of the Civil Service is dealt with more thoroughly in Ch 11.2. This box provides a basic outline of the structure of the Civil Service as a whole.

Service-wide Generalists
These generalists work in various or all departments. The majority work in the Administrative Group which is dealt with on the next page.

Service-wide Specialists
Specialists such as economists and those working in the statisticians group work across the service providing specialist information.

Departmental Groups + Agencies
Some civil servants are tied to particular government departments. Many (75% of the Civil Service in 2005) are hived off into agencies such as the Prisons Service.

The Impact of Civil Service Reform
Growing discontent in the 1950s and early 1960s led to the Fulton Report. The Report criticised the Civil Service for its amateurish approach and tendency to promote on seniority rather than merit. The Report recommended the creation of a Civil Service Department, the abolition of Civil Service Classes, the creation of a unified grade structure with a clear career path, and the establishment of a Civil Service College. The implementation of the Reports recommendations in 1968 was incomplete and short-lived. The grade structure was never full adopted, the College was downgraded and the Civil Service Department was abolished by Thatcher in 1981. Thatcher reduced the size of the Civil Service from 750 000 staff in 1979 to 600 000 in 1990 and 534 000 by the end of 1991. Derek (later Lord) Rayner was given the responsibility of improving financial management. His Efficiency Unit led to the Financial Management Initiative (FMI). Accompanying these developments was a closer scrutiny of top level Civil Service appointments. Some accused Thatcher of politicising the Civil Service. The pace and scale of policy changes during the Thatcher years was also said to have kept the Service on its toes.

'Agencification'
The Ibbs' Report grew out of the failure of earlier reforms to address the root of the problem. Sir Robert Ibbs began work under Thatcher producing the so-called 'Next Steps' programme published in 1988. This report criticised the Civil Service for its size, poor efficiency and conservative outlook. Its recommendations were accepted in February 1988 and have remained influential since. The main impact of the programme has been the hiving-off of Government services into semi-autonomous agencies. This agencification has progressed at great pace. In April 1990 there were 12 agencies. By April 1998 there were 124 a number that had increased to 138 by the autumn (employing 380 000 staff – 75% of the Civil Service). Though the changes have been far-reaching and dramatic not all have been convinced by the results. The Child Support Agency and the Prison Service Agency have been a particular focus of attention and criticism.

How Can Civil Servants Control?
As Tony Benn remarked in 1981

'They [Civil Servants] are always trying to steer incoming Governments back to the policy of the outgoing Government, minus the mistakes that the Civil Servants thought the outgoing Government made. And remember, when a Government is elected it has maximum energy and minimum knowledge. Just before it is defeated it has maximum knowledge and minimum energy.'

There are six distinct advantages that civil servants have over ministers:

1. **Civil Servants control information** (and can either deny ministers essential information or drown the minister in paperwork);
2. **Ministers have other Commitments**;
3. **Top Civil Servants outnumber Ministers** (10:1);
4. **Networking** (civil servants can have informal meetings – often cross-departmental – and outmanoeuvre an awkward minister);
5. **Ministers can go 'native'** (becoming surrounded by the civil service and cut off from the reality outside their departments);
6. **'Outliving' ministers** (top civil servants tend to stay in the department a lot longer than the ministers do).

The Future of the Civil Service
John Major, previously criticised for lacking both vision and a flagship policy, launched his 'big idea' – the Citizen's Charter in 1991. Though it was often criticised at the time, many facets of the scheme were retained under Labour, not least the central emphasis on the quality of provision in public services. Labour has also emphasised the need for greater forward planning and the development of a less risk-averse culture in the Civil Service. Their championing of 'joined-up government' saw encouragement for a more co-operative and collaborative approach across traditional (often departmental) boundaries; as did the trend towards increasing reliance on political advisors and politicisation at the top of the Civil Service. Further changes in the Civil Service may be prompted by the fallout from the programme of devolution started in 1997.

11.2 Departments, ministers and 'their' civil servants

Introduction
Cabinet consists largely of the leading ministers from each Governmental Department. These Secretaries of State head Departments consisting of other Ministers of various ranks and Civil Servants. It is the relationship between top Ministers and their top Civil Servants that has often provoked the most debate.

Departmental Hierarchy
Departments are headed by a Secretary of State under whom there are two ranks of Junior Ministers and the position of Parliamentary Private Secretary. All three ranks serve as apprenticeships or testing grounds for MPs with ambition or potential for higher office.

As of November 2007:

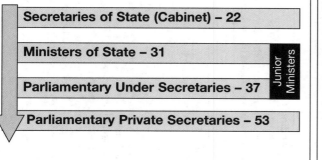

Secretaries of State (Cabinet) – 22

Ministers of State – 31

Parliamentary Under Secretaries – 37

Parliamentary Private Secretaries – 53

Junior Ministers

The Civil Service
As we have seen on the previous page a lot of Civil Servants have no real role in the policy making process. In the top 5 grades of the Administration Group however and particularly amongst those 1000 individuals who make up the top 4 grades there is significant policy input.

Administration Group Civil Servants
The top 5 Grades in the Administration Group have been known as the Senior Civil Service (SCS) since 1996. In 2005 this SCS consisted of 4640 staff with the top 4 Grades (those with key policy input) numbering about 1000.

Grade	Title
1	First Permanent Secretary
1a	Second Permanent Secretary
2	Deputy Secretary
3	Under Secretary
4	Executive Directing Bands
5	Assistant Secretary

Models of Ministerial – Civil Service Relations
Theakston, in his article 'Ministers and Mandarins' (Talking Politics Vol.4 no. 2 1991/2) outlined four models of ministerial-civil servant relationship:

The Formal Constitutional Model
This model views the Civil Service as what it was always expected to be – a service, providing the information that Ministers need, making them aware of the various permutations and problems, yet essentially remaining non-political. This model would allow for the three principles traditionally attached to the Civil Service – neutrality, anonymity and permanence. Whilst this model fits in nicely with the traditional view, it is at best only theoretical.

The Adversarial Model
This model characterises the relationship as something of a struggle for power and control. In the 1960s and 1970s Labour Ministers such as Richard Crossman and Tony Benn felt that the Civil Service was obstructing the Government's policy programme (see the quotation from Benn on the previous page). In the 1980s Margaret Thatcher felt that the Service was similarly unwilling to move ahead quickly on her radical policy programme. She, like Benn before her, accused them of having their own agenda.

The Village Life in the Whitehall Community Model
This model affords the Civil Service a greater input than that offered in the Formal Constitutional Model outlined above, yet essentially retains the idea of a close and co-operative relationship. The Ministers within the Department would provide the vision and drive, the Civil Servants would put the whole thing together based upon their long knowledge and experience of what would work. Thus, when questioned over the Maastricht Treaty, Kenneth Clarke defended the fact that he had not read the Treaty by highlighting the role of the Civil Service in addressing the detail of such legislation.

The Bureaucratic Expansionism Model
This model shares some of its suspicion of the Civil Service with the Adversarial Model, yet moves further. In the Bureaucratic Expansionism Model the Civil Servants are trying to serve their own interests by creating bureaucratic empires which are financially inefficient and get in the way of clear and effective government. It was partly a belief in this view that led to the appointment of Derek Rayner in the 1980s and the launch of the Financial Management Initiative.

Ministerial and Collective Responsibility
In theory Ministers are bound by a number of doctrines and codes of behaviour. Under the doctrine of Collective Responsibility all Cabinet Ministers are bound to publicly stand by decisions taken collectively in Cabinet – regardless of their own personal views. Thus Michael Heseltine resigned from Cabinet over his unwillingness to remain publicly silent over the Westland Affair and Nigel Lawson and Geoffrey Howe also made high profile exits under Thatcher. In reality, however ministers now rarely resign on matters of principle, favouring instead the tactic of briefing the press against their opponents within Cabinet. The doctrine of Ministerial Responsibility can be divided into two distinct strands: role responsibility and personal responsibility. The former dictates that Ministers are responsible for what goes on in their Departments and should resign if they fail in their job. The latter concerns their personal conduct and might, for example, demand resignation over sexual or financial scandals. In reality, both aspects of Ministerial Responsibility have been undermined in recent years – not least by the unwillingness of ministers to go. Norman Lamont's failure to resign over Black Wednesday in 1992 (or by what followed) could be taken as a case in point.

11.3 Quangos

What are Quangos?

The term quango is normally taken to mean …

quasi autonomous non-governmental organisation

quasi (or semi) autonomous (independent) because they tend to work with a degree of independence, non-governmental because their members are not normally drawn from the ranks of elected politicians or the Civil Service. While this may appear straightforward, there is a good deal of debate concerning precisely which groups fall inside this definition. Some take a more **exclusive** view, preferring to use the term NDPB (non-departmental public body) whereas others adopt a more **inclusive** definition and include many more groups under the broader term EGO (extra-governmental organisation). Which interpretation one favours has a dramatic affect on the numbers of quangos that one sees as existing and on attempts to discover whether overall numbers are going up or down. The narrower (exclusive) view would support the idea that there had been a fall in the number of quangos (NDPBs) from around 2000 in 1979 to around 1200 by 2002. The broader (inclusive) definition would place the number at nearer 7000, perhaps more.

Quangos and Party Politics

Though parties in opposition are often critical of the use of quangos, they invariably become more sympathetic towards them once they are in government. In 1979, for example, Margaret Thatcher criticised the number of quangos in existence, seeing them as yet another unnecessary layer of bureaucracy. By 1994, however, quangos accounted for nearly a fifth of all government expenditure and by 1997 the Labour Party was actually accusing the Conservatives of creating a 'quango-state' (or 'quangocracy'). In 1998, the new Labour Government produced two documents, *Opening up the Doors* and *Opening up Public Appointments*, following their 1997 consultation paper, *Opening Up Quangos*. Both initiatives were, however, limited in their scope and in terms of the number of quangos affected. In addition, Labour created almost as many quangos as they removed between 1997 and 1999.

Classification of Quangos

1. Advisory Quangos

Bodies that are formed from specialists with a view to providing advice and guidance to government. Examples include the CRE (the Commission for Racial Equality) or SEAC (The Spongiform Encephalopathy Advisory Committee that advised the government on BSE, 'mad-cow disease').

2. Regulatory Quangos

Bodies that apply and in some cases formulate regulations governing particular areas of activity. Examples include OFSTED (the Office for Standards in Education that organises the inspection of state schools) and the Monopolies and Mergers Commission.

3. Administrative Quangos

Bodies that manage or administer certain activities or services on behalf of the government. A good example is QCA (the Qualifications and Curriculum Authority that manages various aspects of assessment in education).

4. Spending Quangos

Bodies that are set up to spend or distribute funds on the behalf of government. Examples include the Sports Council and the various National Lottery Boards that allocate the money raised by the Lottery for good causes.

Limitations

1. Quangos are not accountable to voters for their decisions. There is, therefore, a democratic deficit – especially when jobs are transferred from elected bodies to quangos.
2. Membership can be problematic. Quangos are often appointed in an atmosphere of secrecy and there have been accusations of nepotism. Sometimes key individuals are left out and there is a sense that this may be for political reasons. For example, the omission of Professor Richard Lacey from SEAC (see above) raised some concerns.
3. Quangos' meetings are often secretive and their recommendations are often not fully made public. There is a lack of transparency.
4. The proliferation of quangos has created a further unnecessary level of bureaucracy.
5. Some quangos have been accused of waste, inefficiency or corruption.

Quangos – A Balance Sheet

Positive Uses

1. Their virtual independence from government and the secrecy in which they often work allows quangos to make the right decisions rather than politically motivated or expedient ones.
2. In certain areas, regulation for example, a certain degree of independence is particularly helpful.
3. The appointment process **can** allow the creation of bodies that are more socially representative than would be achieved through election.
4. Specialists are more suited to dealing with many areas of policy than ministers or most top civil servants.
5. By focusing on one area, quangos often avoid problems caused by conflicting priorities in government.
6. Quangos reduce the workload of ministers and departments.
7. Many quangos operate at a local level where decisions can be made more relevant to those that they affect.

12.1 Unitary and federal systems

Introduction

The UK is traditionally said to be a **unitary state** as opposed to a **federal one**. This means that **ultimate power** in the UK is held by the central government at Westminster. Any power that local government, regional government or Europe appears to have, is merely delegated or **'devolved'** to it and can be withdrawn at any time.

Federal systems are different in that ultimate power (**sovereignty**) is divided between a **central government** and a number of **regions** or **individual states**. Each **tier** of government has ultimate authority over certain areas of policy i.e. they have **separate spheres of authority.**

The relationship between the central government and the various states is **entrenched** i.e. the central government cannot take away the powers of individual states without their consent.

In recent years, however, some commentators have questioned just how different the UK and US systems really are i.e. the extent to which the UK system has become 'more federal' and the US system has become 'more unitary'.

In reality, however, though this may appear to be the case, the two systems remain fundamentally different.

Unitary Systems

Central Government — Exercises wide ranging powers over → **The People**

Central Government — Delegates limited powers to → **Sub-national Gov.**

The People — Grant wide ranging powers to → Central Government

Sub-national Gov. — Exercises limited powers over → The People

The People — Elect → Sub-national Gov.

Federal Systems

Central Government — Exercises wide ranging powers over → **The People**

The People — Grant wide ranging powers to → Central Government

State Governments — Exercises wide ranging powers over → **The People**

The People — Grant wide ranging powers to → State Governments

Is the UK becoming 'more federal'?

YES

New Labour's devolution programme saw real power transferred from Westminster to the new institutions.

In the case of Scotland these powers were extensive i.e. primary legislative powers.

It would be difficult for Westminster to take back devolved powers without a further referendum.

The ongoing process of EU integration has also seen significant power transferred from Westminster to a supra-national level.

NO

Although the primary legislative powers given to Scotland are indeed significant, many of the other bodies created after 1997 are not nearly so powerful.

The Westminster Parliament always retains the right to take power back – as with the suspension of power-sharing in Northern Ireland between 2002 and 2007.

There is no legal requirement to hold a referendum before dissolving devolved institutions as Parliament is still sovereign.

As such, the UK can also withdraw from the EU with a regular act of parliament.

Is the USA becoming 'more unitary'?

YES

The massive expansion of the Federal (i.e. central) Government since 1789. The US Federal Bureaucracy now has as many employees per head of population as the UK Civil Service.

The Federal Government's use of grants as a way of controlling the States e.g. the imposition of a national drinking age.

The willingness of States to give up power to the Federal Government in times of emergency, e.g. at the time of the New Deal or post 9/11.

The US Supreme Court's failure to protect State rights over time.

NO

The States still have significant powers under the 10th Amendment (reserved powers).

These powers cannot be taken away without their consent and major changes would normally require a constitutional amendment.

The Federal Government does not have the will or the resources to control every aspect of government at State level.

Before 9/11 there was actually a move to return power to the States and get the Federal Government out of people's lives (i.e. New Federalism).

12.2 Local government

Introduction

The basic units of local government – parish, county and borough – date back to the end of the Middle Ages. Even in the 1960s, however, there was little uniformity. In some areas authorities were too small to provide services effectively or efficiently, in others they were too big to allow a good degree of democratic accountability. This problem of accountability was also emphasised by the unclear division of roles between different tiers of local government – the voters simply did not know who was responsible for what. Although the introduction of more unitary authorities and the innovation of directly elected mayors has served to address some of these concerns, low levels of turnout and high levels of protest voting at local elections would suggest that citizens do not hold local government in high regard.

Central government controls

Legislation

Central government has power to extend or limit the range and extent of local government activities by statute or through delegated legislation. If it wanted to it could abolish local government outright.

Finance

Central government can regulate the level of central government grant to local government. Central government can also cap the levels of local taxation.

Inspections

Central government can inspect the delivery of local government services directly, or through organisations such as Ofsted.

The Doctrine of *Ultra Vires*

Local authorities are only allowed to do what is authorised by law. Anything else is *ultra vires* (beyond their authority). Individual councillors can be prosecuted and fined (surcharged) to pay for the costs incurred in pursuing such policies.

Acting in Default

Ultimately, central government can act in default, taking a particular local service under the direct control of central government.

During the 1980s, faced with an extended period of Conservative government at Westminster, many Labour-controlled councils in urban areas sought to pursue a socialist agenda at a local level. This so-called municipal socialism provoked legal action and threats of default proceedings in a number of areas, e.g. in 1985 several councillors on the Labour-controlled Liverpool City Council were surcharged £106 000, having set an illegal deficit budget. They included Derek Hatton, the Deputy Leader of the Council, who was expelled from the Labour Party the following year as part of Neil Kinnock's purge on members of the 'outlawed' Militant Tendency.

Local government finance

Most of local government revenue has traditionally been provided in the form of a central government revenue grant and nationally distributed business rates. It is the issue of local taxation, however, that remains the most controversial:

Firstly, because it comes as a highly visible annual bill and must be met from disposable income; and

Secondly, because people do not really understand what local taxation is for.

The changing face of local taxation

The Rates: until 1989 all UK local authorities levied rates. This was a property based tax under which the owner of each property was charged an annual tax based upon the size and standard of the property.

The Community Charge ('Poll Tax'): the Poll Tax, so-called because everyone over 18 was eligible, was introduced in 1990 in England and Wales (1989 in Scotland). The Conservatives argued that by making everyone pay the same, the policy would make local authorities more accountable for the services provided. The unprecedented opposition to the Poll Tax – in terms of mass demonstrations, non-registration and non-payment – contributed to Margaret Thatcher's demise in 1990. New Environment Secretary Michael Heseltine announced plans to scrap the tax in 1991 and the Council Tax was introduced in 1993.

The Council Tax: This was a property-based tax – like the rates – but with significant concessions for those who were living alone or less able to pay.

Do we need local government?

The debate over local government usually focuses on the extent to which it continues to serve a useful function within the UK system:

	Representation	Relevance
Political participation		
The existence of local government encourages people to get involved in making the decisions that will affect them the most...	Local government can represent local people more effectively than Westminster...	Local councils know what the local area needs. It makes sense to delegate power...
BUT ...participation rates in local government are extremely low and voter turnout is poor.	BUT ... councillors rarely have the resources or the time to represent local people properly. Local government is amateurish.	BUT ... local governments often get lost in the detail and fail to see the bigger picture. Central government can often be more objective and, therefore, more appropriate.

Regardless of this debate, however, it is inevitable that some form of local government will persist; if only because of the existing pressures on the Westminster government.

12.3 Devolution: the Scottish Parliament and the Welsh Assembly

Introduction

For many, devolution was one of the 'hot' issues of the 1970s. The successes of the nationalists in Scotland in the 1974 elections put the issue firmly on the agenda, and the referendums of March 1979 offered both the Scots and the Welsh the opportunity to achieve a degree of devolved government. In the event, the referendum showed little support for such a move in Wales. In Scotland the 'yes-campaign' won the majority of votes but the regulations governing the referendum stated that there needed to be support from 40% of the electorate for the plans to go ahead. Though the 'yes' camp had the majority of votes cast, the turnout was not sufficient to take them over the 40% of electorate threshold. The failure in the referendums took some steam out of the campaign for devolution but support grew again in the late 1980s, and by the time of the 1997 general election the Labour Party was committed to new referendums in Scotland and in Wales. In September 1997 these referendums ran on the basis of a simple majority of those voting; that is, without the 40% of the electorate requirement that had caused so many problems in the 1979 Scottish Referendum.

The Scottish Parliament

The Referendum

In its 1997 election manifesto the Labour Party had committed itself to a referendum on the question of devolution for Scotland. The Referendum that took place in September 1997 presented the Scottish electorate with two questions: whether there should be a Scottish Parliament and whether the Parliament should have tax-varying powers. The questions offered voters the chance to vote 'no, no', 'yes, no' or 'yes, yes':

Parliament	Yes 74.3%	No 25.7%	Tax-varying	Yes 63.5%	No 36.5%

Election and composition

Elections are completed under an AMS (FPTP-TU) system	Party	FPTP seats			List top-up			Total MSPs		
		1999	2003	2007	1999	2003	2007	1999	2003	2007
	Conservative	0	3	4	18	15	13	18	18	17
	Labour	53	46	37	3	4	9	56	50	46
	LibDem	12	13	11	5	4	5	17	17	16
	SNP	7	9	21	28	18	26	35	27	47
	Others	1	2	0	2	15	3	3	17	3
	Totals	73	73	73	56	56	56	129	129	129

Function and effectiveness

The Scottish Parliament had significant power devolved to it at the time of its creation. Though areas such as foreign policy, employment legislation and control of the monetary system were reserved for the Westminster Parliament, Scotland took total primary legislative control of areas such as education, agriculture, and law and home affairs. The second 'yes' in the 'yes, yes' referendum result also gave the Parliament income tax-varying powers.

No party won an overall majority in the Parliament elections so the LibDem and Labour groups went into coalition to form an administration headed by First Minister Donald Dewar (later Henry McLeish and Jack McConnell). Though the administration has been criticised in some areas (for example, the debacle over Scottish public examination results) it has made significant moves in other areas (for example, addressing the issue of student loans). Following the 2007 election the SNP formed a minority administration.

NB From 2005, the number of Scottish MPs in the **Westminster Parliament** was reduced from 72 to 59 as a partial remedy for what was once called the 'West Lothian Question' – the problem of what to do about the 'double representation' of Scottish voters once devolution had occurred.

The Welsh Assembly

The Referendum

As was the case with Scottish devolution, the Labour Party had a 1997 manifesto commitment to bring forward proposals for and a referendum on devolving power to a Welsh Assembly. The election of the Labour government led, therefore, to the 1997 Referendum. Unlike in Scotland, where voters were faced with two questions, Welsh voters simply had to decide whether or not they supported the government's proposals:

Yes	50.3% (559 419 votes)	No	49.7% (552 698 votes)

Election and composition

Elections are completed under an AMS (FPTP-TU) system	Party	FPTP seats			List top-up			Total MWAs		
		1999	2003	2007	1999	2003	2007	1999	2003	2007
	Conservative	1	1	5	8	10	7	9	11	12
	Labour	27	30	24	1	0	2	28	30	26
	LibDem	3	3	3	3	3	3	6	6	6
	Plaid Cymru	9	5	7	8	7	8	17	12	15
	Others	0	1	1	0	0	0	0	1	1
	Totals	40	40	40	20	20	20	60	60	60

Function and effectiveness

The Assembly was not given the same powers as the Scottish Parliament. The Assembly has no primary legislative powers but can recommend legislation to the UK Parliament and has a role in overseeing Welsh quangos. It can also implement Westminster legislation in Wales. The Assembly does not have the income tax-varying powers afforded the Scottish Parliament.

As was the case in Scotland, the Assembly Elections did not provide any one party with an overall majority. Unusually, however, the Labour group under Alun Michael decided to go it alone in a minority administration. Michael was widely regarded as someone who had been imposed on the Welsh Labour Party from Westminster and he struggled to achieve any real degree of control. In 2000 he resigned and was replaced as First Secretary by Rhodri Morgan, the man who many felt should have been given the job at the outset. Morgan took the Labour group into coalition with the LibDems though Labour took sole control once more following the 2003 Assembly elections. In the wake of the 2007 elections Labour went into coalition with Plaid Cymru.

12.4 Northern Ireland

The Good Friday Agreement

The Good Friday Agreement came at the end of more than a decade of negotiations, reviews and proposals. The Anglo-Irish Agreement of 1985 established the right of the Republic of Ireland to have a say in policy making in Northern Ireland and this paved the way for the Downing Street Declaration in 1993. This joint declaration from the British and Irish Governments and the framework document that followed in 1995 provided the basis for further negotiations. The IRA restored its cease-fire on July 19, 1997 and this opened the way for the all-party talks that resulted in the Good Friday Agreement of April 1998. The Agreement was confirmed by referendum. In Northern Ireland, 71.1% voted in favour of the Agreement and in the Republic support was at 94.4% for an agreement that involved giving up their Constitutional claims to the North.

The Terms of the Good Friday Agreement

1. An *Elected Northern Ireland Assembly*: made up of 108 elected members and holding legislative powers.
2. A *Governing Executive Committee*: made up of 12 ministers and headed by a First Minister.
3. A *North-South Ministerial Council*: allowing ministers from Dublin and Belfast to co-ordinate and promote joint policies.
4. A *Prisoner Release Programme*: in light of the peace process, terrorist prisoners from both sides of the divide were to be released on license.
5. A *Council of the Isles*: drawing together representatives from Dublin, Belfast, Westminster, Scottish Parliament and Welsh Assembly.
6. *RUC Reform*: eventually the subject of the Independent Commission on Policing under Chris Patten. Included, symbolically, changing the name of the force.
7. *Arms Decommissioning*: to be supervised by an international commission.

Political Parties in Northern Ireland

Unionist

Ulster Unionist Party (UUP)

The UUP was the Party that effectively governed the North from 1922–1972. The Party's members at Westminster tend to vote with the Conservative Party with whom they were closely aligned before the decision to bring in direct rule in 1972. They signed up to the Good Friday Agreement and are generally regarded as the more moderate of the two unionist parties.

Democratic Unionist Party (DUP)

Ian Paisley formed the DUP in 1971 as an offshoot of the UUP. The Party opposed the Good Friday Agreement and traditionally took the more extreme unionist stance, being less willing to make concessions to the Catholic community in the North.

Election Performance in Northern Ireland % vote (seats won)

	2005 General Election	2007 NI Assembly
DUP	33.7% (9)	30.1% (36)
UUP	17.7% (1)	14.9% (18)
	18 seats available	108 seats available

Republican (Nationalist)

Social Democratic and Labour Party (SDLP)

The Party was founded in 1970 as a nationalist rather than a Catholic party but it is fair to say that the vast bulk of its support comes from the Catholic community. The SDLP played a leading role in brokering the Good Friday Agreement and they are widely regarded as the more moderate of the two nationalist groups.

Sinn Fein

Sinn Fein's military wing is the IRA and prior to the 1980s it refused to offer Westminster elections legitimacy by putting up candidates. Since then, however, they have stood in elections and in recent years – particularly as they have taken a more active role in the peace process – their support has increased significantly.

Election Performance in Northern Ireland % vote (seats won)

	2005 General Election	2007 NI Assembly
SF	24.3% (5)	26.2% (28)
SDLP	17.5% (3)	15.2% (16)
	18 seats available	108 seats available

The 2007 Northern Ireland Executive: power-sharing arrangements were restored in 2007, having been suspended from 2002–2007 as a result of renewed paramilitary violence. The Assembly elections held in 2007 (see above) resulted in the DUP and Sinn Fein taking 9 of the 12 positions available on the Executive. The DUP leader, the Rev. Ian Paisley, subsequently took on the role of First Minister with Sinn Fein's Martin McGuinness as Deputy First Minister. In 2008 Peter Robinson succeeded Ian Paisley as DUP leader.

13.1 The origins and organisation of the European Union

Historical context

At the end of the Second World War there was a widely-held desire to bind states together in some kind of economic organisation in order to prevent Europe from descending into war once again. The European Coal and Steel Community was formed in 1952 and included France, Germany, Italy, Belgium, the Netherlands and Luxembourg. In 1957 these six member states signed the Treaty of Rome, creating the European Economic Community (EEC) and the European Atomic Energy Community. This treaty broadened the Coal and Steel Community to include foreign trade and agriculture. At that time the UK favoured retaining close trading links with the US ('the special relationship') and the newly-formed Commonwealth.

Economic union into European Union

By the 1980s it was widely accepted that the EEC had achieved many of its initial objectives. Peace between the major European powers had been preserved for over 35 years and the Common Agricultural Policy had, for the most part, succeeded in regulating production of key 'products' through the use of subsidies and quotas. Many felt that the EEC needed to set itself new targets; ones that reflected how far Europe had come since the war.

In 1986 the Single European Act created a single European market where the 'four freedoms' of goods, persons, services and capital could be preserved; all four would be able to move freely across the borders of European Community states. The Maastricht Treaty of 1992 took things a stage further. It created the European Union (EU), extending the Community beyond the economic into areas such as justice and home affairs, foreign and security policy. The EU was, therefore, to be based on three pillars:

The European Community	Foreign and security policy	Justice and home affairs

The Treaty of Amsterdam built upon Maastricht, extending cooperation. This left the Treaty of Nice, the EU constitution (2004) and the Lisbon Treaty which replaced it to address EU enlargement and the reform of EU institutions.

Key Steps

1952	Coal and Steel Community
1958	Treaty of Rome – EEC formed
1973	UK joined
1986	Single European Act
1992	Maastricht Treaty
1997	Amsterdam Treaty
2001	The Nice Treaty
2004	Accession of 10 new states brings total to 25
2005	French and Dutch rejection of new EU constitution
2007	Lisbon Treaty agreed

The main institutions of the European Union

The Council of the European Union

Often referred to as the Council of Ministers, this body consists of ministers from the 27 member states. The actual minister involved will depend on the nature of the issues being discussed. If, for example, defence policy were being discussed then the 27 national defence ministers might meet. The presidency of the Council operates on a rota. The Council is the main decision-making institution. Its work is supported by COREPER (the Committee of Permanent Representatives). COREPER is made up of officials from each country and it undertakes the necessary preparation in between the various Council meetings. COREPER oversees the work of around 100 more specialised working groups. Some decisions must be taken unanimously but others operate under qualified majority voting (see right).

The European Commission

Until 2005 the Commission consisted of 20 commissioners: two from each of the larger countries (France, Germany, Spain, Italy and the UK) and one from each of the remaining ten member states. Each commissioner was responsible for a certain area. Britain's commissioners were Neil Kinnock (Vice-President of the Commission and Commissioner for Administrative Reform) and Chris Patten (Commissioner for External Relations). The commissioners are appointed for a fixed term of five years. The Commission was reformed in 2005 following the accession of 10 new member states. Under the commissioners work a staff of around 15 000 people divided up into over 30 Directorates-General. Around one-fifth of the staff are employed in the translation and interpreting services. These people ensure that the texts of treaties and directives are available in the native languages of all member states. The Commission has the role of initiating legislation and making proposals to the Council and the Parliament. It also acts as the guardian (enforcer) of EU treaties and holds power to execute agreed policies.

Qualified majority voting

In areas such as foreign and security matters and enlargement of the EU, a unanimous vote is required in the Council of Ministers. This means that states effectively have a veto over such issues. In most areas, however, a system of QMV operates. Under this system, countries' votes are weighted roughly in relation to their population. Under the Treaty of Nice, for example, the UK had 29 votes to Malta's 3. In any vote under QMV a successful proposal must secure a fixed proportion of votes. No one country, therefore, can reject proposals under QMV. Under Nice, QMV was extended into far more areas.

Other EU institutions

Court of Justice; Court of Auditors; European Central Bank; Economic and Social Committee; Committee of the Regions; European Investment Bank; European Ombudsman.

The European Parliament

The European Parliament is the only EU institution that is democratically elected by citizens in each of its member states. In the UK elections now operate under the regional party list system. The Parliament had a total of 731 members in June 2005, with the larger states electing more than the smaller. The UK had 78 members, for example, whereas Luxembourg only has six. Initially, Parliament only had the power to advise, but in recent years it has been given some powers to amend legislation. This increased power – the co-decision procedure – sees the Parliament on an equal footing in some areas of policy; for example, health and the environment, where Parliament has been able to secure improvements in fuel quality with a view to reducing pollution (from 2000). The Parliament also has control of the purse strings: each year, the President of the Parliament has to approve the budget before it can come into effect. As a result the EU can, in theory, reject the EU budget. MEPs also have a role in approving the Commission President and the Commission, and can censure the entire Commission – forcing it to resign. This might well have happened in 1999, following allegations of corruption, had not the 20 commissioners resigned en masse on March 15 – removing the need for Parliamentary censure.

13.2   The EU since Maastricht

The Treaty of Nice and EU Institutions

The European Parliament
The Treaty of Nice limited the number of MEPs to 732; apportioned between the 25 member states (post-enlargement) in broad proportion to population. In 2005 the UK had 78 seats (previously 87), Germany had 99 (99), and the largest and smallest of the 10 new member states, Poland and Malta, had 54 and 5 respectively. The Treaty also enhanced the European Parliament's legislative powers (the co-decision procedure). The organisation and funding of political parties at European level came under the scrutiny of the Council of Ministers.

The European Commission
If the EU enlargement envisaged under Nice had gone ahead without reform of the system by which Commissioners were allocated, the Commission would have numbered over 30 from 2005. Under the Treaty of Nice, therefore, the Commission was reduced to one Commissioner per member state up to a maximum of 27. The Treaty mandated the Council of Ministers to revisit the question of Commission size once EU membership had exceeded 27. In June 2005 the EU and, therefore, the Commission was 25 strong. Britain's appointee was Trade Commissioner Peter Mandelson.

As well as dealing with questions of size and composition, the Treaty of Nice offered enhanced executive powers for the Commission's President; José Manuel Barroso in June 2005.

These included the powers to:
- allocate and change Commissioner's portfolios at will
- demand the resignation of a Commissioner, subject to the Commission's approval.

The Council of Ministers
The enlargement of the EU in 2005, from 15 to 25 members, made it virtually impossible for the Council to work on the basis of unanimity. The Treaty of Nice foresaw this and consequently proposed the extension of QMV into over 30 areas previously decided on the basis of unanimity. The weighting of each state's votes also had to change as states joined. The Treaty of Nice proposed that the UK would hold 29 votes, as would Germany, France and Italy. Poland, the largest of the states to join in 2005, was given 27, with Malta (the smallest of the new states) getting 3. The number of votes required to pass a measure under QMV was also changed under Nice, but member states were given the right to insist that ministers representing 62% of the EU population approved a measure before it could pass.

A New Constitution for the EU?
The proposed constitution, running to over 400 pages, sought to bring together the various existing treaties into a single authoritative (codified) document that set out the rules of the Union. In the UK the Labour Government argued that the document was merely a 'tidying up' exercise, after decades of EU enlargement and widening powers. Others saw it as a step towards a 'United States of Europe'.

The proposed Constitution did not grant the EU any additional powers but it would have:
- strengthened the role of the European Parliament
- enhanced the role of national parliaments in revising EU law
- extended QMV into 26 policy areas that previously allowed the national veto (e.g. asylum)

The ratification of the Constitution was suspended in June 2005, following the decision of French and Dutch voters to reject the proposals in referendums on May 29 and June 1 respectively. However, many elements of the constitution were revived in the Lisbon Treaty (2007).

The Future of the Common Agricultural Policy (CAP)
The CAP was introduced in the 1960s. It worked on the principle that when market prices were low, the EEC would buy up surplus production; thus stabilising prices. Some foodstuffs were stored; the so-called grain-mountains, butter-mountains and wine-lakes. When goods were in short supply, the EEC would release stored goods or offer subsidies to encourage production. In some areas, a farmer would need to hold a 'quota' in order to start production (e.g. milk); in others the EEC would pay farmers to farm nothing (set-aside).

Some CAP reform took place in the 1990s, but EU expansion has necessitated further changes in the programme. According to the Guardian, the CAP still accounted for around 40% of the EU's budget (€45.09 billion) in 2003, despite the fact that the industry only accounted for around 5% of employment and 1.6% of output.

Britain's Budget Rebate
The difference between what Britain pays into the EU and what it gets back in EU funding led Margaret Thatcher to negotiate the UK's budget rebate at Fontainebleau in 1984. In the wake of the French rejection of the new EU Constitution in May 2005 (see above), several countries, including France, argued for a significant cut, if not an outright abolition of the rebate (which amounted to €5.18 billion in 2003). Britain argued that any cut in the rebate should be dependent on CAP reform; as it was the operation of the latter that necessitated the former. Though the UK and France each paid €15.15 billion into the EU in 2003, France received €6.45 billion more in CAP funding than the UK.

The Single Currency
In January 2002 the Euro became the legal currency in 12 EU member states. On February 28, 2002 their old national currencies became obsolete. The UK, Sweden and Denmark did not join the single currency at this point.

Deepening the Union
The Treaty of Nice encouraged greater co-operation by requiring only 8 EU states to agree before so-called 'enhanced co-operation' could take place. Other states are then free to join as and when they see fit; creating a 'multi-track Europe'.

Common Foreign and Security Policy
A series of events in the 1990s, including the fallout from the collapse of Yugoslavia, led some European leaders to believe that a European-wide peace-keeping force or rapid-reaction force might be the best way to deal with problems on the continent. Concerns regarding the chain of command, however, make foreign policy co-operation in the form of Europe-wide economic sanctions against suspect regimes far more likely.

Home Affairs and Justice
Some progress already (for example the Social Chapter and increased cross-border co-operation on crime). The Union is likely to develop further in this area.

14.1 Rights

Introduction

As is often stated, the UK does not have a formal 'Bill of Rights' in the US sense – that is, a codified and entrenched (i.e. not easily amended or repealed) document setting out the various rights afforded to citizens. Citizens' rights in the UK have traditionally been protected by a combination of existing statutes, common law and case law. Many saw the Human Rights Act as a step towards a more formal declaration of rights, but it falls short of allowing courts to void conflicting statute and – as we have seen with the recent anti-terrorism legislation – is too easily brushed aside by government in times of apparent crisis.

What are rights?

Natural rights

Philosophers such as John Locke have identified so-called natural rights; universal God-given and inalienable rights including life, liberty and property. Such ideas are echoed in documents such as the US Declaration of Independence (1776). A belief in 'natural rights' rests on the concept of a 'natural human state' (pre-dating political structures and society).

Citizens' rights

More commonly when we refer to rights, we are referring to those rights granted to citizens by the state. Such **positive rights** should, in theory, be more tangible because they have been set out and recorded by an institution rather than being part of an attempt philosophically to reconstruct pre-history.

The rights of British citizens (?)

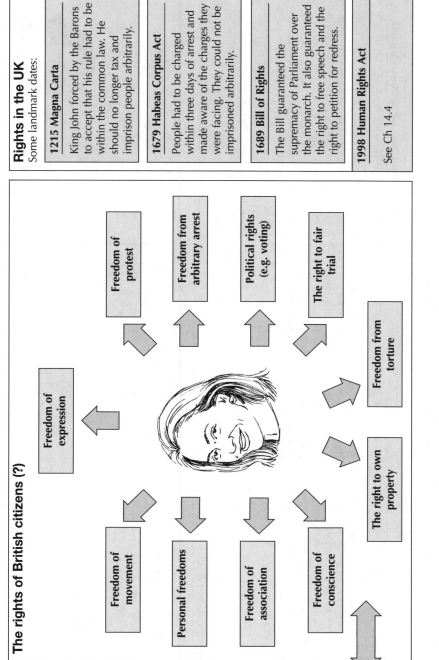

Freedom of expression

Freedom of protest

Freedom from arbitrary arrest

Political rights (e.g. voting)

The right to fair trial

Freedom from torture

The right to own property

Freedom of conscience

Freedom of association

Personal freedoms

Freedom of movement

The reality?

While the rights outlined above might be available to citizens in most cases, there have been numerous examples of such rights being violated in recent years. During the Miners' Strike in 1984–85, for example, free movement for many non-miners was prevented by police efforts to stop striking miners entering Nottingham to picket pits that were still working. Terrorist suspects (especially following the recent measures) are not afforded the same rights as those suspected of other violent crimes. Our freedom of speech is restricted by – amongst other things – laws outlawing certain inflammatory forms of racism and blasphemy. The Criminal Justice Act (1994) gave the police massive discretionary powers to stop and search and to regulate (and in many cases make illegal) certain forms of protest. In the same act the government effectively removed the right to silence by allowing judges to direct juries to take note of a defendant's decision to remain silent where, previously, no inference was supposed to be drawn from a failure to answer questions. The suggestion that the government is looking to further limit access to trial by jury has led to calls for a codified and entrenched Bill of Rights for Britain.

Rights in the UK
Some landmark dates:

1215 Magna Carta

King John forced by the Barons to accept that his rule had to be within the common law. He should no longer tax and imprison people arbitrarily.

1679 Habeas Corpus Act

People had to be charged within three days of arrest and made aware of the charges they were facing. They could not be imprisoned arbitrarily.

1689 Bill of Rights

The Bill guaranteed the supremacy of Parliament over the monarch. It also guaranteed the right to free speech and the right to petition for redress.

1998 Human Rights Act

See Ch 14.4

14.2 Redress of grievances

The nature of grievances

Government is an imprecise science and it is inevitable that many individuals will find themselves in a position where they feel that they have a justifiable grievance against some agency or tier of government. An individual might feel that their planning application has been dealt with unfairly, or that their tax allowances have been calculated incorrectly. They may feel that they are being victimised by a government agency or that a local authority is failing to discharge a particular aspect of its duties effectively. Any number of serious grievances might motivate a citizen to seek redress. What avenues are open to them?

The Citizen's Charter

The Citizen's Charter – John Major's 'big idea' – was launched in 1991. Charters were to be drawn up setting out the levels of service citizens could expect from public bodies. Such bodies would be expected to meet these target levels. Citizens were, therefore, presented with something concrete to measure services against. The Citizen's Charter also gave the service providers something to aim at – an aspect of the policy enhanced by the issuing of Charter Marks for excellence in public service.

Channels for redressing grievances

Tribunals

Tribunals sometimes offer a source of redress where there is no real remedy through the courts, whether because the complainant does not have the ability (perhaps the money) to pursue the case legally or because they have been denied the right to judicial review. Tribunals offer a relatively cheap and easy way of having a grievance considered. Hundreds of different types of tribunals exist to mediate in disputes not only between citizens and the various agencies of the state but also between employers and employees.

The courts

The courts do not generally deal with the merits of particular act or decision. They tend to look more at the way in which the decision was taken – whether the correct procedures were followed or whether the minister was acting within their authority when making a decision. Judicial review in the UK is not, therefore, the same as that in the US where courts can strike down acts and regulations. Access to the legal system is also limited by the cost of embarking on such actions and on the difficulty in being granted judicial review in your case.

Judicial review

In the UK judicial review normally takes place where unreasonableness, illegality or procedural impropriety can be found. The High Court, for example, found that the Foreign Office had illegally decided to spend £34 million on the Malaysian Pergau Dam project. It ordered that a further £65.6 million set aside for similar projects should be paid back into the overseas aid budget.

Inquiries

Public inquiries exist to take in views about proposed projects or to investigate particular events (e.g. the 'arms for Iraq' inquiry). Inquiries are often very long and expensive. The Heathrow Terminal 5 inquiry, for example, ran from 1995 to 1999 costing taxpayers £80 million. Some feel that inquiries are often PR exercises and that governments generally pick and choose which, if any, inquiry recommendations to accept. At the time of writing the government is planning to do away with inquiries for airport and roads projects.

The European Court of Human Rights

The Court was set up in 1950 to enforce the various guarantees set out in the European Convention on Human Rights (EHCR). Cases from Britain could be taken to the Court where the domestic appeals procedures had been exhausted. Up to 1998 the European Commission on Human Rights received about 800 cases each year from British citizens and, by 1997, the Court had found violations of human rights in 50 out of the 98 cases referred to it. Under the Human Rights Act (1998) which came into force in October 2000 many of the protections set out in the ECHR are now available to citizens in British courts. This act is dealt with more fully in Ch 14.4.

Elected representatives

Individuals can approach their elected representatives for help in redressing their grievances. MPs can speak or write to ministers and civil servants, ask parliamentary questions and seek to initiate debates in the House on behalf of their constituents. Local representatives might also be able to address grievances and facilitate some remedy. In many ways, working through one's elected representatives was the traditional way of having one's concerns addressed. In recent years, however, many citizens have come to see MPs as too controlled by their party and special interests to provide effective help. Such feelings were brought in to focus by the 'cash for questions' scandal and the subsequent activities and findings of the Parliamentary Commissioner for Standards (Gordon Downey and later Elizabeth Filkin).

Ombudsmen (see ombudsman.org.uk)

An ombudsman ('people's friend') has the role of investigating complaints made by the public and suggesting possible redress where they find maladministration. Though ombudsmen have little real power, they do have a certain authority and the ability to shame.

Example: On November 1, 2001 Michael Buckley in his capacity as Health Service Ombudsman found in favour of a woman who had complained about the way in which she had been treated by St Mary's NHS Trust following a miscarriage. He was particularly critical of the Hospital's 'insensitive disposal of the foetus'.

14.3 The UK judiciary

The structure of the judiciary in England and Wales

The term 'judiciary' is a collective noun referring to all UK judges, from Lay Magistrates right the way up to the Law Lords. In a wider sense it can also be taken to mean all of those who are directly involved in the administration and application of justice.

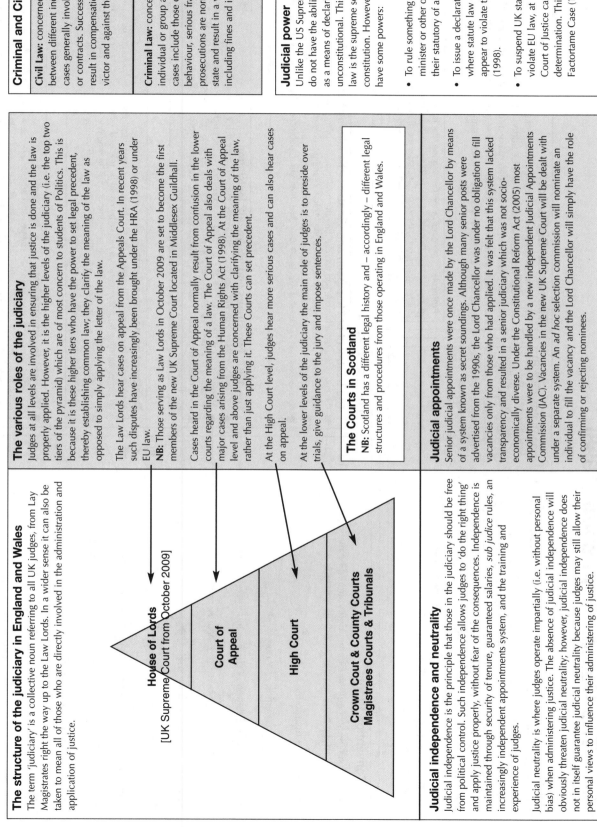

House of Lords

[UK Supreme Court from October 2009]

Court of Appeal

High Court

Crown Cout & County Courts Magistraes Courts & Tribunals

The various roles of the judiciary

Judges at all levels are involved in ensuring that justice is done and the law is properly applied. However, it is the higher levels of the judiciary (i.e. the top two tiers of the pyramid) which are of most concern to students of Politics. This is because it is these higher tiers who have the power to set legal precedent, thereby establishing common law; they clarify the meaning of the law as opposed to simply applying the letter of the law.

The Law Lords hear cases on appeal from the Appeals Court. In recent years such disputes have increasingly been brought under the HRA (1998) or under EU law.

NB: Those serving as Law Lords in October 2009 are set to become the first members of the new UK Supreme Court located in Middlesex Guildhall.

Cases heard in the Court of Appeal normally result from confusion in the lower courts regarding the meaning of a law. The Court of Appeal also deals with major cases arising from the Human Rights Act (1998). At the Court of Appeal level and above judges are concerned with clarifying the meaning of the law, rather than just applying it. These Courts can set precedent.

At the High Court level, judges hear more serious cases and can also hear cases on appeal.

At the lower levels of the judiciary the main role of judges is to preside over trials, give guidance to the jury and impose sentences.

The Courts in Scotland

NB: Scotland has a different legal history and – accordingly – different legal structures and procedures from those operating in England and Wales.

Judicial appointments

Senior judicial appointments were once made by the Lord Chancellor by means of a system known as secret soundings. Although many senior posts were advertised from the 1990s, the Lord Chancellor was under no obligation to fill vacancies only from those who had applied. It was felt that this system lacked transparency and resulted in a senior judiciary which was not socio-economically diverse. Under the Constitutional Reform Act (2005) most appointments were to be handled by a new independent Judicial Appointments Commission (JAC). Vacancies in the new UK Supreme Court will be dealt with under a separate system. An *ad hoc* selection commission will nominate an individual to fill the vacancy and the Lord Chancellor will simply have the role of confirming or rejecting nominees.

Judicial independence and neutrality

Judicial independence is the principle that those in the judiciary should be free from political control. Such independence allows judges to 'do the right thing' and apply justice properly, without fear of the consequences. Independence is maintained through security of tenure, guaranteed salaries, *sub judice* rules, an increasingly independent appointments system, and the training and experience of judges.

Judicial neutrality is where judges operate impartially (i.e. without personal bias) when administering justice. The absence of judicial independence will obviously threaten judicial neutrality; however, judicial independence does not in itself guarantee judicial neutrality because judges may still allow their personal views to influence their administering of justice.

Criminal and Civil Law

Civil Law: concerned with interrelationships between different individuals and groups. Civil cases generally involve matters such as wills or contracts. Successful civil cases generally result in compensation awards in favour of the victor and against those losing the case.

Criminal Law: concerned with crimes by an individual or group against the state. Criminal cases include those concerning violent behaviour, serious fraud or burglary. These prosecutions are normally conducted by the state and result in a variety of punishments including fines and imprisonment.

Judicial power

Unlike the US Supreme Court, UK courts do not have the ability to use judicial review as a means of declaring acts of the legislature unconstitutional. This is because statute law is the supreme source of the UK constitution. However, the Courts do have some powers:

- To rule something *ultra vires* where a minister or other official has acted beyond their statutory of authority.

- To issue a declaration of incompatibility where statute law or actions of the executive appear to violate the Human Rights Act (1998).

- To suspend UK statute where it appears to violate EU law, at least until the European Court of Justice can make a final determination. This power resulted from the Factortame Case (1990).

14.4 The Human Rights Act (1998)

Context

The European Convention on Human Rights, signed in 1950, set up a Commission of Human Rights and a European Court of Human Rights (not to be confused with the European Court of Justice) to enforce the Articles of the Convention; some of which are now incorporated into the Human Rights Act. This Act was passed in 1998 and came into force in October 2000.

The European Court of Human Rights (ECHR)

The ECHR sits in Strasbourg and was established by the Convention to hear cases where governments were accused of violating the Convention's terms. Appeals by individuals could only take place when the national appeals process had been exhausted and when the Commission of Rights declared cases admissible. This was an extremely long process. The passing of the HRA has allowed individuals the opportunity of using the Articles in the British courts.

The Human Rights Act

The Act itself does not bring all of the rights or protocols of the Convention into British law – though those areas left out can be added later if necessary. If acts of Parliament conflict with the HRA then the courts can make a 'declaration of incompatibility'. Government and Parliament then have to consider whether the law needs changing and in the meantime the courts have to enforce the law as it stands.

Protocols … are parts of the Convention that have been added since the Convention was first drafted. Some, though not all, of these are incorporated into the HRA. Others are already catered for in existing laws. Protocol 1 includes the right to protection of property, free elections and education. Protocol 6 abolishes the death penalty.

Mini case studies

The treatment of Thompson and Venables (the killers of Jamie Bulger)

The courts granted a lifetime ban on revealing the new identities of the two boys. This ban was granted on the grounds that identifying them might threaten their life (Article 2) and possibly subject them to inhuman and degrading treatment (Article 3). It was also argued that such a ban might help protect their right to a private and family life (Article 8). Newspapers had argued that Article 10 gave them the right to publish details but the court disagreed.

The 1997 'Two strikes and you're out' legislation

Four individuals serving life sentences challenged the legislation that gave mandatory life sentences for second-time serious offences. They argued that it constituted a violation of their right to liberty (Article 5), constituted inhuman and degrading treatment (Article 3) and compromised the ban on making law retrospective (Article 7). The appeal court in effect disabled the law by allowing judges to use their discretion when sentencing (as had been the case before the Act was passed).

Treatment of mental patients

A paranoid schizophrenic killer being held in Broadmoor argued that the onus should not be on him to prove that he was no longer suffering from the condition before he could be released, but on the authorities to prove that he was still dangerous enough for them to detain him against his will. In requiring him to prove his health, the Mental Health Act of 1983 reversed the burden of proof (protected by Article 6) and infringed his liberty (Article 5). The appeal court agreed and ruled the Act incompatible with the Convention.

The right to remain silent

A woman, Margaret Brown, who was charged after admitting being drunk in charge of a vehicle, argued that section 172 of the Road Traffic Act (1988), which makes it an offence not to name the driver of a vehicle, violated her right against self-incrimination – i.e. her right to silence (Article 6). This section also applied to vehicles caught on speed cameras. Scotland's High Court threw out the prosecution against her on the grounds that section 172 violated her right to a fair trial (Article 6). The Privy Council later reversed this decision.

The Convention Rights

Article 1 simply sets out the fact that rights should be made available. The detail concerning protected rights starts in Article 2.

Article 2 – the right to life

Article 3 – the prohibition of torture

Article 4 – the prohibition of slavery and forced labour

Article 5 – the right to liberty and security

Article 6 – the right to a fair trial

Article 7 – no punishment without law

Article 8 – the right to respect for private and family life

Article 9 – the freedom of thought, conscience and religion

Article 10 – the freedom of expression

Article 11 – the freedom of association and assembly

Article 12 – the right to marry and found a family

Article 14 – prohibition of discrimination

14.5 How effectively are rights protected in the UK?

What rights are commonly protected in a liberal democracy?

The right to life, the freedom of expression, the freedom of worship, the rights of association and assembly, the right to protest and to petition the government for redress of grievances, and the freedom of movement have traditionally been upheld under the limited form of government present in most western liberal democracies. Such rights are not, of course, absolute. The freedom of speech, for example, has always been limited both in practical terms and – more recently – in statute also, e.g. the restrictions on inciting racial hatred in the Race Relations Act (1976) and the Public Order Act (1986). As well as these basic or natural rights, liberal democracies offer their citizens political rights, e.g. the right to vote.

Rights in the UK

Where are the rights of UK citizens set out?

Before the passage of the Human Rights Act (HRA, 1998) there was no clearly codified list of rights available to UK citizens. This did not mean, however, that those in the UK had no rights. Firstly, there were what were referred to as negative rights. These were based on the notion that UK citizens were free do all that was not explicitly prohibited by law. Secondly, specific rights had been established under common law (e.g. the freedom of speech) and others had been set out in statute (e.g. the right to vote or the right to abortion). UK citizens had also benefited from a number of rights available to citizens of the EU since the Union was established under the Maastricht Treaty (1990), e.g. the right to live and work in other EU states. That said, the passage of the HRA (1998) and the Freedom of Information Act (FOI, 2000) were clearly significant.

The status of such rights

Although the passage of the HRA (1998) and FOI (2000) served to make the rights of UK citizens more immediately visible and readily accessible, the status of many of those rights remains uncertain at best. In the absence of a properly entrenched and superior bill of rights, any of the freedoms currently guaranteed through statute law, in common law or under various treaties and international agreements can be removed by a regular piece of statute. Though the difficulty of removing the UK from the EU means that the rights those in the UK have as European citizens are relatively well protected, this is not true in the case of the HRA (1998). This is because the European Convention on Human Rights (ECHR, 1950) on which the HRA (1998) is based was not an EU initiative, originating instead with the Council of Europe. The UK Government can therefore formally derogate or circumvent its provisions.

The judiciary and rights

The importance of judicial review

The UK judiciary was not traditionally said to have a highly political role. This is because the absence of a codified and entrenched constitution which is superior to regular statute meant that courts were largely restricted to ensuring that the law was properly applied (i.e. *ultra vires* rulings), as opposed to using their power of judicial review to challenge the very basis of individual acts of parliament.

In recent years, however, judicial review in the UK has taken on a greater political significance. This change has resulted from three broad factors: the enhanced role of UK courts in respect of EU law following the Factortame Case (1990); the passage of the HRA (1998) and FOI (2000); and government restrictions on individual liberties post-9/11.

Case Study: the Courts, the HRA and the detention of terrorist suspects

- The passage of the UK's Anti-Terrorism, Crime and Security Act (2001), part 4, allowed the indefinite detention, without trial, of foreign nationals whom the Home Secretary judged were involved in terrorism.
- This measure could only be passed because the Government was able to derogate Article 5 of the Human Rights Act on the grounds that there was a 'public emergency threatening the life of the nation', a form of words which met the requirements set out in Article 15.
- In December 2004, an appellate committee of nine Law Lords ruled (8:1) that the indefinite detention of suspects under the Anti-Terrorism, Crime and Security Act (2001) was incompatible with Articles 5 and 14 of the HRA.
- In June and August 2006 the High Court found that the control orders brought in as part of the 2005 Prevention of Terrorism Act also violated Article 5 as they were tantamount to imprisonment without trial – though the Government chose to persist with such control orders.

Source: P. A. FAIRCLOUGH (2007) *UK Government & Politics Annual Survey* (Philip Allan Updates)

14.6 How democratic is the UK system of government?

What is democracy?

As we saw earlier in this book, the term democracy comes from the Greek – *demos* (meaning 'the people') and *kratos* ('power'). Literally, therefore, democracy is 'rule by the people' or 'people power'. In the 20th century the term democracy was applied so broadly that it lost all real meaning. As a result it is now more common to use the term liberal democracy to describe the style of limited government commonly practiced in most western democracies; where government intervention is kept to a minimum and basic civil rights are guaranteed.

Positive and negative features of UK democracy

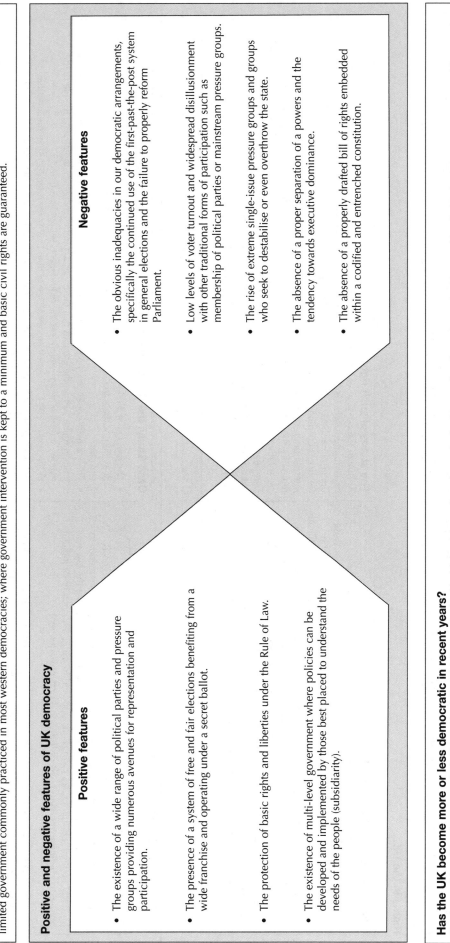

Positive features

- The existence of a wide range of political parties and pressure groups providing numerous avenues for representation and participation.

- The presence of a system of free and fair elections benefiting from a wide franchise and operating under a secret ballot.

- The protection of basic rights and liberties under the Rule of Law.

- The existence of multi-level government where policies can be developed and implemented by those best placed to understand the needs of the people (subsidiarity).

Negative features

- The obvious inadequacies in our democratic arrangements, specifically the continued use of the first-past-the-post system in general elections and the failure to properly reform Parliament.

- Low levels of voter turnout and widespread disillusionment with other traditional forms of participation such as membership of political parties or mainstream pressure groups.

- The rise of extreme single-issue pressure groups and groups who seek to destabilise or even overthrow the state.

- The absence of a proper separation of a powers and the tendency towards executive dominance.

- The absence of a properly drafted bill of rights embedded within a codified and entrenched constitution.

Has the UK become more or less democratic in recent years?

On the positive side, the removal of all but 92 of the 759 Peers who had held the right to sit and vote in the Upper chamber prior to the House of Lords Act (1999) was seen as a positive step in terms of democracy, as was the passage of the Human Rights Act (1998) and the Freedom of Information Act (2000). The devolution programme and the introduction of directly elected local mayors in many areas was also said to have made government closer to the people. The increased use of referendums after 1997 could also be said to have enhanced democracy.

On the negative side, historically low levels of electoral turnout in the 2001 and 2005 General Elections, the collapse of confidence in the integrity of politicians between 1995 and 2008, and the erosion of civil liberties in the wake of 9/11 could be used to support the view that UK democracy is rather less healthy now than it once was.

15.1   The electorate

Extension of the franchise

In order to vote, Americans must be registered to vote in the state in which they live. Over the last 40 years, however, there have been many changes to the rules that govern who precisely may register.

The original constitutional document gave states the right to control many of the rules governing elections within their territory. Following their defeat in the Civil War, many southern states introduced complicated rules that prevented Blacks from voting in the elections. These rules could not be explicit (i.e. 'Blacks can't vote') because such measures would have fallen foul of the 14th Amendment's equal protection clause. Instead, many states introduced poll taxes (which most Blacks did not pay), literacy tests (which many Blacks could not pass) or introduced mechanisms such as the Grandfather Clause (which stated that you could only vote if your grandfather had been an American citizen). The federal government eventually moved to confront these restrictions with the 24th Amendment of 1964 (removing the various clauses and abolishing poll taxes) and the Voting Rights Act of 1965 (giving the federal government the power to register voters in states where literacy tests were used).

These reforms had a dramatic impact. For example:

State	% Blacks registered pre-1964	% Blacks registered 1968
Alabama	19.3%	51%
Mississippi	6.7%	59.8%

These measures were followed by:

1970	The Voting Rights Act which gave all 18-year-olds the vote in federal elections
1971	The 26th Amendment which extended the 18-year-old rule to all elections.

These two reforms increased the size of the electorate by 11 million.

Population profile

Population

According to the US Census in 2000 the population of the US was then 281.4 million. The official population estimate for 2008 was 304 282 000. California remains the most populous state with 34.5 million people (12.1% of the total US population) and Nevada had the fastest-growing population (5.4% between Census 2000 and July 2001). During the same period several states experienced falling populations: North Dakota (−1.2%) and West Virginia (−0.4%), for example. Such changes in population will eventually be reflected in changes in the states' seat allocation in the House of Representatives and, consequently, their vote allocation in the electoral college. In 2004, for example, California had 55 votes (54 in 2000), Florida had 27 (25 in 2000) and Pennsylvania had 21 (23 in 2000).

Ethnicity

The US has often been described as a multi-variant or pluralist society. Wave after wave of immigration has led to an incredibly diverse population ethnically. Between 1820 and 1914 an effective 'open door policy' operated and around 30 million immigrants arrived in the US (48 million between 1820 and 1978). Even today, immigration is a significant feature. Since the 1980s over one million immigrants per year have arrived in the US. There is a clear correlation between ethnicity and voting patterns.

Single race or mixed race (total 281 421 906)		
Single race	274 595 678	97.6%
Mixed race	6 826 228	2.4%

Single race breakdown (total 274 595 678)		
White	211 460 626	75.1%
Black	34 419 434	12.9%
Asian	10 242 998	3.6%
Other	18 472 620	8.4%
NB all figures in this table include Hispanics and Latinos (White Hispanics, Black Hispanics etc.)		

Hispanic and Latino (including those of mixed race)		
Mexican	20 640 711	7.3%
Puerto Rican	3 406 178	1.2%
Cuban	1 241 685	0.4%
Other Hispanic and Latino	10 017 244	3.6%
Total Hispanic or Latino	35 305 818	12.5%

% population by geographical region

East	23%
Midwest	26%
South	31%
West	20%

For 'Geography and voting' see Ch 16.1

Gender

There have been some attempts by **psephologists** to link gender with voting behaviour.

Male	138 053 563	49.1%
Female	143 368 343	50.9%

Age

As is the case with gender, age has often been linked to voting behaviour.

Age group as % of population		
Under 5	19 175 798	6.8%
5 to 9	20 549 505	7.3%
10 to 14	20 528 072	7.3%
15 to 19	20 219 890	7.2%
20 to 24	18 964 001	6.7%
25 to 34	39 891 724	14.2%
35 to 44	45 148 527	16.0%
45 to 54	37 677 952	13.4%
55 to 59	13 469 237	4.8%
60 to 64	10 805 447	3.8%
65 to 74	18 390 180	6.5%
75 to 84	12 361 180	4.4%
Over 84	4 239 587	1.5%

Potential electorate (18+) as % of population		
Male	100 994 367	35.9%
Female	108 133 727	38.4%

15.2 How elections work

Presidential elections

Introduction

The quadrennial presidential election is a constant and invariable restating of democratic values. In the UK, during times of extreme national crisis (e.g. during the Second World War) elections are cancelled and the parties work together against the common enemy. In the US, however, little has got in the way of the presidential election since the framing of the Constitution. In November 1864, as the North fought the South in the American Civil War, Lincoln (then President) had to stand for re-election. As he later remarked,

> 'The Presidential Election, occurring in regular course during the rebellion added not a little to the strain, but the election was a necessity. We cannot have free government without election and if the rebellion could force us to forgo or postpone a national election it might fairly claim to have already conquered and ruined us.'

The race for the White House is divided into a number of distinct stages.

Primaries (the pre-nomination stage)

During this stage:

1. *Delegates are selected to go to the National Party Conventions;*
2. *The public are made aware of the candidates and in many cases get to have a say in which one will be chosen.*

Two broad types of system are used at this stage: **primaries** and **caucuses**

Primaries

Primaries give the broader public a chance to express a preference for one or more of the candidates seeking the party nominations for the presidential election race proper. In **'open primaries'** anyone can vote in either or both of the parties' primaries or but in recent years **'closed primaries'** – where only registered supporters of the party can have a say – have become more widely used.

Caucuses

Under this system the power to select delegates rests with party activists who meet first at local, then at county and finally at state level to make their choices. Most states have now moved away from caucuses towards primaries but some, including Iowa and North Dakota, persevere with caucuses.

Party Conventions (the nomination stage)

The Conventions are where the final decisions are taken regarding each party's **'ticket'** (its Presidential and Vice-Presidential candidate) and its **'platform'** (the policies on which the candidates will stand). The ticket is normally a foregone conclusion because most of the convention's delegates are committed to vote in a certain way, at least in the first ballot (supporters of Edward Kennedy tried to remove this first ballot pledge in 1980). If there is no winner after the first ballot, delegates are free to switch their support to one of the other candidates or vote for a new 'unity candidate' in order to ensure a speedy resolution to the impasse. In a situation where a second ballot occurs, a candidate running third or lower might 'trade' the support of their delegates in return for the assimilation of some of his/her policy ideas into the platform of the former. Jesse Jackson might have been in this position in 1988 had the result at the Democratic Convention been a little closer. It should be remembered, however, that no vote has gone beyond the first ballot since 1952 when the Democrats took three ballots to select Adlai Stevenson.

The general election

The 'general election' itself puts the two parties' presidential candidates head to head, though often with the added distraction of 'third party' candidates. The election takes place on the first Tuesday after the first Monday in November and is a public holiday. The election is indirect as voters are, in reality, voting for the people who will vote for the President as part of the electoral college.

The other half of the ticket and the platform

Though the conventions theoretically also choose the other half of the ticket, the reality is that since the 1950s, in both parties, nominated presidential candidates have chosen their own running mates. In some cases there is an attempt to balance the ticket. Gerald Ford, for example, was believed to have been asked to be the running mate for the former actor Reagan in 1980, in order that he might add political weight; Cheney added experience and a certain authority to the George W Bush ticket in 2000 but other nominations are less easily explained. Some questioned whether Bush's choice of Dan Quayle as his running mate in 1988 wasn't simply 'impeachment insurance'.

The Convention's role in influencing the 'platform' is also limited by the fact that the winning candidate will often come ready with a set of policies of his own or be unwilling to be too specific about policies prior to election, for fear of alienating potential support.

The electoral college

The electoral college is a relic of the Founding Father's fear of popular power or 'mobocracy'. The candidate who wins the vote in each state receives all of the so-called electoral college votes assigned to that state. Each state has a number of electoral college votes equal to the number of Senators it has (two) plus the number of members of the House of Representatives it has (which will depend upon the population of the state). Three additional Electors represent Washington DC. The Electors (not the actual Congressmen and Senators) chosen to represent the state can then vote for the new President. There are 538 votes in the electoral college. The winning candidate needs to secure 270 votes in order to become President.

See Ch 15.4

Congressional elections

Members of the Senate (two from each state) represent the whole state. Members of the House of Representatives, in contrast, represent districts within states; each district having a population of around 500 000. The entire House is elected every two years, as is one-third of the Senate. As in presidential elections, hopefuls normally have to compete in primaries in order to be selected as their party's candidate.

In a leap year (1992, 1996, 2000 etc.), presidential elections coincide with congressional elections. Mid-term elections are those congressional elections that occur in the middle of the four-year presidential term (1994, 1998, and 2002). These mid-term elections can be very important because they can change the whole balance of the legislature in the middle of the four-year presidential term and, therefore, dramatically affect the President's chances of being able to secure favourable legislation. In 1994, for example, the mid-term elections saw the Republicans – fighting on the national platform of the 'Contract with America' – win control of both the House and the Senate. This signalled that start of a difficult period for Bill Clinton from 1995, with Newt Gingrich (the new Speaker of the House) providing a serious check on the President's agenda.

15.3 Direct democracy in the USA

Introduction

Many US states employ mechanisms that allow for a degree of direct democracy. Some states, Washington for example (see right), have amended their state constitutions to allow citizens the right to initiate legislation. Others prefer to allow public consultation only on measures proposed or passed by the state legislature. Three such mechanisms are dealt with on this page: referendums, initiatives, and recalls.

Referendums

A referendum is a popular vote on a measure passed or proposed by a legislature (as opposed to a measure proposed by the people). Though regulations vary from state to state, referendums generally take place where:

- the legislature decides to put a measure or policy to a public vote;
- the legislature is required by law to put certain measures to a public vote; or
- the people have the right to force a referendum on a law passed by the legislature (known as a petition referendum).

Initiatives

Initiatives differ from referendums in that they allow voters to propose (initiate) laws themselves. They operate – in some form or another – in 24 states. The normal procedure is as follows:

1. Those proposing the law must produce a petition carrying the support of a predetermined percentage of the population (normally 5–15%).
2. If it gains enough support, the issue will be placed on the ballot automatically (in some states) or via the legislature (in others).
3. Registered voters in the state then get the chance to vote on the proposal.
4. The measure fails or becomes law.

Recalls

A recall is a procedure that allows registered voters in a state to remove an elected official from office before the end of their term where there is evidence of corruption, negligence or, in some cases, incompetence. Around one-quarter of US states offer this power to voters, though in practice such recalls are often difficult to execute, e.g. California Governor Gray Davis' replacement by Arnold Schwarzenegger in 2003.

Case studies

Washington State

Washington was one of the first states to allow initiatives and referendums. In 1912 voters approved an amendment to the state constitution that guaranteed the right of voters to initiate legislation:

'The first power reserved by the people is the initiative.'
Article II, Section 1(a), Washington State Constitution.

Measures (1912–2002)	Filed	Balloted	Passed
Initiatives (of all types)	1035	143	74
Referendums (referred by legislature)	49	47	38
Referendums (referred by petition of voters)	49	32	4

California's Proposition 13

California has long been associated with direct democracy. When they went to the polls in 1988, for example, Californians were not only electing a president but also having a say on decisions as wide-ranging as car insurance and water conservation. More controversial were California's 1994 Proposition 187, cutting off state-funded public services to those classified as illegal immigrants and its 1996 Proposition 209 effectively banning affirmative action.

Most famous of all, however, was Proposition 13 (the Jarvis–Gann initiative) passed by Californian voters in 1978. This measure cut property taxes by almost two-thirds and forced the state government into spending its surplus in order to protect vital services.

Initiatives in Action

When they went to the polls in November 2000, voters in many states had the opportunity to have their say on a range of initiatives as well as who should become the next President, House member, Senator, state politician or official. *Time Magazine* (November 20, 2000) reported the results of these votes.

Background checks at gun shows?

These votes came in the wake of the Columbine school killings. The measure would allow checks to be made on those buying weapons.

State	Yes	No
Colorado	70%	30%
Oregon	60%	40%

Ban gay marriage?

State	Yes	No
Nebraska	70%	30%
Nevada	70%	30%

Legalise cannabis (marijuana)?

Several states had already allowed cannabis use for medical use. This initiative went further still.

State	Yes	No
Alaska	39%	61%
Colorado	54%	46%
Nevada	65%	35%

School vouchers?

This scheme would see parents given vouchers for private schools in the face of a perceived deterioration in state-sector education provision.

State	Yes	No
California	29%	71%
Michigan	31%	69%

15.4 Some key issues and debates

Campaign Finance and Reform

Where do candidates get their money from?

1. Personal funds: Most candidates are fairly well off and they therefore spend large amounts of their own money.
2. Individual donations: Credit card donations by telephone spiralled in the 1990s.
3. Donations from interest groups: Business/occupational groups might support a particular candidate.
4. Federal funding ('matching funds'): The Federal Government provides money for the candidates who can demonstrate a broad-based support – see below.

The 1974 Federal Election Campaign Act (FECA)

FECA was introduced in the wake of Watergate. It sought to limit candidate spending and ease the financial burden on the candidates themselves.

(1) Spending in Primaries, Caucuses and State Conventions:

*   Each candidate could spend $10 million (index linked).
*   If a candidate raised at least $100 000 dollars including at least $5000 from 20 different states, the Federal Government would provide matching funds. Candidates didn't have to take the money, but it made sense.
*   A limit of $5 million on public funding for any one candidate.

(2) Spending in the 'General Election'

*   Each candidate could spend $20 million, index-linked (e.g. in 1996 Clinton and Dole each received $62 million).
*   Matching funds were available (see above).
*   The party itself could collect a further $2.9 million for organisation and, in addition, both parties were given $2 million to pay for their National Conventions.

NB In *Buckley v. Valeo* (1976) the Supreme Court struck down the compulsory spending limits unconstitutional but allowed voluntary spending limits as a condition of receiving matching funds.

(3) Limits on contributions

*   The Act placed a limit of $1000 per individual citizen to a single election campaign (Primaries and General Election are considered separate).
*   No one could spend more than $25 000 in one year supporting candidates.
*   Political Action Committees (PACs) were limited to contributions of $5000 per candidate.

The Bipartisan Campaign Reform Act (BCRA) of 2002

From 1979 Congress allowed money to be collected and spent on voter-registration drives and 'get out the votes' programmes. This 'soft money' was outside of FECA's scope. The blurring of the lines between 'hard' (regulated) and 'soft' money (unregulated) eventually led to the passing of the BCRA (2002). This Act:

1. Banned soft money contributions to the national political parties;
2. Increased the hard money contribution limits on individuals donations from $1000 per candidate per election to $2000;
3. Left PAC contribution limits unchanged ($5000); and
4. Restricted the use of electioneering ads by companies, corporations or unions featuring the likenesses or names of candidates within 30 days of a primary election or 60 days of a general election.

In *McConnell v. Federal Electoral Commission* (2003), the US Supreme Court upheld all of the BCRA's main provisions; though the rise of 527 groups such as the Swift Boat Veterans in the 2004 Presidential Election re-ignited the debate over group-funded campaign ads.

Primaries

For	Against
Primaries put power into the hands of ordinary voters rather than the party bosses – the 'fat cats' in their 'smoke-filled rooms'.	The party bosses, or at least experienced politicians, are better placed to choose candidates than the public. Primaries often become straightforward beauty contests and the candidates selected are not necessarily the best for the job – simply the lowest common denominator.
Primaries can encourage higher levels of political participation because people feel that they can have a real input into the decision-making process. Some primaries (e.g. Michigan) saw significantly increased turnout in 2000 compared to 1996.	Of the people who are eligible to vote, only about one in five turn out. This shows that people don't take primaries seriously while, at the same time, undermining the legitimacy of the process.
The primaries are physically and mentally demanding. This is good because it mirrors some of the demands that a President will face in office.	The primary season is too long. With the serious preparation for primaries starting the year before the elections, members of the House are in a perpetual state of election preparation. Some candidates do not stand because they can't afford to waste a year or more of their life seeking nomination and then election.
Primaries allow Washington outsiders such as Carter and Clinton to get in on the presidential election act. These individuals might not have been chosen under a system of caucuses.	Though opening up the field is probably a good thing, one should be wary of seeing 'outsiders' as a 'good thing'. Presidents with inside experience of the federal government are much better placed to achieve legislative success.

The electoral college

For	Against
It works effectively and is well understood. The fact that it is an anachronism is no reason to get rid of it.	It was created as a check on the power of the people and is therefore an anachronism.
The winning President can normally claim the support of 50% of the voters because the electoral college promotes a two-horse race.	Sometimes Presidents are elected with less than 50% of the popular vote (George W Bush, for example, won 540 000 votes fewer than Gore in 2000).
It prevents the voices of the smaller states being drowned out.	It statistically over-represents smaller states because each state is rewarded in the electoral college for the fact that it has two Senators.
Most Electors in the college vote as instructed by their states. Many are bound by legal contract. It is little more than a rubber stamp.	There is nothing that can stop Electors from voting for a candidate other than the one they are supposed to vote for. One Elector voted for no-one in 2000 and in 1988 one Democratic ('Dukakis') Elector voted for Lloyd Bentsen.
The college rarely makes any difference to the outcome of the election.	The winner-takes-all system operating in states exaggerates the winning margin in the electoral college.
Unless third party candidates can amass a massive national support they are never going to win anyway even without an electoral college.	The winner-takes-all system makes life hard for third party candidates. Ros Perot, for example, secured 19% of the popular vote in 1992 but gained no electoral college votes.

Introduction

A lot of what we said about voting behaviour theory in UK elections can also be applied to elections in the US. This page does not, therefore, aim to repeat this. Instead, it looks at a number of important factors, illustrating them with examples from the elections in 2004. You should use the material provided here and on the next page in conjunction with the page on 'The electorate' (Population profile).

Partisan alignment

In the UK we have seen a decline in partisan alignment. This has been attributed partly to the rise of a strong third party and partly to the tendency for major parties to compete for the centre ground; 'middle England'.

In the US we might also expect to see low levels of party identification and loyalty because of the nature of US society and the nature of American political parties. In the 2008 presidential election, however, there appears to have been significant evidence of party identification.

% who identified with a party

Total	71%
Democrats	39%
Republicans	32%

% who voted in-line with their party identification

Democrats	89%
Republicans	90%

Split-ticket voting . . .

is where voters do not vote consistently for one party's candidates on election day. They may vote for a Democrat as President, a Republican as Senator and an independent as State Governor, where all three elections coincide. The result of split-ticket voting has been a situation where the President is often from one party whereas another controls one or both chambers in Congress. Sometimes, this leads to 'gridlock'. In the 1980s, in contrast, writers spoke of a 'coat-tails effect' where Reagan's massive popularity got Republican Congressmen elected 'on his coat-tails'. The Democrats benefitted from a similar coat-tails effect in 2008, winning control of the House and Senate as well as the White House.

Urban/rural residency and voting

% voting by residential type

Area	McCain (R)	Obama (D)
Rural	53%	45%
Suburbs	48%	50%
Urban	35%	63%

Commentary

The Democrats have, in recent years, achieved far greater success in urban areas than in rural areas and the suburbs. In rural areas in particular, the Republican Party appears to have a clear lead.

Many attribute this to the fact that urban areas tend to benefit from the kind of 'big government' social/welfare spending programmes favoured more by Democratic administrations than Republican ones. In contrast, the gun lobby has campaigned hard in rural areas in support of Republican candidates over the last ten years.

Geography and voting

% voting by geographical area

Area	McCain (R)	Obama (D)
East	40%	59%
Midwest	44%	54%
South	54%	45%
West	40%	57%

Commentary

Well into the second half of the twentieth century it was possible to talk about the Democrats' control of the 'solid South'. This support had resulted largely from the fact that it had been a Republican – Lincoln – who had waged war against the Southern states and ended slavery.

As the figures show, the solid South appears more solid for the Republicans now than the Democrats, and they have now won majority support in the region in the last five presidential elections.

Ethnicity and voting

% voting by race

Race	McCain (R)	Obama (D)
White	55%	43%
Black	4%	95%
Hispanic	31%	67%
Asian	35%	62%
Other	31%	66%

Commentary

The figures above are largely self-explanatory and reflect broad and longstanding trends in the ethnic support for the two parties. There has, however, been some movement in recent years. As in 2000, George W Bush campaigned hard in pursuit of the Hispanic vote in 2004 and achieved an estimated 9% increase in support amongst this group for the Republicans as compared to 2000. These gains were lost in 2008.

Religion and voting

% voting by religion

Religion	McCain (R)	Obama (D)
Protestant/Christian	54%	45%
Catholic	45%	54%
Jewish	21%	78%
Other	22%	73%
None	23%	75%

Commentary

The Democrats traditionally far better than Republicans amongst those in the 'other' or 'no' religion category. They also tend to do better amongst the Jewish community. Gore's choice of Jew Joe Lieberman in 2000 as his vice-presidential candidate no doubt firmed up this support but Clinton had also achieved 78% support amongst Jews in 1992 and 1996.

As a rule, those who attended religious services weekly or daily tended to support Bush more than those who attended less frequently.

16.2 Influences on voting behaviour (part 2)

Issues, policies, events and voting

Issues, policies and events in the public eye in the months running up to the election can have a significant impact on voting behaviour. Commentators on both sides of the Atlantic in recent years have highlighted the increasing importance of short-term factors in elections and the increasing trend towards issue-led politics.

Ford v. Carter in 1976

Ford was appointed Nixon's Vice-President in 1974 following Spiro Agnew's resignation, and then became President following Nixon's own resignation over the Watergate scandal in 1974.

In the 1976 election, Ford faced significant difficulties:

- *He was tainted by Watergate, however unfairly.*
- *He was seen as a rather ineffectual and weak President.*
- *He had previously said that he would not run in 1976.*

Carter, on the other hand, had advantages:

- *There was a desire for change.*
- *He was seen as a 'Washington outsider'.*
- *As a 'born-again Christian', he was seen as being morally sound.*

Bush v. Clinton in 1992

If the election had taken place in 1991, Bush would have been the likely winner because of the incredibly high opinion poll ratings he was achieving in the light of US action in the Gulf War.

By 1992, however, things had moved on but Bush was still trying to play the foreign policy card. This led Clinton famously to launch the slogan 'It's the economy, stupid!' Such sentiments were echoed in car bumper stickers seen at the time of the New Hampshire Primary. They read 'Saddam Hussein still has a job; do you?'.

Candidates and voting

The candidates themselves clearly have a role in affecting voting behaviour. A particularly effective or an inadequate candidate can swing the voters one way or the other. This importance is emphasised by factors such as:

- The relative weakness of the parties;
- The increasing importance of image rather than policy in elections;
- The role of the modern media.

See next page for 'focus on the image'

The importance of money

Candidates need an enormous amount of money for, amongst other things:

producing adverts and buying airtime; travelling (not just for them but for their campaign teams); acquiring office space and office staff (offices cost money and administering donations; issuing mail-shots (sending out information to the voters); co-ordinating merchandising (shirts, banners, badges, mugs etc.)

Though candidates can take donations they need to be relatively wealthy themselves before embarking on the campaign trail. Even in 1992 the average incumbent in the House spent $580 000 on their re-election campaigns and, in the presidential campaign of the same year, the independent Ros Perot spent $23.9 million, nearly all his own money.

Spending money doesn't guarantee success. For example:

- Perot lost in 1992 and in 1996 when he spent more than the federal limit (over $50 million of his own money) and therefore received no matching funds;
- Michael Huffington spend $26 million trying to win a Senate seat (California) in 1994 and still lost to incumbent Dianne Feinstein

… but it nearly always helps raise a candidates profile and it is difficult for a candidate to stay on the campaign trail for over a year and hold down a job! As political consultant Raymond Strother noted, 'poor people can't be elected now'. This would appear to be born out by the fact that over one quarter of all Senators are said to be millionaires. The 2008 election campaign was said to be the first $1 billion election.

Income and union membership

% voting by income group

Family income	McCain (R)	Obama (D)
< $15 000	25%	73%
$15 000–$29 999	37%	60%
$30 000–$49 999	43%	55%
$50 000–$74 999	49%	48%
> $200 000 +	52%	46%

% voting by unionisation

	McCain (R)	Obama (D)
Union members	38%	61%

Commentary

Lower-income and more highly-unionised households are more likely to vote Democrat than Republican. This should come as no surprise. The Republicans have long been associated with business interests (think of the recent Enron scandal) whereas the Democrats have been seen as more the party of the common man. It should be remembered, of course, that there is also a strong correlation **between race and average income.**

Gender and voting

% voting by gender

Gender	McCain (R)	Obama (D)
Male	48%	49%
Female	43%	56%

Commentary

In Britain those studying electoral behaviour have charted the closing of the so-called 'gender gap'. In the US, however, it is alive and well. Some have attributed such massive differences in gender voting to candidate appeal or to the platforms of the two parties (the fact that the Democrats have been firmly pro-choice on abortion since 1992, for example).

16.3 Influences on voting behaviour (part 3): the media

What is the modern campaign like?

In the nineteenth century, candidates travelled around the country gaining support and exchanging ideas with opponents and audiences in a series of two-way public meetings. When Lincoln and Douglas spoke to audiences on the campaign trail in 1858, they were reinforcing one of the most important principles underlying American politics: that people need to be and feel involved. The modern election campaign is, however, much more of a one-way process; the candidate presenting himself or herself to the voters in contexts where the majority of those watching cannot have an input. For example:

- on **whistle-stop tours** of the country . . .
  where the focus is on 'population coverage' rather than engagement or dialogue; or
- on **television** . . .
  where, as H G Nicholas noted, 'a candidate draws no sustenance from his unseen millions; the millions meet not a man but an image'.

Such changes have resulted in a campaign where:

- **individuals feel less involved**, possibly even **disaffected**
- **candidates themselves become increasingly lightweight**, because their ideas are not as thoroughly tested as they might have been previously.
- there is a **focus on the image** and even the **physical appearance** of the candidate. As political consultant Raymond Strother noted, there are some 'people that are not electable. . . . Lincoln [due to his appearance] could not have been elected in today's politics'. In 1976 Walter Mondale withdrew from the Democratic Party primaries saying, 'Nationally it is more theatre than the politics I know. I kept getting constant suggestions that I needed to buy different clothes and go to speech instructors. I hated that.'

The press

There are no major national newspapers apart from *USA Today*. The *Washington Post* and the *New York Times* are, however, both widely read and have strong editorials. Local newspapers also back and attack particular candidates.

Television broadcasting

Television time can be broadly divided into two types: paid and unpaid. Naturally, any candidate will want as much 'airtime' as possible, but with limited budgets it is important that the candidates get as much unpaid exposure as possible.

Unpaid coverage (standard programming)

Though unpaid coverage does not offer the candidate the same degree of control over programme content and tone, it is important that the candidate gets as much unpaid media coverage as possible due to the financial demands of any campaign. The candidate's campaign team is crucial in terms of locating and managing such opportunities:

1 Candidates might be pursued by camera crews to give their 'on-the-spot' feelings on given issues. This is fine if you are a candidate who can think on your feet but not if you are one who is used to having every word you say written for you. Reagan's communications advisor Michael Deaver certainly protected his candidate from this kind of exposure.

2 Presidential candidates are normally invited to take part in three major televised debates. This is a little better because you usually get a chance to reel off some pre-prepared sound-bites in response to a question.

3 Candidates might be the targets of investigative journalism. In 1992 Bill Clinton was constantly on the television being quizzed about his avoiding fighting in the Vietnam War, his smoking pot (though apparently 'not inhaling'!) at college and his supposed affair with Gennifer Flowers. Is it true that 'all publicity is good publicity'?

Paid coverage (commercial advertising)

If a candidate is paying for the airtime then obviously they have complete control over the content. Having said that, television time is so expensive that candidates normally have to cram the essence of what they want to say into a few seconds. When using paid media the candidate can adopt one of two broad strategies:

Positive advertising

Today's positive advertising can take a number of forms:

1. **Biographical ads** – ads that seek to tell the voter something about the candidate's life and put a face to a name. For example, the ad by Frank Greer that helped Gaston Caperton III become Governor of West Virginia in 1988, despite his obvious lack of political experience.

2. **Subliminal ads** – those that rarely mention the candidate but instead focus on creating a positive mood and allowing voters to make their own connections to a large extent. For example, the 'It's Morning in America' ads deployed by Reagan's team in 1984.

3. **Infomercials** – almost unique to Ros Perot, the man who spent $2 million a day in the latter stages of the campaign buying up 30-minute TV slots and then broadcasting lengthy party political programmes that he presented himself. In October 2008 Obama spent $3 million on a single 30-minute infomercial.

Negative campaigning

As Larry Sabato observed 'many advertisers have made the mistake of believing that in 30 to 60 seconds you can change someone's mind. What you can do is crystallise a feeling that is already there.'

It was in this belief that Tony Schwartz produced his infamous 'daisy girl ad' on behalf of Lyndon Johnson against Barry Goldwater in the 1964 presidential race. Goldwater was seen as an extremist and the ad showed a girl counting the petals of a daisy as she removed them, with her voice gradually being replaced by the countdown to a nuclear detonation. Johnson won a landslide victory and Goldwater at least felt that such negative propaganda had been crucial.

Following such ads, negative advertising became endemic in the US system. In recent years, however, there has been something of a public backlash against overtly negative ads and, as a result, some consultants have even started making negative ads that accuse the other side of making negative ads.

How low is turnout?

Turnout in US elections is measured as a percentage of voting age population. According to the Federal Election Commission:

'The term Voting Age Population (VAP), refers to the total number of persons in the United States who are 18 years of age or older regardless of citizenship, military status, felony conviction, or mental state.'

This definition of turnout creates a number of problems:

- Firstly, not all of those who are voting age are entitled to vote. A large number are not US citizens.
- Secondly, many of those who are entitled to vote are not registered to vote.

These two factors mean that any measurement of turnout by voting age will be artificially low (see below)

NB: There are slight inconsistencies in some of the figures provided on this page because different US agencies sometimes use different measures.

It is, however, also possible to measure levels of voter registration and then show turnout as a percentage of registered voters.

% of VAP registered (1988–2008)

Year	Presidential	Mid-term
1988	69	
1990		65
1992	71	
1994		67
1996	74	
1998		71
2000	76	
2002		71
2004	79	
2006		62
2008	81	

% of registered who voted (1988–2008)

Year	Presidential	Mid-term
1988	72	
1990		56
1992	78	
1994		58
1996	66	
1998		52
2000	68	
2002		53
2004	70	
2006		59
2008	79	

Source: Federal Election Commission.

Study these statistics carefully.

1. *What do they tell us about turnout in general?*
2. *What do they tell us about the differences in turnout in presidential and mid-term election years?*
3. *What do they tell us about registration?*

Turnout as a % of VAP (1986–2006)

Year	Presidential	Mid-term
1986		36.4
1988	50.1	
1990		36.5
1992	55.1	
1994		38.8
1996	49.1	
1998		36.0
2000	51.3	
2002		37.0
2004	55.3	
2006		43.6

Focus on voter registration

Variation by region (2000)

Different states enforce different deadlines and procedures governing voter registration. Levels of voter registration also vary markedly from state to state.

State	% VAP Reg.	Registration deadline
Missouri	94%	28 days before
New York	81.6%	25 days before
Idaho	79.1%	25 days before by mail, 24 days before in person. On the day at the poll.
Alabama	75.9%	10 days before
Connecticut	75%	14 days before
California	63.2%	29 days before
Arizona	59%	29 days before

Variation by race and gender (2004)

The percentage of citizens registering and voting can also vary significantly by race and gender.

Race	% Registration	% Voting
White (alone)	73.6%	65.4%
Black (alone)	68.7%	60%
Hispanic (of any race)	57.9%	47.2%

Gender	% Registration	% Voting
Male	70.5%	62.1%
Female	73.6%	65.4%

Source: US Census Bureau.

Recent efforts to increase registration rates

The National Voter Registration Act (NVRA) passed in 1993 took effect in 1995. It aimed to extend voter registration across the board. Known as the 'motor voter' law it required states to make registration available at facilities more easily accessible to voters. Forty-three states implemented 'motor voter' regulations, one (South Dakota) already had no registration requirements, and the six others either already had or chose to introduce election day registration for those that wanted to vote. Though the results have been far from clear-cut, states with more voter-friendly systems tend to achieve higher average turnout figures. In 2008 many states allowed early voting. It was estimated that over 29 million votes were cast before election day (November 4). Of these 11% were first time voters.

The 2004 Presidential Election

The 2004 Presidential Election

As the **incumbent** President, George W Bush was always likely to be unchallenged in the race to secure the Republican nomination in 2004. The Democratic race, therefore, provided the interest early in the year.

Pre-Nomination

Former Governor of Vermont **Howard Dean** had been the Democratic front-runner in the **'invisible primary'**. His anti-War stance attracted support as the situation in Iraq deteriorated and he also benefited from a strong **grass-roots** campaign. Many leading Democrats, however, were fearful of a Dean candidacy. Though a *Time* poll reflected a public sense that Dean was 'patriotic' (81%) and 'not too liberal' (78%) many insiders felt that Dean might simply not be **likable** enough amongst voters. His reputation as a **maverick** and his open opposition to **Party elders** – including his labelling of Clinton and other **New Democrats** as the **Republican wing of the Party** – had fuelled a strong **'anyone but Dean'** movement within the Party.

Senator **John Kerry**, however, came through strongly in the primary season proper; taking both **Iowa** and **New Hampshire** as he built up a momentum that effectively saw the race over before **Super Tuesday** on March 2.

Conventions

Democratic candidate-elect Kerry named primary runner-up **John Edwards** as his running mate **before** the Convention. Bush did likewise with **Cheney**. Both parties maintained a **united front** at Convention, with both benefiting from a **'post convention bounce'** in the polls.

General Election

The early campaign centred on the ongoing US involvement in **Iraq**, but the campaign quickly refocussed on the **economy**. Kerry was said to have won the early Presidential debates with Bush appearing uncomfortable. As the campaign neared its end Bush and Kerry were neck-and-neck in the polls, but Bush secured a second term – due at least in part to his advisor, Karl Rove's, targeting of key voters in swing-states.

Most important issues for voters in 2004

Top Issue	%Voters	Bush	Kerry
Moral Values	22%	80%	18%
Economy/Jobs	20%	18%	80%
Terrorism	19%	86%	14%
Iraq	15%	26%	73%
Healthcare	8%	23%	77%
Taxes	5%	57%	43%
Education	4%	26%	73%

The 2008 Presidential Election

The main candidates

Democrats
Hillary Clinton
John Edwards
Barack Obama

Republicans
Rudolph Giuliani
Mike Huckabee
John McCain
Ron Paul
Mitt Romney

The 2008 Conventions

The Democrat convention in Denver confirmed the Obama-Biden ticket. The Republican convention in Minnesota saw McCain spring a surprise, choosing Sarah Palin as his running mate. Neither party achieved a major post-convention poll-boost, though the Republicans gained a short[lived 'Palin bounce'.

Pre-nomination

Iowa (January 3)

For the Democrats, Barack Obama (37.6%) claimed victory in the first contest of the election season, with John Edwards (29.8%) narrowly beating Hillary Clinton (29.5%) into third place. For the Republicans, Mike Huckabee (34.3%) won with Mitt Romney (25.3%) second. John McCain (13.1%) came fourth.

New Hampshire (January 8) Democrat Hillary Clinton and Republican John McCain both fought back well (see right) after disappointing in Iowa. For the Democrats, Clinton secured the suport of 46% of women and 48% of the over-65s. Obama secured the support of 60% of those aged 18–24.

Super Tuesday (February 5) For the Democrats, Barack Obama won in 14 of the 22 States contested - though the loss of several larger states such as California and New York to Clinton meant that the two candidates were still neck-and-neck in terms of the total delegates won. For the Republicans, John McCain won 9 of the 21 states contested, with Mitt Romney taking 7 and Mike Huckabee 5. These results left McCain with more than twice as many delegates as his nearest rival and over half way towards the 1191 needed to secure his Party's nomination.

New Hampshire in 2008

Democrats

Clinton 39.0%
Edwards 16.9%
Others 7.7%
Obama 36.4%

Republicans

McCain 37.0%
Others 4.1%
Paul 7.6%
Giuliani 8.5%
Huckabee 11.2%
Romney 31.5%

The General Election

The Campaign

The presumptive candidates began campaigning long before the conventions. The emerging global economic crisis made Obama's offer of 'change' more appealing. Obama's superior fundraising also meant that he was able to outspend McCain by $4 to $1 in the run-up to Election Day: spending £3m on a single 30-minute Perot-style infomercial on network TV in October. According to the *Guardian*, Obama's superior finances also meant that he was able to maintain 770 offices nationwide to McCain's 370.

The Televised Debates

Obama was clearly more comfortable in the media spotlight than McCain. Although some commentators scored the first debae as a draw, polls suggested that Obama had won all three contests. McCain tried to draw attention to Obama's inexperience on foreign policy. Obama suggested that vote for McCain was a vote for 'four more years of Bush'.

The Result

Obama eventually won 364:174 in the Electoral College: 53%:46% in the popular vote. 57% of voters identified the economy as the key election issue. The turnout of 64% was a record for the modern era. 11% were first-time voters.

17.1 Political parties (outline)

Introduction

The Founding Fathers were suspicious of political parties; as George Washington observed, '[Parties] serve to organise faction ... to put in place of the delegated will of the nation, the will of a party.'

The United States is a pluralist society and most of the Founding Fathers would have agreed with Alexander Hamilton when he said that the aim of the Constitution should be to establish a system of government in which 'no alliance of interests could ever gain control of the whole'. The Constitution was designed, therefore, to break up rather than unite political power through its institutionalisation of the separation of powers and of checks and balances. James Madison acknowledged this fact when he wrote in the *The Federalist* that the Constitution had a 'tendency to break and control the violence of faction'.

The emergence of political parties therefore, was something that the Founding Fathers would probably never have envisaged and certainly never intended.

The rise, decline and revival of political parties

Rise

It was the very fact that many Americans had so little in common that made the parties such an attractive proposition. With so much immigration during the early years of the new Constitution, political parties actually gave many Americans:

- *something to belong to*
- *practical help; they offered a safety net for those facing hard times*

As a result, parties quickly took control of the political organisation of many regions and, in particular, cities. As H G Nicholas noted 'It was elemental like gravity, the sun, the stars, the ocean ... One became in Urbana and in Ohio for many years, a Republican just as the Eskimo dons fur clothes'.

This almost total control of certain areas by the party machine became known as **'machine politics'**. Inside these cities the 'machine' creamed off the surplus profit from private enterprise. The 'liberals' hated the 'machine' system, because they craved 'open government'. Local 'machine politics' was not about open meetings, it was about the city **'fat cats'** in the **'smoke-filled rooms'** where the deals were cut.

Though they controlled all of this power, however, the parties were still essentially local institutions: they came together once every four years for the presidential election but 'win or lose, the national party was a bloodless skeleton between the quadrennial Presidential tourneys' (H G Nicholas). Indeed, parties were decentralised not only to a state but also to a city or county level. Brooklyn Democrats' battle cry, 'the tiger shall not cross the bridge', was directed not at their Republican opponents but at their Democratic neighbours across the river in Manhattan.

Decline

Commentators attribute the decline of 'machine politics' to a number of factors:

1. *The expansion and increasing complication of legislation made parties increasingly weak and irrelevant in Congress.*
2. *The role which the parties played in terms of providing some kind of 'welfare provision', was undermined by the introduction of national welfare schemes.*
3. *State initiatives allowed registered voters to by-pass the parties.*
4. *The rise of primaries over caucuses undermined the parties' role in candidate selection.*
5. *Federal 'matching funds' undermined the role of parties in presidential elections.*
6. *The media increasingly by-passed the party in candidate-centred campaigns.*
7. *The increased importance of presidential aides has distanced the President from his party in Congress.*
8. *The rise of the independent or floating voter.*
9. *The increasing influence of pressure groups, particularly through their use of Political Action Committees.*

Revival?

Some of the factors that have led to a decline in the role of political parties are due to changes in the nature of American society and government and are unlikely to be reversed. In one or two areas, however, the parties have attempted to reverse their decline:

1. Campaign finance
The role of parties in elections was enhanced by Congressional legislation in 1979 that saw the emergence of 'soft money'. This money was not covered by the limits imposed by the 1974 Campaign Finance Act and was supposed to be focused on initiatives reviving grass-roots politics. The blurring of the lines between 'hard' and 'soft' money led to the 2002 BCRA.

2. Candidate selection
Parties still have a significant role in influencing the choice of presidential candidates. For example, around 20% of Democratic Convention delegates are so-called super delegates – elected politicians sent to the Convention because of their position rather than as a result of primaries.

3. Improvements in party organisation
Both parties have made efforts to strengthen their national organisations. The National Committees of each party are now more permanent organisations with offices in Washington DC, rather than simply quadrennial election-organising committees.

17.2 Democrats and Republicans

Structure and organisation

CHAIR → NATIONAL COMMITTEE → STATE COMMITTEE → COUNTY COMMITTEE → WARD COMMITTEES AND PRECINCTS

The chairperson
Each party has a 'chair' who chairs the meetings of the national committee. The chairperson acts as a spokesperson for the national party and oversees the day-to-day running of the party.

The national committees
Each party has a national committee elected by the previous national Party Convention; the Republican National Committee (RNC) and the Democratic National Committee (DNC). They organise the election effort and the parties' national Convention in presidential election years. Though the national committees meet twice a year and have permanent offices in Washington DC, they have only a limited role outside the quadrennial party conventions that they organise.

State party organisations
Organisations differ from state to state as regulated by state laws. State parties have a state general committee which co-ordinates the parties' state activities. The committee is chaired by a state party chairperson. The state party committee organises the state party convention and organises the selection of candidates for state office.

County committees
County committees are important because acting at a local level they exercise a good deal of patronage over local party jobs. Delegates from the various county committees make up the state general committee.

Wards and precincts
There are around 180 000 precincts or voting districts. They are normally organised by a precinct chairperson (or captain) and tend to focus on activities such as local fundraising and mobilising the vote on polling day. Ward committees are at the next level up, representing a number of precincts.

Ideology and outlook

General

US political parties have to be broad churches in order to be elected. The result is a situation in which the two parties often appear to have more entrenched differences within them than between them.

Critics have often picked up on this feature of American politics:

Ogden Nash, for example, wrote 'Some politicians are Republican, some Democratic and their feud is dramatic, but except for the name they are identically the same'

Lord James Bryce, in his book *The American Commonwealth*, famously said that the two major parties were 'like two bottles. Each bore a label denoting the kind of liquor it contained, but each was empty.'

The Democrats

For most of the twentieth century the Party had the broadest possible range of support, being popular: in the South amongst those who still resented the Republicans' historic role in the Civil War and the subsequent abolition of slavery, with the 'common man' (perhaps a legacy of the New Deal Democratic Party of the 1930s), and amongst ethnic minorities.

The reality is, as outlined earlier, that the word 'Democrat' means very little without the addition of a qualifying prefix ('liberal', 'conservative' etc.). Clinton was able to maintain a broad base of support for the Party by appealing to independent voters who would normally be fearful of the Democrats' reputation for big government programmes. In the 2000 election, some of Gore's speeches were too left wing for these groups, as were Kerry's in 2004.

The Republicans

Traditionally, the Republicans have been seen as the more conservative of the two parties. Both Reagan (in 1980 and 1984) and Bush senior (1988) ran on platforms promising low personal taxation. During the 1980s the Party also became associated with the 'New Right' and right wing evangelical groups such as Jerry Falwell's 'Moral Majority' (with their anti-abortion and anti-gay beliefs).

In the 2000 presidential election, however, George W. Bush adopted a more inclusive approach in an attempt to broaden the appeal of the Party and get it back into government. He adopted the phrase 'compassionate conservatism' and pushed more extreme members of the Party (the anti-abortionist Henry Hyde, for example) to the fringes of the Party Convention.

17.3 The two-party system and third party candidacy

Introduction to the party system

There have been two major political parties in the US from the time of Jefferson, though the names have changed over the years: Democrats, Whigs, Republicans, Democratic Republicans, or the Federalists. This is partly the result of a natural need for a clear choice and partly due to factors such as:

1. the electoral system
2. issues and debates that have polarised American opinion through time, such as

the issue of ratifying the Constitution;
the interests of industrial/financial North v. the agricultural South;
anti-slavery v. pro-slavery;
(after the New Deal) the Democrats representing the 'common man', the Republicans representing 'business'.

Third party candidates

The United States does not have permanent national third parties capable of achieving significant shares of the popular vote in elections. This is due to a number of factors including:

the difficulty in securing funding, the first past the post electoral system, the difficulty in getting one's name onto the ballot, the lack of media coverage, public ignorance or lack of awareness.

This does not, however, mean that third party presidential challenges are not worthy of note. They can:

(a) Affect the result of the election

(i) by depriving the major parties of votes. In Florida in 2000, for example, Ralph Nader secured 87 974 votes on the first count while the original margin between Bush and Gore was only 1784 votes. Nader voters would have been unlikely to vote for Bush had their man not stood.
(ii) by winning electoral college votes (ECVs), stopping a major party achieving 270.

(b) Get some of their policies into the programmes of the main parties

Perot, for example, put financial management and the deficit onto the agenda.

Major third party results

Year	Candidates		% vote	ECVs
1968	G Wallace	American Ind.	13	46
1980	J Anderson	National Unity	7	0
1992	R Perot	Independent	19	0
1996	R Perot	Reform	9	0

Third parties in Congress in 2005

Senate		
Bernie Sanders	2007–	Independent
Joe Lieberman	2007–	Independent

Breaking down the party labels

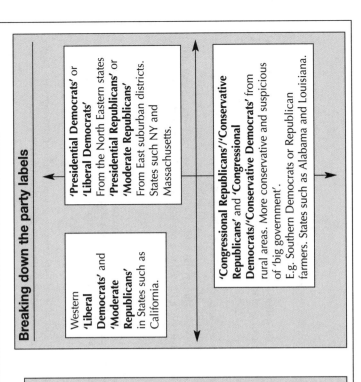

Western 'Liberal Democrats' and 'Moderate Republicans' in States such as California.

'Presidential Democrats' or 'Liberal Democrats' From the North Eastern states 'Presidential Republicans' or 'Moderate Republicans' From East suburban districts. States such NY and Massachusetts.

'Congressional Republicans'/'Conservative Republicans' and 'Congressional Democrats'/'Conservative Democrats' from rural areas. More conservative and suspicious of 'big government'.
E.g. Southern Democrats or Republican farmers. States such as Alabama and Louisiana.

Is the US really a two-party system?

Yes

1. The last President elected from outside of the two main parties was Martin Fillmore (Whig) in 1850.
2. All but two of the members of the 110th Congress (both Senators) belonged to one of the two major parties.
3. The combined Republican and Democrat vote in presidential elections invariably exceeds 80% and is often over 90% (99% in 1984 and 1988).
4. All 50 state governors were Democrats or Republicans in 2008.

No

1. Clearly, the competition between the two parties is not everywhere: there are still states which always support one party.
2. Some authors have gone as far as to say that rather than a two-party system, the United States in fact has **51 party systems**, each unique: one system of parties at the federal level and another unique party system in each and every one of the 50 states of the Union.
3. Both parties are really broad churches and include within their folds an enormous diversity of attitude and opinion: the words 'Democrat' and 'Republican' disguise a massive range of ideas.
4. Writers such as James McGregor Burns have suggested more complicated models. In McGregor Burn's construct Republicans from rural areas really have more in common with Democrats from rural areas than they do with their urban Republican 'brothers'. Democrats from urban areas, in contrast, might align with Republicans from districts facing similar social problems in order to support Presidents trying to force through policies that will help these areas. Others have used terms such as 'liberal Democrats', 'conservative Democrats', 'moderate' and 'conservative Republicans' and identified these different shades as being located in particular geographic areas.

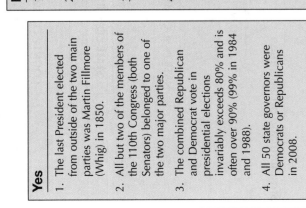

18.1 Definitions and classification

Pressure groups in the US

Definitions and context
As we observed in the UK section of the book, pressure groups are groups of like-minded individuals who campaign for their own interests and/or to achieve goals or pursue common causes.

The heterogeneous (or multi-variant) society and the proliferation of pressure groups
The United States is a heterogeneous society – that is to say it is massively varied in terms of population (ethnicity, religion, culture etc.), geographically, climatically and economically. There are, in fact, so many different interests that parties cannot possibly hope to encompass all interests effectively. In this context, pressure groups flourish and proliferate.

Points of leverage
The structure of the US Government both reflects this diversity and reinforces it. As Alexander Hamilton noted, the Constitution aimed to establish a system of government in which 'no alliance of interests could ever gain control of the whole'. Such a fragmentation of power was achieved through:

1. *the separation of powers between legislative, executive and judicial branches;*
2. *establishing checks and balances; and*
3. *identifying the division between federal and state governments.*

This fragmentation of power presents pressure groups with numerous points of leverage: they can exert pressure at federal or state level; on any or all of the branches of government.

Classifying pressure groups

The obvious question to ask here is 'can we use the same typologies for classifying US pressure groups that we employed when classifying groups in the UK?'

Can we apply the sectional/cause typology to our study of US pressure groups?

There is no reason why we cannot apply the sectional/cause classification model to US pressure groups.

Sectional groups
(represent the interests of a particular section of society)
For example, the *American Medical Association*, the *American Bar Association*, the *AFL-CIO*

Cause groups
(campaign for a particular cause or objective)

Sectional cause groups (protect a section of society beyond their membership: they do not stand to benefit individually)
For example, anti-abortion groups would argue that they were campaigning for the rights of the unborn.

Attitude cause groups (aim to change people's attitudes on a particular issue)
For example, *Friends of the Earth*.

Political cause groups (aim to achieve certain political goals)
For example, the *American Civil Liberties Union (ACLU)*

Does the insider/outsider typology work here?

The insider/outsider typology assumes that there is a clear focus for policy-making – a certain centralisation of power around the core executive. This is not *as* true in the US as it is in the UK. The fragmentation of power and the federal/state division in the US creates a situation in which it is possible to be 'inside' or 'outside' on a number of different levels in a number of different contexts. A group might, for example, be very much 'inside' Congress, frustrating the legislative plans of the President, or 'inside the White House' influencing the agenda. On those issues where the state controls policy, pressure groups might focus all of their efforts on one or more branches of the state government. Some groups are, however, clearly 'inside' the policy-making loop in Washington (see right).

Case study – the collapse of Enron (2002)
The collapse of the energy-trading firm Enron and the ensuing scandal revealed the extent of inside influence afforded to some groups in Washington. Enron had made campaign contributions to 71 out of 100 Senators as well as 188 out of 435 House members. It had made phone calls to at least six key members of the Bush team in the run-up to the collapse. Five others had received cash from the company (some as directors or consultants) and four had met with Enron executives. According to *The Guardian*, Cheney had been involved in six such meetings in the year before the collapse.

Other ways of classifying groups

Some US specialists have advanced other typologies Robert McKeever, for example, divides groups into eight types:

Business/trade	Agriculture	Unions	Professional
Single issue	Ideological	Group rights	Public interest

18.2   Methods

Pressure group methods in the US context

US pressure groups share many of their methods and tactics with their UK counterparts. As we have seen, however, a number of factors affect the range of methods adopted by groups in the US. For example:

1. the US Constitution, through the separation of powers and checks and balances, serves to divide up power. This gives pressure groups many potential points of leverage;
2. the US system is federal. For many pressure groups, therefore, they can achieve their objectives at state level because the states retain control over so many aspects of government. The sheer scale of the US also encourages the proliferation of local groups

Pressure group tactics

Influencing the legislative process directly

Pressure groups are massively involved in the work of Congress. Most will:
- *testify at the committee hearing stage, where appropriate;*
- *lobby Congressmen directly, highlighting the impact of certain measures on the voters in the Congressmen's states or encouraging log-rolling for 'pork'.*

Some anti-abortion groups have also used publicity stunts such as sending Congressmen life-size plastic foetuses.

Negating legislative efforts

It is often easier to stop things happening in Congress than to force them through. Pressure groups have numerous opportunities to apply pressure for a bill to be killed or pigeon-holed during its passage through the legislature. A single Senator can talk a measure out of time if they engage in filibustering.

At state level

If the aims of a group are confined to a state or are achievable at state level through a number of state-based campaigns, the group might focus their attention on state governments rather than the federal government. The use of initiatives and referendums in some states also allows groups to initiate legislation or pass final judgement on it. These mechanisms have been particularly popular amongst groups campaigning for lower taxes.

Influencing the legislative process indirectly through elections

Pressure groups are massively involved in providing finance for congressional election campaigns. For example:

The collapse of the Enron energy-trading firm led to criticisms of Congress. According to *The Guardian*, 71 of the 100 Senators and 188 of the 435 House Members had received campaign contributions from the company (Enron spent $5.8 million on federal election campaigns over 12 years). The same Congress had blocked President Clinton's attempts to close financial loopholes that were allowing companies like Enron to conceal the scale of their debts. Such apparent conflicts of interest contributed to the calls for reform that resulted in the BCRA (2002) (15.4).

Influencing the executive

In the last page we looked at the links between Enron and the Bush Administration. Pressure groups can also get inside executive agencies and independent regulatory commissions, with the effect of limiting the effectiveness of regulation in the areas that concern the group.

Influencing political parties

As we have seen, political parties are not as central to the whole policy-making process as they are in Britain. That said, many pressure groups have worked within parties with a view to getting their policies onto the parties' approved election platform. Within the Republican Party, for example, the 'pro-life' Christian Right groups were able to maintain the Party's 'pro-life' credentials throughout the 1980s and 1990s – though George W Bush sought to marginalise such elements in the 2000 Convention for fear of alienating independent voters. The Democrats, in contrast, have become the home for 'pro-choice' groups and have had a platform commitment to abortion rights since the 1992 Convention. The extent to which this really matters once the candidates are elected is, however, questionable. After all, neither Reagan nor Bush made any real attempts to act decisively on the abortion issue.

Embarking on legal action

Groups are often invited to brief the courts before formal arguments are heard. This allows them to put their case in areas where they have a legitimate interest. These so-called *amicus curiae* briefings are also important for the courts because groups can often provide specialist knowledge or a different perspective. Some groups also become involved in their own legal actions in pursuit of their aims. In the case of Reno v. American Civil Liberties Union (1997) for example, the Supreme Court struck down two provisions of the 1996 Communications Decency Act, which sought to protect minors from harmful material available on the internet. The Court maintained that these sections violated the First Amendment protection of freedom of speech (7:2).

Mobilising public pressure

Public campaigns

The constant demands of re-election make Congressmen extremely receptive to popular campaigns. Petitions or letter-writing campaigns (where groups encourage people to literally bury elected representatives and officials with mail-sacks full of support for the group's goal) are especially popular with groups. Acts of civil disobedience and direct action (see right), sometimes violent, have also been evident in the last 40 years.

Direct action

Picketing of abortion clinics, for example, became commonplace during the 1980s and continues. The intimidatory effect of such picketing has been heightened by the upsurge in related bomb attacks against buildings and violence against staff at such facilities. In 1994, for example, Paul Hill (the leader of the Defensive Action League) used a shotgun to kill Dr John Britton and his bodyguard (James Herman Barrett) outside a clinic in Pensacola, Florida. In 1994 there was a total of four murders and eight attempted murders. In October 1998 Buffalo-based obstetrician Dr Barnett Slepian was murdered, by a sniper who shot him through his kitchen window.

18.3 Political Action Committees

What are Political Action Committees?

Political Action Committees (PACs) are organisations that collect and channel money to candidates running for political office. The expansion in PACs took place following the campaign finance reform of the early 1970s, particularly after the 1974 Campaign Finance Act. This reform prevented unions, corporations and trade associations from making campaign contributions directly to candidates. PACs, therefore, became the middlemen; collecting together contributions from such groups as well as other individuals and then channelling the monies towards the candidates that might best serve the interests of the contributors.

PAC Funding of Federal Candidates 1998–2004

The tables below show the amounts contributed in millions of dollars. Again, all figures are from the Federal Election Commission.

	2004	2002	2000	1998
Senate	$63.7	$59.2	$51.9	$48.1
House	$225.4	$206.9	$193.4	$158.7

$Millions going to incumbents and challengers (rounded)

	2004	2002	2000	1998
Incumbents				
House	$187.1	$160.9	$150.0	$123.9
Senate	$39.3	$37.0	$33.5	$34.3
Challengers				
House	$15.6	$13.8	$19.8	$14.8
Senate	$5.6	$14.2	$7.1	$6.6

$Millions going to candidates by party (rounded)

	2004	2002	2000	1998
Senate				
Democrat	$28.4	$25.4	$18.7	$20.7
Republican	$35.3	$33.8	$33.2	$27.3
House				
Democrat	$98.6	$102.6	$98.2	$77.7
Republican	$126.6	$104.2	$94.7	$80.9

Numbers of Political Action Committees 1974 and 1997–2005

The table below shows the total number of political action committees operating in each year according to the Federal Election Commission.

1974	608
1997	3884
1998	3798
1999	3835
2000	4499
2005	4867

Top five PACs by total contributions to candidates (2004)

The table below shows the top five PACs by total contributions to candidate campaigns.

Name	Total amount
Realtors (estate agents)	$3 771 083
National Automobile Dealers' Association	$2 584 800
International Brotherhood of Electrical Workers' Committee on Political Education	$2 304 600
National Beer Wholesalers' Association	$2 289 000
Laborers' Political League	$2 249 000

Top five PACs by receipts (January 2003–December 2004)

The table below shows the top five PACs by receipts (i.e. monies raised)

Name	Receipts
America Coming Together	$33 715 898
Move On PAC	$31 870 607
Emily's List	$27 547 122
Service Employers' International Union Committee on Political Education (SEIU COPE)	$14 716 632
American Federation of State, County and Municipal Employees – PEOPLE Qualified	$13 880 683

How does the US public feel about Political Action Committee activity?

According to a Harris Poll (May 16, 2001) a large majority of Americans feel that big companies and PACs have too much influence.

'Big companies have too much power and influence in Washington'	86%
'PACs have too much power and influence in Washington'	83%
'Small business has too little power and influence in Washington'	88%
'Public opinion has too little power and influence in Washington'	73%

18.4 Special interests in Congress

Power centres

The process of government is increasingly complex. As a result special interest groups often seek to gain influence by forming close working relationships with key figures in congressional committees, executive departments and regulatory agencies. Richard L. Kolbe (*American Political Parties*, 1985) noted that such special interest groups are particularly keen to develop such contacts where:

1. the potential benefits for or costs to the group are **large**;
2. the potential benefits for or costs to the group are clearly **recognisable**;
3. the potential benefits for or costs to the group are **immediate**.

Thus a farming interest group seeking an increase in federal subsidies would be chasing **large**, **obvious** and more **immediate** benefits than an individual taxpayer – for whom the costs of the subsidies would be **small** and **hidden**.

'Iron Triangles'

The term 'iron triangle' is applied to the close relationships that can form between the key pressure in a particular field, the appropriate congressional committee and the executive agency or bureau of the department with overview of the area. As such triangles are formed, other interested parties are excluded from the 'policy-loop', to their detriment. Kolbe uses the example of a triangle concerning wheat production (see right), but such relationships probably exist in most areas of policy.

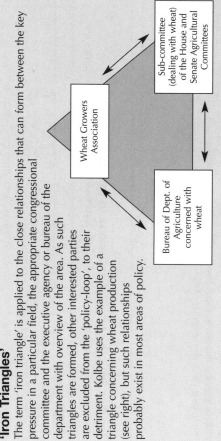

Wheat Growers Association

Bureau of Dept. of Agriculture concerned with wheat

Sub-committee (dealing with wheat) of the House and Senate Agricultural Committees

'Revolving Doors'

When we talk about the revolving door syndrome we are referring to the way in which individuals in Congress or in the executive often walk out of office into well paid consultancy jobs with special interest groups and, at the same time, former consultants find themselves being offered key positions in the administration of the day. *The Guardian*, for example, reported that Robert Rubin, Clinton's treasury chief, later became a senior figure at Enron creditors Citigroup and lobbied the Bush administration on behalf of Enron.

'Agency Capture'

Agency capture is said to have occurred when a special interest group is able to exert a degree of control over the government agency that should be overseeing or regulating the area of policy with which the group is concerned. Once in such a position, the group can often exclude other interested parties from the administration of policy.

Money in Congress

The perception that PAC contributions are increasingly influencing the process of policy formation has led Senator Barbara Mikulski and others to speak of a 'coin-operated congress'. 2000 Presidential Candidate Bill Bradley echoed this sentiment, remarking that 'money is to politics as acid is to cloth. It eats away the fabric of democracy'. Though it is difficult to gauge the extent to which Senator Edward Kennedy was fair in characterising the legislature as 'the best congress that money can buy', a number of case studies illustrate the nature of the problem.

NB: The subject of campaign finance and the role of Political Action Committees in particular is dealt with more fully in Chapters 16.2 and 18.3. Efforts to regulate contributions are dealt with in Chapter 15.4. The Enron scandal is dealt with in Chapters 18.1 and 18.2.

Mini case studies

The 'Keating Five'

Charles Keating was investigated by Federal Regulators following the collapse of his *Lincoln Savings and Loans Association*. Five Senators (later dubbed 'the Keating Five') were accused of improperly interfering with the investigation and it was alleged that the five had collectively received more than $1 million in campaign contributions from Keating. In 1991 four of the five were cited for questionable conduct. The fifth, Senator Alan Cranston (D, California), was censured for reprehensible conduct.

The Lemon Law

In the US the term 'lemon' is often applied to used cars that are repaired and sold despite having previously been 'written-off' in accidents. Many states traditionally had 'lemon laws' guaranteeing consumers certain rights with regard to such vehicles. In 1997 the US Consumers' Union reported that the House of Representatives had passed a law (336 to 72) that would allow used car dealers to sell cars over seven years old without full disclosure of the vehicle's history and would also limit the rights of consumers to gain compensation if they discovered that they had been sold a 'lemon'. NADA (the National Automobile Dealers' Association) had been at work behind the scenes on behalf of used car dealers. It was subsequently reported that 90% of those who had received $4000 or more in campaign contributions from related interest groups voted for the bill whereas only 32% of those receiving no money or contributions below $4000 had done so.

Clinton's Health Security Reform Plan of 1993

Clinton's 1993 health care reform package had been the flagship policy of his 1992 election platform. Within five days of entering the White House, the new administration had set up a task force on health reform – headed by Hilary Clinton. The plan produced by this task force envisaged universal coverage for all uninsured Americans (around 37 million individuals). From the start, however, the programme faced opposition within Congress. The HIAA (Health Insurers Association of America) feared the collapse of the private health insurance market in the face of the reforms and lobbied hard against it. Healthcare providers and physicians were also concerned that the programme could impact on their work practices and their incomes. The AMA (American Medical Association), representing over 300 000 members, acted on their behalf and they had friends in the right places. Between 1990 and 1992 they had given $977 704 in congressional campaign contributions. Some consumer groups such as the AARP (American Association of Retired People) were concerned that the plan might have a detrimental affect on existing Medicare/Medicaid programmes. Others, confused by the detail, fell victim to strong negative campaigns that fed off the confusion surrounding what exactly the package involved.

18.5 Are pressure groups 'good' or 'bad' for US democracy?

A r g u m e n t s   f o r

1. Pressure groups occur naturally under any system of government. People have a natural desire to unite in protection of their own interests or in advancing a particular cause.

2. Pressure groups are particularly necessary in the US because America is a heterogeneous society with a massive range of views and interests. It would be impossible for any political party to represent the full range of opinion effectively. This is what pluralism is about.

3. Pressure groups allow a greater degree of public participation in the political process, particularly between elections when governments can become complacent.

4. Groups play an essential role in moderating the views of their more extreme members. Without such groups, individuals with extreme views might never have their views challenged and moderated.

5. Groups play a vital role in educating the general public. Many necessary changes have been brought about as a result of public pressure resulting from the activities of pressure groups in raising awareness of issues.

6. Groups provide valuable information to governments. Governments must have access to the best possible information on which to base policy. Pressure groups are often in a position to provide detailed information on specific issues because they tend to be specialised. Many groups also have significant research programmes.

7. Groups can hold the government accountable. They can act as watchdogs, monitoring the impact of policies and bringing public pressure to bear where governments fail to live up to their promises or their obligations under the law.

8. Minority views, often drowned out within political parties or in Congress, can be articulated within pressure groups. People with such views are, therefore, allowed to 'let off steam' without becoming disaffected and adopting very extreme methods.

A r g u m e n t s   a g a i n s t

1. Some groups are far more powerful than others are. We should really be talking about elites theory rather than pluralist theory.

2. Many groups are disadvantaged by a lack of financial clout. For example, it is difficult for groups representing poorer people to compete with groups representing business interests. As US political consultant Raymond Strother noted, 'poor people don't often have rich friends'.

3. Human resources are also an issue. Groups tend to be more successful where they have articulate, educated leading members. Many have argued that this tends to favour groups run by the middle classes over those set up by the working class.

4. Groups often have an effect on government that is disproportionate to their size or to the merit of their cause. By using direct action, even illegal tactics, groups can defeat the efforts of popularly-elected governments and change policy. This has been apparent over abortion where anti-abortion groups have used intimidation at clinics and have deliberately jammed free-phone lines in order to shut abortion facilities down de facto.

5. Some groups have worryingly close contacts with government. In the case of Enron, for example, leading members of the federal executive had either worked for the company as consultants or had received monies from the company. Many more politicians and officials take positions as consultants after they leave office. This raises the question of how even-handedly they can act whilst in office.

6. In the US, many business interests often have too cosy a relationship with the independent regulatory commissions that are supposed to be objectively assessing their compliance with the various laws and regulations.

The historical context

The Declaration of Independence

In 1776 the 13 colonies on the east coast of North America issued the Declaration of Independence. This act resulted from a deterioration in relations between the colonies and Britain that had seen such landmark historical events as the Boston Tea Party in 1773. The key issue for many in the colonies was the British insistence on demanding taxation without granting any meaningful representation. The Declaration, drafted by Thomas Jefferson, formally put into words the colonies' justification for their rejection of British rule as well as setting out some of the principles upon which a new government could be formed.

'We hold these truths to be self-evident, that all Men are created equal, that they are endowed by their Creator with certain unalienable Rights, that among these are Life, Liberty and the Pursuit of Happiness. That to secure these Rights, Governments are instituted among Men, deriving their just Powers from the Consent of the Governed that whenever any Form of Government becomes destructive of these Ends, it is the Rights of the People to alter or to abolish it, and to constitute new Government, laying its foundation on such principles, and organising its powers in such form, as to them shall seem most likely to effect their safety and happiness.'

The American War of Independence (1776–83)

The War of Independence, or American Revolution as it is sometimes referred to, dates back to at least 1775 when fighting broke out between colonial militia and the British. In 1774 the various colonial assemblies had sent delegates to a first national 'Continental Congress'. In 1775 the 'Second Continental Congress' appointed George Washington to command their army and, in July, adopted the Declaration of Independence. After seven years the War was over and the Treaty of Paris was signed in 1783. In this Treaty Britain recognised American independence.

The Articles of Confederation (1781)

In 1781 the former American colonies formed a loose confederacy. Under this system there was to be no national executive (such as a president) or any national judiciary. There would simply be a Congress consisting of representatives from each state. Under the Articles of Confederation this 'central government' only had power over the following areas:

Foreign policy and defence	Territorial disputes between states	Coinage
Weights and measures	Postal services	Relations with Indians

All other matters were left to the states

Preparations for the Philadelphia Convention

By 1786 there was widespread disillusionment with the form of government created by the Articles of Confederation. Many, including Hamilton (see below), called for a convention to discuss reform of the Articles. This Convention was eventually called in 1787. Fifty-five representatives, out of the 74 who were invited from the various states, turned up at the Constitutional Convention in Philadelphia. Only one state, Rhode Island, sent no representatives. Many of the leading figures present were from Virginia, at that time the largest of the states. George Washington, a unifying figurehead following his leadership in the Revolution, was asked to preside over the meetings, but individuals such as James Madison provided the real driving force.

Key participants

George Washington (1732–99)
Washington had represented Virginia in the First (1774) and Second (1775) Continental Congress. In 1775 the Congress had given him control of American forces and in 1787 he presided over the Philadelphia Convention. He was the first US President (1789–97).

James Madison (1751–1836)
Madison had been involved in Virginia politics since 1776 and became a real driving force at the Convention. He collaborated with Hamilton in the writing of the Federalist Papers, supporting the ratification of the finished Constitution. He was a strong advocate of a Bill of Rights.

Thomas Jefferson (1743–1826)
Jefferson was another Virginian. He had served on the Second Continental Congress in 1775 and then drafted the Declaration of Independence issued in July 1776. He was a keen advocate of the separation of powers and limited government.

Alexander Hamilton (1755–1804)
Hamilton was Washington's aide-de-camp in the American Revolution (between 1777 and 1781). He co-authored the Federalist Papers (with Madison) and was the founder and the leader of the Federalist Party until the time of his death in a duel in 1804. Hamilton was a firm believer in a strong federal government. He believed, however, that pure democracy would lead to mob-rule.

19.2 Framing the Constitution

The Philadelphia Convention, 1787

Who were the Founding Fathers?

The Founding Fathers were the 55 delegates who wrote the new Constitution in 1787. Most of them were fairly young, wealthy landowners, lawyers and businessmen with a good level of education. When they met at Philadelphia in 1787 they were supposed to discuss reforms to the Articles of Confederation that had been in force since 1781. In the event, they decided to go beyond this remit and start afresh on a new constitutional settlement. Throughout the summer of 1787 the delegates debated and argued the detail of the new arrangements. No small difficulty was the need to balance the need for strong and effective central government with the need to protect the rights of states and individual citizens. Under British rule, the remoteness and unitary nature of government had been seen to impinge upon individual rights. The confederacy arising from the Articles of Confederation had been to the other extreme – weak and ineffective.

Conflicting interests and compromise

The Virginia Plan

This plan set out the interests of most of the larger states. There would be a bicameral legislature, with representatives in each house apportioned to each state in relation to the state's population. There would be an elected national executive and national courts. The central (federal) government would have power to declare acts of state governments invalid and could use the federal army to quell problems within states.

The New Jersey Plan

This placed a greater emphasis on the needs of the smaller states who feared that their voices might be lost amongst the larger states. The plan provided greater detail on the power of the legislature. This legislature would, for example, appoint the President, and its laws would be the supreme law in the land. The real sticking point, however, came over the way in which seats in the legislature would be apportioned between states.

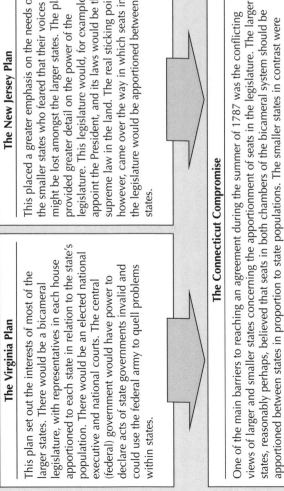

The Connecticut Compromise

One of the main barriers to reaching an agreement during the summer of 1787 was the conflicting views of larger and smaller states concerning the apportionment of seats in the legislature. The larger states, reasonably perhaps, believed that seats in both chambers of the bicameral system should be apportioned between states in proportion to state populations. The smaller states in contrast were worried that this would see their voices lost in the new Congress and were unwilling to agree to a constitution that would result in such a situation. The so-called Connecticut Compromise, proposed by Connecticut delegate Roger Sherman, offered a solution. One chamber (the House) would be apportioned in relation to a state's population and the other (the Senate) would comprise two representatives from each state regardless of state population. Thus, the deadlock was broken.

Key issues at Philadelphia

Centralisation or fragmentation?

As we have seen, by 1786 it was clear that a more effective balance had to be struck between the need for effective government and the need for the protection of state rights and individual liberties. Under the British (King George III), the colonies had experienced a particularly centralised 'unitary' system of government. Under the Articles of Confederation they had experienced an unusually loose and disparate form of Government, a 'confederal' system. Both had proven unacceptable for different reasons. The key was, therefore, to create a truly 'federal' system where the powers of federal (central) and state governments would be clearly defined and in balance.

Democracy or 'mobocracy'?

As we have seen the majority of the delegates at the Convention – the Founding Fathers – were relatively well educated and wealthy. Many were landowners, all were white men. Many of them – Hamilton included – feared that democracy, unchecked, could reel out of control and become the rule of the uneducated, politically ignorant mob – 'mobocracy'. As a result they put in place mechanisms to avoid such an eventuality, including the electoral college.

The end product

After four months of deliberations the final draft of the new Constitution was signed by 39 of the 55 delegates who had attended the Convention. As George Washington wrote to Patrick Henry in 1787:

'I wish the Constitution, which is offered, had been made more perfect, but I sincerely believe it is the best that could be obtained at this time.'

The new Constitution established a federal government with a bicameral Congress (composition, conditions of office and powers were set out in Article 1), a President (Article 2) and a Supreme Court (Article 3). The constitutional positions of each of these institutions and other aspects of the political process are dealt with in context on their respective pages.

19.3 Principles

Introduction

As we have seen, the Founding Fathers were – for the most part – well-educated men. In such circles the influence of the social contract theorists such as Locke and Rousseau spread, along with the ideas of other writers such as Thomas Paine and the French writer Baron Montesquieu. They developed an understanding of natural rights, limited government and the separation of powers, taking such ideas with them when they attended the Constitutional Convention in Philadelphia in 1787.

Federalism

The key issue at the 1787 Philadelphia Convention was the role that the central government was to play in relation to the state governments. Some would have preferred to retain something closer to the loose confederation created by the Articles of Confederation; others would have wanted the amalgamation of all of the states into a single unitary national government. As was so often the case at the Convention, a compromise was reached. Certain powers (**the enumerated powers**) were given to the federal government. Others were **inherent** or **implied** because the federal government would not have been able to discharge its enumerated powers without them. Some powers were **denied** the federal government. In addition, the Tenth Amendment to the Constitution stated that 'the powers not delegated to the United States by the Constitution, nor prohibited by it to the States, are reserved to the States respectively, or to the people.' These then are the **reserved** or **residual** powers. Finally, some powers were to be held jointly – the **concurrent** powers.

Dual federalism (1780s–1920s)

Under this manifestation of federalism, the federal (central) and various state governments each had separate spheres of authority. Within their own areas they were sovereign and they were, therefore, equal in status. This system operated fairly well as long as the federal government was small and was not interventionist. In the 1930s, however, things changed significantly.

Co-operative federalism or intergovernmentalism (1930s–1960s)

Until the end of the 1920s the various states were reasonably powerful and the federal government's powers to intervene were fairly narrowly interpreted. Following the Wall Street Crash (1929), however, the federal government was forced to become more involved in the co-ordinating the effort to get the economy moving again. Franklin D Roosevelt's New Deal policy brought the federal government into Americans' lives, wherever they lived in the US. Truman's 'Fair Deal', Kennedy's 'New Frontier' and Johnson's 'Great Society' continued this interventionist trend, particularly in their use of targeted grants.

New Federalism (1970s–present)

Criticism of federal government intervention/interference led to calls for 'smaller government'. Reagan's 'New Federalism' was a stated desire to return power to the states. Reagan was critical of the way in which the Tenth Amendment's guarantee of state rights had been ignored since the 1930s. Republican domination of the White House in the period 1970–93 led to plans to reduce federal grants as part of the budget-balancing programme The Supreme Court also took the lead by, for example, allowing states to pass statutes undermining Roe v. Wade locally, by limiting access to abortion (e.g. Webster v. Reproductive Health Services, 1989).

Republicanism

Their experiences under British rule had led many Founding Fathers to oppose the idea of establishing a US monarchy in principle. For them, the tyranny visited on the 13 colonies by George III was reason enough to establish a republic. Though some, Hamilton for example, felt that a monarchy could work in the US, the republicans won the day. Congress was also prevented from granting other titles of nobility in Article 1, Section 8.

Separation of powers

This was the principle outlined by the French writer Baron Montesquieu. Essentially, Montesquieu argued that a concentration of the three key elements of state power could lead to tyranny. These three elements (see right) should, therefore, be separated in the three branches of government. In the US this principle means, for example, that no individual can hold office in more than one of the three branches simultaneously. This is a far cry from the situation in the UK where the Prime Minister is head of the executive and sits in the legislature, and the Lord Chancellor was still part of the government (executive), the House of Lords (legislature) and at the apex of the legal system at the start of 2005.

Executive
The executive branch has the role of executing – putting the laws into effect.

Legislature
The legislature has the role of legislating – this means that it makes the laws.

Judiciary
The judiciary has the role of enforcing and interpreting the laws. The US Supreme Court has to interpret the meaning of the Constitution – the supreme law of the land.

Checks and balances

A total separation of power and an absence of co-operation between branches would lead to 'gridlock' in government. As a result, the Constitution forces co-operation between the three separated branches by instituting checks and balances. Those in each branch know that they can achieve little without the other branches but, by negotiation, can go some way towards achieving their goals. In order to avoid the dangers of branches co-operating too much or simply capitulating, the Founding Fathers also staggered the length of terms of office for President (four years), Supreme Court (life), House of Representatives (two years) and Senate (six years with one-third elected every two years). This means that those in different branches often have different ideological perspectives.

19.4 Checks and balances

Introduction

The separation of powers was central to the Constitution framed at Philadelphia but, as we saw on the last page, a total separation of the powers to make laws, to execute laws and to enforce laws would have left government permanently gridlocked and unworkable. As a result interconnections, 'checks and balances', were built into the system of government. These checks and balances provided enough linkage for the government to be effective while, at the same time, providing barriers to any one branch dominating the political process.

What checks exist between the three branches of the federal government?

	President	
	Checks on Congress	**Checks on Supreme Court (and the federal judiciary)**
	(1) The President effectively recommends/proposes legislation though the 'State of the Union Message'.	(1) The President can appoint top federal judges including Supreme Court Justices.
	(2) The President can veto legislation and also has a 'pocket veto' in certain circumstances (see Ch 16.2).	(2) The President can issue pardons, thus reversing judicial action.
	(3) The President can call special sessions of Congress.	

	Congress	
	Checks on President	**Checks on Supreme Court**
	(1) Congress can reject, amend or delay the President's legislative proposals.	(1) Congress (the Senate) confirms Supreme Court appointments by majority vote.
	(2) The President's Budget has to be approved by Congress.	(2) Congress controls the size and appellate jurisdiction of the Court and can set up inferior courts as it sees fit.
	(3) Congress can override the President's veto (with a two-thirds majority in each house).	(3) Congress can initiate constitutional amendments with a view to changing the passages of the Constitution upon which the Court is basing the judgements that Congress disapproves of.
	(4) Many Presidential appointments have to be approved by a majority vote in the Senate.	
	(5) A two-thirds majority is required in the Senate for treaties to be ratified.	
	(6) Congress retains the War Power and can, in theory, prevent the President entering a war or force him into one against his will.	
	(7) Congress can initiate impeachment proceedings against the President as it did in the case of Bill Clinton.	

	Supreme Court	
	Checks on President	**Checks on Congress**
	(1) Through judicial review, the Supreme Court can declare the actions of the President unconstitutional.	(1) Through judicial review, the Court can declare acts of Congress unconstitutional, thus making them void.
		(2) The Court can also interpret the meaning of acts, affecting the way in which they are implemented.

19.5 The Bill of Rights

Introduction

The first ten amendments to the Constitution are referred to collectively as the Bill of Rights. They were ratified in 1791 as part of the deal that ensured some states accepted the Constitution itself.

The Bill of Rights outlines a number of key constitutional guarantees and the majority, if not all, of these ten amendments still have a direct relevance to the lives of Americans today. The important thing to remember is that although many of the protected rights appear unambiguous and clear cut (**absolute**), in reality the Supreme Court and inferior courts have had to **balance** the rights of one individual against another and balance the rights of all individuals against the legitimate interests of the state in regulating human activity.

The Bill of Rights

1. Protects the freedom of religion, the press, speech and assembly (see right)
2. Protects the right to bear arms
3. Protects the privacy of property owners
4. Guarantees freedom from unreasonable searches and seizures
5. Guarantees the rights of the accused and includes the 'due process clause'
6. Sets out rights for those standing trial
7. Deals with common law suits
8. Bans excessive bail and 'cruel and unusual' punishments
9. Deals with rights reserved to the people
10. Deals with rights reserved to the states

Case study: the First Amendment

Introduction

The majority of Americans are familiar with the First Amendment; if not 'word-for-word', then for what it represents. This first plank of the Bill of Rights has become, as Lee C. Bollinger noted, 'one of the nation's foremost normative and cultural symbols' because it 'reflects the vital attributes of the American character'. What, then, is the basis of this 'cultural symbol'? For all of the heat it generates, the First Amendment is a remarkably compact piece of prose:

'Congress shall make no law respecting an establishment of religion, or prohibiting the free exercise thereof; or abridging the **freedom of speech**, or of the press; or the right of the people peaceably to assembly and to petition the Government for a redress of grievances.'

To the reader many of these guarantees appear absolute. What the Supreme Court has had to do, however, is to 'draw a line between constitutionally and legally appropriate application of the quintet of First Amendment guarantees' (Henry Abraham) in order to decide whether they should be taken as absolute or subject to some *balancing* (against the rights of others and the interests of the state).

The limits of speech

The free-speech clause has been used to defend a wide range of practices. Though the decision that upheld the right to burn the US flag (Texas v. Johnson, 1989) is still considered significant, the protection of free speech has gone far further. The Court has ruled, for example, that the guarantee of free speech protects the right of women to strip (expressive conduct), though they allow some regulation of this non-pure form of 'speech'!

CITY OF ERIE *et al.* v. PAP'S A.M, tdba 'Kandyland' (2000)

Controversy:	Decision:
Dancers in Erie were supposed to wear G-strings and 'pasties' (fake jewel – 'paste' – nipple tassels). PAP's A.M, however, operated 'Kandyland', an establishment offering *totally* nude erotic dancing by women.	The Court argued that the overall loss of expression (in wearing G-strings and 'pasties') was insignificant, and that small losses of expression could not be used to justify invalidating Erie's otherwise constitutional measure. Erie's regulation was therefore upheld.

Freedom of speech

In protecting this right, the US Supreme Court has had to consider what precisely constitutes speech.

Protected speech

The Court has identified two types of speech which are protected by the First Amendment. The first is **pure speech** – the right of people to say or write things. The second is what is known as **expressive conduct**. Expressive conduct generally consists of non-verbal communication (burning the flag, for example) that is expressing a view. Expressive conduct is not granted the same protection as pure speech but it is, in the Court's eyes worthy of some protection.

Unprotected speech

The Court sees some forms of speech as unprotected. Justice Frank Murphy explained that obscenity, libel and fighting words are unprotected under the First Amendment because 'such utterances are no essential part of an exposition of ideas, and are of such slight social value as a step to truth that any benefit that may be derived from them is clearly outweighed by the social interest in order and morality.'

In many cases the line between expressive conduct worthy of some protection and unprotected speech is a fine one. This is particularly true over the question of what constitutes obscenity.

Conclusions

Barbara Jordan observed in 1990 that 'The Bill of Rights was not ordained by nature or God. It's very human, very fragile'. If this were true, we might expect the First Amendment, given its language and scope, to be particularly vulnerable to attack. In reality, however, the 45 words that constitute these five key guarantees have proven incredibly resilient; providing threads of continuity, yet leaving enough flexibility for the Supreme Court to shape the Amendment to the demands of each new age. This is crucial. While 'the great thing about the First Amendment' may well be 'that it extends its rights to everyone. The wise and the foolish' (Samuel J. Ervin), no state can protect the rights of *all* individuals, at *all* costs, at *all* times. The Court has to find a balance between the *liberal* interest of individual freedom and the *democratic* need to regulate some activities.

19.6 The living Constitution

Introduction

The fact that the US Constitution is **codified** often leads people to suggest that it is **rigid** rather than **flexible**. However, while the amendment process is tortuous, the Constitution is anything but rigid. Indeed, it has shown itself to be incredibly flexible and adaptable in the 216 years since it was framed. This flexibility has been provided not only by the possibility of amendment but also by the ability of the Courts – ultimately the US Supreme Court – to interpret the document and apply it to each new age. The legality of practices never dreamt of at the time that the Constitution was written has been assessed through this process of interpretation and – at the same time – the Supreme Court has been able to update its own interpretations of the same constitutional passage over a period of time. In this sense the Constitution is a truly living document.

Amending the Constitution

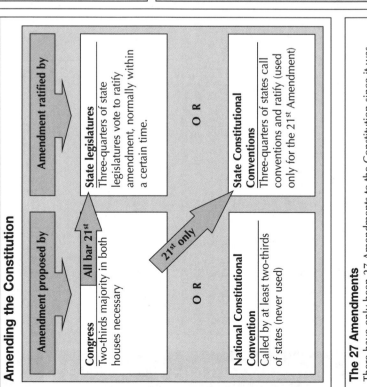

The 27 Amendments

There have only been 27 Amendments to the Constitution since it was framed and the first ten of those, the 'Bill of Rights' were ratified together in 1791.

Updating the Constitution through judicial action

The Supreme Court updating interpretations over time

Arthur J. Goldberg stated that 'the Supreme Court, when it decides a new legal question, does not make illegal what was previously legal; it gives a final authoritative determination of whether an action was legal when it took place'. However, while in theory the Court is only interpreting the Constitution, in practice the differences between interpretations of the same constitutional passage over as short a time as 60 years (Plessy v. Ferguson, 1896 to Brown v. Board of Education, Topeka, 1954) may often appear tantamount to legislative action (see below). Indeed, James F Byrnes referring to just that transformation in interpretation took a radically different view of the Court's role to that taken by Goldberg, remarking that 'the Court did not interpret the Constitution – the Court amended it'.

PLESSY v. FERGUSON, 1896 (MAJORITY 7:1)

Controversy:	Decision:
Whether the 13th and 14th Amendments allowed the segregation of races on trains.	The Court argued that for there to be a violation of the 13th Amendment, there would have had to be some attempt to reintroduce slavery and that this had not occurred. Under the 14th Amendment segregation was acceptable as long as the result was 'separate but equal'.

BROWN v. BOARD OF EDUCATION, TOPEKA (KANSAS), 1954 (MAJORITY (9:0)

Controversy:	Decision:
Was it a violation of the 14th Amendment to prevent a black girl (Linda Brown) from attending a white school?	Looked at the merits of the case and used (then) controversial sociological research to show that the separation of races created inequalities. Separate was, therefore, always unequal and unacceptable under the 14th Amendment. 'In the field of public education, separate but equal has no place.' Plessy was thus out of date.

The Supreme Court addressing a new phenomenon (in this case, the internet)

RENO v. AMERICAN CIVIL LIBERTIES UNION, 1997 (MAJORITY 7:2)

The Supreme Court struck down two provisions of the 1996 Communications Decency Act, which sought to protect minors from harmful material available on the internet. The Court maintained that these sections violated the First Amendment protection of freedom of speech.

The majority:	The dissent:
Stevens, Scalia, Kennedy, Souter, Thomas, Ginsburg, Breyer	O'Connor, Rehnquist
'At issue is the constitutionality of two statutory provisions enacted to protect minors from 'indecent' and 'patently offensive' communications on the Internet. Not withstanding the legitimacy and importance of the congressional goal of protecting children from harmful materials, we agree with the three judge District Court that the statute abridges "the freedom of speech" protected by the First Amendment.' (Stevens)	'I write separately to explain why I view the Communications Decency Act of 1996 (CDA) as little more than an attempt by Congress to create 'adult zones' on the Internet. Our precedent indicates that the creation of such zones can be constitutionally sound. Despite the soundness of its purpose, however, portions of the CDA are unconstitutional because they stray from the blueprint our prior cases have developed for constructing a "zoning law" that passes constitutional muster.' (O'Connor)

House of Representatives

Composition (110th Congress)

Size
There are 435 members in the House. Each state has a number of Representatives in proportion to its population. In January 2007 there were 233 Democrats and 202 Republicans.

Election and term
The term of office is two years. The whole House is re-elected every two years. Candidates must be 25+, a citizen of the US for 7+ years and resident in the state for which they are standing.

Background of Representatives (Jan. 2007)
74 women, 42 Black members, 26 Hispanics, 162 lawyers, 101 prior military service. Average age of 55.93 years.

Powers exclusive to House

1. To consider all 'money bills' first
This power was originally given to the House because it was the only directly elected chamber (until the 17th Amendment, 1913).

2. To impeach …
any member of the federal government, executive or judicial branches

3. To choose a President …
in the event that no candidate has received a majority in the electoral college.

Power held by Congress (as a whole)

1. To pass laws
2. To pass the budget
3. To undertake investigations into the actions of the executive branch
3. To start constitutional amendments by a two-thirds majority in each House
5. To declare war
6. To confirm the appointment of a newly elected Vice-President

Key figures
The Speaker (see below) is *the* key figure in the House of Representatives. There is also a Majority and a Minority Leader, elected by their respective party groups. These individuals play a key role of co-ordinating the day to day activities of the House as well as representing the views of the Chamber in meetings with the President.

The Speaker
The role of the Speaker of the House is compared to the role of British Prime Minister more often than it is to the role of the Speaker in the House of Commons. This is because the US Speaker is a partisan player rather than an umpire. Speaker Newt Gingrich, for example, – with his party's 'Contract with America' – took a real lead in politics from 1995.

Roles: refers bills to committee, appoints select committee and conference committee chairs while influencing the appointment of standing committee chairs, appoints majority party contingent on the House Rules Committee, and presides over the House, enforcing the rules.

Senate

Composition (110th Congress)

Size
There are 100 members in the Senate. Each state has two Senators. In January 2007 there were 49 Democrats, 49 Republicans and two Democrat-leaning independents.

Election and term
The term of office is six years. One-third of the Senate is elected every two years. Candidates must be 30+, a citizen of the US for 9+ years and a resident in the state for which they are standing.

Background of Senators (Jan. 2007)
16 women, 1 Black member, 3 Hispanics, 58 lawyers, 29 prior military service. Average age of 61.73 years.

Powers exclusive to Senate

1. To ratify treaties by a two-thirds majority

2. To confirm many federal appointments
… by simple majority (e.g. Supreme Court Justices)

3. To try cases of impeachment
… brought by Congress (two-thirds majority needed for conviction)

4. To elect a Vice-President
… where two or more candidates are tied

Key figures
The Vice-President is the President of the Senate and has the right to preside over the chamber and control the casting vote in the event of a tie. Normally, however, the Senates elect a President pro tempore – a senior figure of the majority party – to chair the chamber in the Vice-President's absence. Majority and Minority Leaders are also important (see above). The Senate – in the absence of a 'Rules Committee' – timetables bills though **unanimous consent agreements.**

'Filibustering'
The right of Senators to speak freely throws up the curious spectacle of the filibuster – a unique brand of procrastination. Through this practice of talking at length on virtually any subject, a single-minded minority – indeed one – can succeed in 'talking a bill' out of time and therefore out of existence. Senator Strom Thurmond of South Carolina, for example, spoke for 24 hours and 18 minutes against the 1957 Civil Rights Act, and a group of Southern Democrats conducted an 83-day group filibuster against the 1964 Civil Rights Act. A filibuster can be ended by a cloture motion, requiring the support of three-fifths of the entire Senate (60).

20.2 The passage of legislation

Introduction

The legislative process in the US is not vastly different from that in the UK. One difference, however, is that both houses have equal legislative power. One feature of this is that bills pass through the House and Senate at the same time. As a result, conference committees are sometimes needed at the end of the third reading stage in order to iron out any differences that exist between the House and Senate versions of a bill.

Presidential action

1. **Sign** – If the President signs the bill then it can become law.

2. **Veto** – The President can veto the **entire bill** within ten days of receiving it as long as he sends it back with note explaining his reasons for using the veto.

3. **Pocket veto** – If the congressional session ends before the end of the ten days, the President can 'pocket' the bill, killing it.

The line-item veto – In 1997 Congress passed a law granting the President the right to delete individual parts of a bill (see Ch 16.2). This was declared unconstitutional in 1998. The President, therefore, has no line-item veto.

The passage of legislation

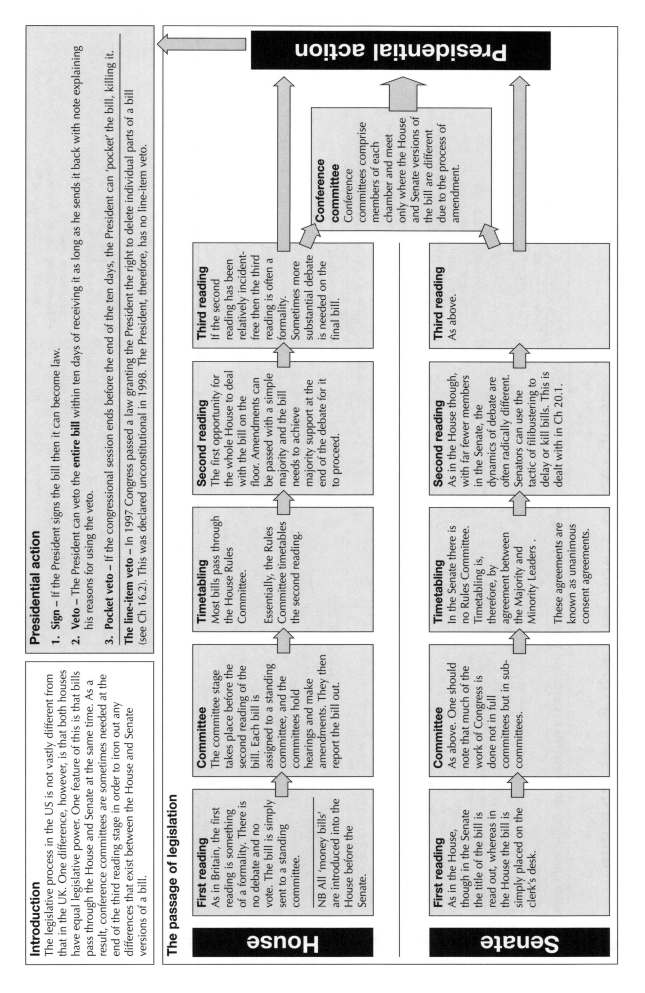

Presidential action

House

First reading

As in Britain, the first reading is something of a formality. There is no debate and no vote. The bill is simply sent to a standing committee.

NB All 'money bills' are introduced into the House before the Senate.

Committee

The committee stage takes place before the second reading of the bill. Each bill is assigned to a standing committee, and the committees hold hearings and make amendments. They then report the bill out.

Timetabling

Most bills pass through the House Rules Committee.

Essentially, the Rules Committee timetables the second reading.

Second reading

The first opportunity for the whole House to deal with the bill on the floor. Amendments can be passed with a simple majority and the bill needs to achieve majority support at the end of the debate for it to proceed.

Third reading

If the second reading has been relatively incident-free then the third reading is often a formality. Sometimes more substantial debate is needed on the final bill.

Senate

First reading

As in the House, though in the Senate the title of the bill is read out, whereas in the House the bill is simply placed on the clerk's desk.

Committee

As above. One should note that much of the work of Congress is done not in full committees but in sub-committees.

Timetabling

In the Senate there is no Rules Committee. Timetabling is, therefore, by agreement between the Majority and Minority Leaders .

These agreements are known as unanimous consent agreements.

Second reading

As in the House though, with far fewer members in the Senate, the dynamics of debate are often radically different. Senators can use the tactic of filibustering to delay or kill bills. This is dealt with in Ch 20.1.

Third reading

As above.

Conference committee

Conference committees comprise members of each chamber and meet only where the House and Senate versions of the bill are different due to the process of amendment.

What factors are the most important in determining outcomes in Congress?

Pressure group action

The issue of abortion provides an excellent illustration of pressure group influence on Congressmen. Though Kay Orr remarked that '[it would be] a disservice to our political system if we allow … [abortion] to be the test of every candidate', the 'pro-life' lobby has tried to make it just that. During the 1980s groups such as Jerry Falwell's 'Moral Majority' undertook a series of campaigns not only to raise public awareness, but also to back sympathetic candidates and attack unsympathetic ones. Several liberal Senators – Birch Bayle, George McGovern and Frank Church among them – came under attack for their positions on issues such as abortion, while candidates who backed such groups, it was argued, gained significantly. By forming Political Action Committees (PACs), pressure groups can maximise their financial contributions to candidates' campaigns, circumventing the 1974 Campaign Finance Act.

Constituency pressure

Members of Congress have to take a good deal more notice of their constituents than most MPs in the UK. This is in part because …

1. It is normally constituents who select candidates through congressional primaries.
2. Representatives in the House face election every two years, as do one-third of Senators.

That said, the vast majority of those Members of Congress who seek re-election are successful:

Year	House		Senate	
	% Re-elected*		% Re-elected*	
1998	98.3		89.6	
2000	97.8		82.8	
2002	96.0		86.0	
2004	98.3		96.2	
2006	94.3		79.3	

NB % of those seeking re-election

In 2004, only one of the 26 incumbent Senators seeking re-election was defeated (Tom Daschle). In the House, only 7 of the 404 incumbents standing were defeated. Do these re-election rates suggest that incumbents are re-elected whatever they do, or do they reflect how attentive incumbents are to the needs of their constituents?

Party pressure

Those comparing the influence of US 'party whips' and their namesakes in the UK have often concluded that in the US the whips have no 'sting'. This is partly because of the fact that…

parties cannot threaten to deselect candidates (because constituents have control of this through congressional primaries) and they can't offer promotion to the executive, due to the separation of powers.

Members of Congress, it is argued, are under so much pressure from their constituents that they cannot maintain as slavish an obedience to the party line as MPs generally do in Britain. In addition it should be remembered that…

parties are ideologically weak and decentralised compared to their counterparts in Britain – they are truly 'broad-churches'.

If we take a 'party vote' to be a vote where the majority of one party votes for a measure and the majority of the other party votes against, then only 55.1% of House and 57% of Senate votes were 'party votes' in 2006.

Executive pressure

The President can have significant influence over individual members of Congress. We have outlined this influence in earlier pages. To recap:

1. **The President can use his friends**
   The **Vice-President**, **party leaders** in Congress, the **Chief of Staff** can put the President's case.

2. **The President can use personal persuasion**
   - **Telephone calls** – Johnson is said to have called a Congressman at the time of a crucial vote. 'You might need me some time and I'll remember you if you do this thing for me now'.
   - **Entertaining** – Reagan, for example, used to invite key Congressmen to breakfast at the White House before important votes.
   - **Offering 'pork'** (for example federal contracts or financial help for local projects) or **help in the election campaign.**

Conscience?

Some members of Congress have views on particular issues that will not allow them to follow the party line. On the issue of abortion, for example, some Democrats are committed 'pro-lifers' even though their party has explicitly endorsed a 'pro-choice' position since the 1992 presidential election.

That said, Democrats uneasy over abortion have increasingly been forced to 'toe the line' and it is noticeable that Al Gore, Jesse Jackson and Representative Richard A Gephardt have, as the New York Times noted, 'jettisoned their previous reservations about abortion'. As the paper went on to conclude, 'no Democrat with pretensions to national leadership can afford not to be strictly in favor of abortion rights'.

20.4 Congressional committees

Standing committees

Introduction

There are a variety of committees in Congress: standing committees (meaning they are always present), select or special committees (being set up for more limited and more specific purposes), and conference committees. This box deals with standing committees; select and conference committees are dealt with below.

In 2008 these were 21permanent standing committees in the House and a further 20 in the Senate. Each committee is normally divided into sub-committees dealing with more specific areas of legislation and then reporting back to the full committee.

Composition and membership

The composition of committees in both houses is in proportion to each party's strength in the relevant chamber. Each party produces a list of prospective committee members and these lists are then voted on by each party and then by the House as a whole. In January 2001 the Republicans had 221 members in the House compared to the Democrats' 212. This meant that they had a majority of members in each committee. In the Senate the parties were split 50–50 so they decided to split the membership of each standing committee 50–50. The decision of Senator James Jeffords of Vermont to switch from Republican to Independent left the Democrats with a 50–49 majority. As of June 2001, therefore, Democrats controlled all committees and all committee chairmanships in the Senate.

Decisions over who gets which committee jobs is largely governed by issues such as seniority, partisan regularity, regional dispersion, suitability (perhaps specialism) and, in the Senate, the fact that every Senator is required to be in at least one committee.

Role and powers

At the beginning of each session, each committee has a number of executive meetings to discuss a possible agenda for the session and try to work out a possible order in which the committee will look at the bills presented to it. Committee chairmen (see right) play a key role in prioritising bills. Many bills are simply pigeon-holed (put to one side and effectively killed). Those bills that avoid pigeon-holing are then subject to hearings (see right). Following hearings, the bill is amended (if necessary) in light of the evidence. This is called the marking-up session. It is then reported out of the committee back to the chamber. Committees can be forced to report out a bill that they have 'sat on', but this is rare.

Committee hearings

Once underway, the committee will organise hearings relating to bills. Many Congressmen and women are trained lawyers (37% in the House, 58% in the Senate in 2005) and as a result the committee hearings are similar in format to a trial, with evidence being brought forward by specialists and interested parties alike in the belief that, as Ernest S Griffith observed, 'truth customarily emerges from a battle of protagonists'. Pressure groups with an interest in a particular piece of legislation will send professional lobbyists to the committee hearings and to meet the committee members who they feel might be sympathetic to their case.

Committees also spend a considerable amount of time, and money, conducting independent research. For example, 200 investigators were sent to Europe after the Second World War to check the Marshall Plan. Only after such hearings will the committee consider the fate of the bill being considered.

Importance of committee chairs

The chairmen of committees and sub-committees wield considerable power over the agenda and procedure of the committees and, as a result, committee chairmen can exert a great deal of influence in the House and the Senate. This is particularly true of those chairing major committees.

In the past, committee chairs were filled largely on the basis of seniority – where the member with the longest continuous period of service on the committee became its chair. In the 1960s this resulted in many of the top committee chairmen jobs being permanently occupied by a handful of old, white southern Democrats. During the 1970s, however, the Democrats made some major changes to the committee system including the effective abolition of the old seniority system (1971) and an agreement that if 20% of a committee's members so desired, the committee chair would be elected by the committee.

The House Rules Committee

The Rules Committee is one of the most important committees (along with the Ways and Means Committee, which deals with legislation which requires the raising of new taxes, and the Appropriations Committee, which appropriates the necessary money from federal funds to pay for authorised programmes).

Once reported back to the House of Representatives, the bill must be placed on the calendar for its second reading. Most bills are passed to the Rules Committee to be given a rule which stipulates the date on which they are to be heard and the degree of debate and amendment that they will be subject to. The committee can place a bill under one of three types of 'rule':

an **open rule**, which allows the bill to be amended without limits (i.e. 'to death');
a **closed rule** (which restricts the amendments which can be passed);
and a **special rule** (which demands the House considers the bill immediately).

Like other standing committees, the Rules Committee has the power to pigeon-hole a bill, but the House can force it to release a bill by passing a 'discharge petition' with a simple majority.

Professor William H Riker described the Rules Committee as 'a toll bridge attendant who argues and bargains with each prospective customer: who lets his friends go free, who will not let his enemies pass at any price'.

Select committees

Where investigations fall outside of the normal scope of an existing standing committee or are likely to be on such a large scale as to affect the committee's normal work, a select or special committee may be formed on an ad hoc basis to deal with the issue. A good example is the Joint Select Committee on the Iran–Contra affair.

Conference committees

Once both chambers have considered a bill there is a fair chance that the two finished versions will be slightly different. As a result, the Speaker of the House and the President pro tempore from the Senate choose people from each chamber to sit on a conference committee that can iron out the differences. The compromise bill is then re-entered into both chambers and they must accept it, refer it back again, or kill it.

21.1   An outline of the role and power of the presidency

The intentions of the Founding Fathers

Some have questioned the merit of looking at the intent of the Founding Fathers at all. Arthur Schlesinger (see below) argues that such an endeavour is flawed in two ways:

1. The Constitution's meaning should be determined not by the original intentions of those who drew up the paper but by the exigencies and new aspects of life itself.
2. Assessment of original intent is difficult because, while the role of the President in domestic affairs is reasonably well set out, in foreign policy the division of power was 'ambiguous and unclear'.

Clearly some of the Founding Fathers wanted a strong President. 'Energy in the Executive,' stated Alexander Hamilton, 'is a leading character in the definition of good government.' Others, however, were concerned that the President could become too powerful and become, effectively, a monarch – particularly in times of emergency (see below).

Constitutional position (de jure)

A number of formal presidential powers are set out in Article 2.

Domestic	Foreign
Can make proposals through the 'State of the Union Message', signs or vetoes legislation, acts as chief executive, nominates executive branch domestic policy officials and top judges, can issue pardons.	Acts as Commander in Chief, can negotiate treaties, can appoint executive branch foreign policy staff and foreign ambassadors and envoys.

Emergency powers

Locke had stated that 'in emergency responsible leaders could resort to exceptional power' but this was not included in the Constitution because, as Congressman White of the First Congress noted, it would be better 'to extend his power on some extraordinary occasion, even where he is not strictly justified by the Constitution than the Legislature should grant him an improper power to be exercised at all times'.

Reasons for the growth in presidential power

Several factors have led to an expansion in the role of the President:

1. Congress has been all too willing to delegate unconstitutional powers to the President in times of crisis when public opinion is against it and the President can 'wrap himself in the flag'. It shows a tendency to allow the President to make decisions which they themselves are not prepared to make.

2. The expansion of the federal government: The federal government has grown and is growing. The decline of 'laissez faire' government means that everything is legislated for. A lot of this dates from the time of the New Deal.

3. The Supreme Court has failed to make decisions on critical areas (e.g. Vietnam) and has been scared into submission in other areas (e.g. over the New Deal's Industrial Recovery Act and Agricultural Adjustment Act).

4. The role of head of state has expanded. The international role of the US has increased massively since the time of the Constitution and, as a result, the President has become the representative of the nation, rather than just one part of the tripartite government. This has been emphasised by
   - i) the US's superpower status (the 'black box') – even more so since the collapse of the USSR
   - ii) the rise of the mass media

Actual position (de facto)

The result of these pressures has been a significant increase in the potential power available to modern Presidents. The President is now not only chief executive, chief diplomat, and commander in chief, but also chief legislator, chief war and peacemaker, head of state and head of his party. Some of these areas are dealt with in the pages that follow.

The Imperial Presidency

In his book 'The Imperial Presidency (1973), Arthur Schlesinger outlined what he saw as the monumental increase in presidential power since the framing of the Constitution. Crucially, however, Schlesinger showed that this was not a sudden change but a gradual process that had begun almost as soon as the ink was dry on the Constitution and had accelerated significantly in the 40 years up to the time that the book was published. Schlesinger wrote from a position of some knowledge. As an advisor to President Kennedy he had experienced at first hand the nature of presidential power. Following the fall of Nixon in 1974 and the relatively ineffectual presidencies of Ford and Carter, many felt that talk of 'imperial presidencies' was somewhat overstated. Others suggested that it was more sensible to look on the presidency as carrying with it a potential for power that effective incumbents could tap to great effect if they had the abilities.

Perceptions of presidential power

Other views

'The Power of the Presidency is awesome.' Thomas ('Tip') O'Neill (former Speaker of the House, 1986)

'When the President does it, that means that it is not illegal.' (Richard Nixon, 1977)

'The Buck stops here.' (Harry S. Truman)

'I sit here all day saying do this and do that and nothing ever gets done. Christ! What a job!' (Harry S. Truman)

'All Presidents start out to run a crusade but after a couple of years they find they are running something less heroic and much more intractable: namely a Presidency. The people are well cured by then of election fever, during which they think they are choosing Moses. In the third year, they look on the man as a sinner and a bumbler and begin to poke around for rumours of another Messiah.' Alistair Cooke (1968)

'Weakness is still what I see; weakness in the sense of a great gap between what is expected of a man (or someday woman) and assured capacity to carry through.' Richard Neustadt.

21.2 The Domestic Policy President

Two presidencies (?)

As H G Nicholas remarked in his book *The Nature of American Politics* (OUP, 1992), that 'the power of the President in foreign affairs has received such striking demonstration in the era of the Cold War that it has seemed to some observers that there are, in effect, two Presidencies. Presidents who have been thwarted or defeated by Congress in their domestic programmes have succeeded time and again in persuading Congress to acquiesce in their foreign policy'. In setting out this view Nicholas was, therefore, echoing Aaron Wildavsky (*The Two Presidencies*, 1969) in identifying a 'Domestic Policy President' and a 'Foreign Policy President'. Such a distinction should come as no surprise:

Firstly, the Constitution divided domestic legislative powers between legislature and executive far more clearly than it divides foreign policy powers;

Secondly, members of Congress are far more likely to be concerned about domestic policy because their re-election is more likely to depend upon it; and

Thirdly, successful modern foreign policy is, by its very nature, difficult to formulate in a Congress numbering 535 individuals.

Domestic policy powers

Legislative powers
Given the Founding Fathers' interest in the separation of powers, it is surprising that we should be calling the President chief legislator. The societal changes outlined on the previous page have, however, demanded a greater role of the chief executive.

To sign or to veto
The Constitution grants the President the power of veto over legislation passed by Congress. The President must veto the whole bill, returning it to the house in which it was initiated within ten days of his receiving it. He is also required to include a written explanation of why the veto has been issued. If he does not send it back within ten days then it becomes law. However, if Congress is adjourned within the ten-day period then the President can pocket the bill – killing it. This is known as the pocket veto.

Proposing legislation
The Constitution grants the President the right to address Congress on the State of the Union. This has, in effect, become an agenda-setting exercise. Presidents can then enlist the help of their friends in Congress to introduce legislation.

The 'line-item' veto
In 1997 a law came into effect granting the President a 'line-item' veto. In effect this meant that the President could delete the amounts allocated to specific items in spending bills within five days of the bill being signed. Clinton first used this power in August 1997, and by June 1998 had used the measure on 82 occasions, cutting over $300 million from the federal budget. In June 1998 the Supreme Court ruled the line-item veto unconstitutional (6:3).

The budget
The President has taken on the role of formulating the annual budget proposals; a task completed in the Office of Management and Budget (OMB).

Powers as chief executive
The Constitution gives the President the role of chief executive. In this role he has the responsibility of ensuring that 'the laws be faithfully executed' (Article II, section 3). As chief executive he also has the role of appointing executive branch officials. He also appoints top federal judges (including Supreme Court Justices). These individuals are dealt with more fully in later pages.

Head of state
In the US the head of the executive is also, de facto, head of state. This role can bring with it significant influence because the President can mobilise patriotic feeling in support of his measures by 'wrapping himself in the flag'.

Important note
Because this page focuses on the President, it tends to rather overstate the degree of freedom that the President has to act in domestic policy. You should use this page in conjunction with the pages on 'Recent presidencies' and 'Checks and balances', as well as the chapters on Congress.

Case study
Many Presidents have come into office with visionary domestic policy programmes. For example:

FDR and the 'New Deal'
The Wall Street Crash of 1929 devastated the US economy, and state governments found that they could not deal with the hardship which the Depression brought to their localities. In the Presidential election of 1932 therefore, the electorate looked for a candidate who would bring the federal government in to deal with the economic problems on a national level. The result was the election of Franklin D Roosevelt and the introduction of the policies known collectively as the New Deal.

In 1935 three major Acts were passed:
1) The Social Security Act, which gave assistance to the aged, blind, dependent children and unemployed.

> 'The Act provided a solid, enduring, legal foundation for the Federal grant-in-aid system to reach into almost any are of public concern.'
> C E Barfield (*Rethinking Federalism* 1981)

2) The National Industrial Recovery Act.
3) The Agricultural Adjustment Act.

The Supreme Court ruled that these acts were invalid (e.g. United States v. Butler,1936, which said that the Agricultural Programme was invalid) but when Roosevelt was re-elected with a landslide victory in 1936 he threatened to use Congress to 'pack the Court' with an additional six members (from nine to 15) who would support his policies.

Faced with such opposition the Court thought again and one Justice changed his mind, resulting in the *New York Times* reporting the next day that 'a switch in time' had 'saved nine'.

21.3 The Foreign Policy President

Introduction
Modern foreign policy is, by its very nature, more effective when directed by a relatively small number of individuals because:

Firstly, it demands a degree of secrecy that would be hard to achieve if every detail were discussed on the floor of the House;
Secondly, it requires a speed of response not suited to careful congressional deliberations and amendment; and
Thirdly, it requires a unified and determined approach – difficult to maintain in a group of 535.

It was partly for this reason, and the need for the President to be able to act in emergencies, that the Founding Fathers left foreign policy powers deliberately vague and overlapping when framing the Constitution. They wanted to provide the potential for speed of action and flexibility while at the same time avoiding some permanent grant of major military power into the hands of one man – the President.

The growth of foreign policy powers

War-maker
The power to declare war was placed firmly and clearly in the hands of Congress but – as we have seen – the Founding Fathers were fully aware that emergencies might require the President to take independent action and return to Congress later. It was in the area of war-making that Schlesinger thought the most marked growth of presidential power had occurred, with the rise of so-called presidential wars – wars in all but name that were never formally declared by Congress but justified, most often, on the grounds of emergency or self-defence. The problem was, as Schlesinger recognised, that allowing Presidents the power to defend the US was 'to imply unilateral authority to conduct defences so aggressively that ... those on the receiving end may well be pardoned if they mistook it for aggression'.

Examples
Schlesinger charted abuses of the war-making power back to the early 1800s but saw the major growth as having taken place in 1950s, 1960s and early 1970s. US involvement in Cuba and particularly in Vietnam eventually under the Gulf of Tonkin Resolution (1964) marked a real shift in power from Congress to the President. The secret US air-war against Cambodia (1969–71) was the final insult to a Congress that didn't even know it had been happening.

Peacemaker
The power to ratify treaties was, like the power to declare war, also given to Congress – more specifically, the Senate. Though the President had the right to negotiate treaties, he had to gain the ratification of the Senate (two-thirds support needed) in order for them to come into force legally. This ratification has been no mere formality. For example, the Senate refused to ratify any meaningful treaty between 1871 and 1898 and in 1919 it had refused to ratify the Versailles Peace Treaty that was supposed to ensure long-term peace in Europe. Faced with such opposition, Presidents had begun to make treaties by other names. These so-called executive agreements had the same legal standing as treaties (as underlined in the 1942 Supreme Court case US v. Pink) but – because they were not called treaties – they circumvented the rules, not needing the customary two-thirds Senate majority. Such executive agreements proliferated in the years following the Second World War.

Expansion of executive agreements
Between 1850 and 1900 there were 215 treaties and 238 executive agreements. Between 1889 and 1939 there were 524 treaties and 917 executive agreements. Under Nixon things deteriorated further. In 1971 there were only 17 treaties compared to 214 executive agreements. Since then there have been an average of 30 treaties and 250 executive agreements per year.

The Symington Committee
The Senate Foreign Relations Committee set up this special committee in February 1969 under the chairmanship of Stuart Symington of Missouri. It was charged with the task of investigating secret US security agreements and commitments abroad. Amongst other things, the Committee discovered that:

In 1971 the US had seven air bases, seven generals and 82 000 men in Thailand without congressional authorisation or detailed knowledge; The executive had been fighting a secret war in support of the Vientiane Government against Pathet Lao in Northern Laos since 1964, yet Congress believed that American bombing over Laos was against North Vietnamese troops passing along South East Laos; Since 1953 the US had been subsidising the Ethiopian Army for an electronic communication base at Kagnew. Congress did not know until 1969.

The War Powers Act (War Powers Resolution) of 1973
In 1971 Senator Barry Goldwater remarked that 'we [the US] have only been in five declared wars out of over 150 that we have fought'. In 1973 the War Powers Act was passed. It said that the President could only send troops into battle for 60 days without congressional approval. Congress intended this as a measure limiting presidential power, yet in reality it granted the President unconstitutional powers.

The Case Act of 1972
Like the War Powers Act, the Case Act was designed to limit the power of the President to make executive agreements, while in reality recognising a presidential power not intended by the Constitution. Under the Act, Presidents were free to make such agreements but had to tell Congress within 60 days. This gave Congress the opportunity to vote to cancel such agreement or withhold funding, thus stopping their implementation. In 1977 the time limit was reduced by Congress from 60 to 20 days.

Foreign policy in the 1970s and 1980s
The War Powers Act and the Case Act were not particularly effective in limiting presidential activity in the foreign policy arena. Both measures were more symbolic than anything, not dealing with the fact that the nature of secret wars and secret treaties made it hard for Congress to know whether or not the two acts had, in fact, been broken. Presidents also became adept at completing military engagements within the 60 days or ignored the restrictions: Reagan in Grenada (1983), for example, or Bush in Panama (1989), or when deploying troops in Kuwait (1990). Executive agreements have also continued as 'arrangements' or 'accords'; for example, Nixon with South Vietnam, Ford with regard to Sinai, and Carter over disarmament.

The 'power to persuade'

President Harry S Truman is generally credited with coining this phrase. 'I sit here all day,' he lamented, 'trying to persuade people to do things they ought to have sense enough to do without my persuading them. That's all the powers of the president amount to.' Truman's frustration in the face of what he saw as massive practical limitations on the power of his office was obvious, though not unique. Other recent Presidents, Ford for example, have voiced similar concerns. The central problem that any President faces is that, regardless of the apparent growth in the powers of his office, he needs the help of others to achieve his objectives – and this help is not always forthcoming. The art of persuasion is, therefore, an art that all new Presidents need to master rapidly.

Limitations on presidential power

The sheer scale and complexity of government

As we have already seen, the expansion of the federal government in the last 70 years has been incredible. The very scale of federal operations, however, presents the President with a real problem of co-ordination and overview. He must – by necessity – have a massive staff and he must inevitably delegate a great deal.

The power of Congress

We have already identified many of the congressional checks and balances that operate upon the President. The President can do little that is dramatic and lasting without the agreement of Congress.

The vigilance of the US Supreme Court

The Supreme Court has not been afraid to declare the acts of Presidents unconstitutional. In the case of United States v. Nixon (1974), for example, the Court found that Nixon had acted unconstitutionally in refusing to hand over the so-called 'White House Tapes' to the authorities investigating 'Watergate'.

Public opinion, pressure groups and the media

Public opinion is unlikely to bring down a President, though some argue that Johnson's decision not to run for a second term in 1968 was largely a result of the public reaction to his pursuit of the war in Vietnam ('LBJ, LBJ, how many kids did you kill today?' to quote the anti-war protesters). Pressure groups can aggregate and amplify public concern, and the importance of media coverage is underlined by the numbers of presidential staff permanently assigned to 'media management'.

Means of persuasion (see Ch 20.3)

1. **Using his friends**
   - The **Vice-President, party leaders** in Congress, the **Chief of Staff** can put the President's case.
2. **Personal persuasion**
   - **Telephone calls** – Johnson is said to have called Congressmen late at night, prior to key votes. 'You might need me some time and I'll remember you if you do this thing for me now.'
   - **Entertaining** – Reagan, for example, invited key Congressmen to breakfast at the White House before important votes.
   - **Offering 'pork'** (see above right) or **help in their election campaign.**

'Pork-barrelling' and 'log-rolling'

1. **Pork-barrelling** is where Congressmen appropriate money by adding 'riders' to bills. These riders provide funds for 'pet projects' back in their states. The 'rider' will normally have little to do with the bill that it is riding on (see example below). As such 'rider' amendments would be difficult to effect alone, Congressmen generally have to engage in log-rolling.

2. **Log-rolling** is where groups of Congressmen help each other to add clauses to bills that will benefit each other's constituents. They do this by voting for each other's amendments in a reciprocal fashion.

Some Presidents have been extremely adept at manipulating Congressmen with the lure of 'pork':
- John F. Kennedy, facing problems with his tax legislation, gained the support of Senator Robert Kerr by promising Kerr, in return, his support for the Arkansas River Project;
- Gerald Ford found Congressman Mitchel supportive of his jobs bill when he told Mitchel that he would not allow the closure of an air base in his constituency.

Individual Congressmen in key positions can also reap great rewards for their constituents. L. Mendel Rivers, Chairman of the Armed Services Committee 1965–70, gained 11 major new naval installations for his state (ship yards, missile bases, hospitals and training camps). In addition, the Bureau of Naval Personnel and the Naval Reserve Headquarters were all moved to his state (South Carolina) and he had a complex of buildings named after himself. According to David S. Sorenson, 'it was said of L. Mendel Rivers that if he located one more base near Charleston, the whole district would sink into the sea.'

Case study

On March 20, 1986 the House rejected a bill sponsored by President Reagan, which was designed to provide aid to the 'Contras' fighting against the Communist Sandinistas in Nicaragua. On April 16 the House had to reconsider the bill, as the Senate had been persuaded to support it. The House Rules Committee supported the bill, but added a 'rider' worth $1.7 billion of supplementary spending to it. That is to say, if Reagan wanted to send the aid to the Contras, which the bill offered, he would have had to pay 170 times the value of the aid to the pet projects of Congressmen. The President had no 'line-item veto'. He could not choose which bits of the bill to accept and which to reject. He had to accept the whole bill or none of it. Reagan's aides described the rider as a 'rancid barrel of pork', a 'shabby and shameful trick': but there was little that could be done in the time available.

The presidency of Bill Clinton (1993–2001)

Context

The election of Bill Clinton as the 42nd President of the United States in November 1992 was something of a surprise, as a year before the election few would have given Clinton a chance. At that time George Bush (senior) was riding high in the polls following the success in the Gulf War. By the time of the 1992 presidential election, however, the Gulf War effect had worn off and voters were beginning to turn their attention to domestic policy where Bush had failed to keep to his 1988 'No New Taxes' pledge.. Against this background Clinton was able to win even though allegations of affairs (Gennifer Flowers), student drug use, and draft-dodging (Vietnam) followed him everywhere.

Personality and character

Though Clinton proved adept at capturing the public mood – keeping the public largely on-side throughout his two terms – the ongoing scandals did little to enhance the institution of the presidency. The accusations of an affair with Gennifer Flowers paled into insignificance when set against the legal action initiated by Paula Jones and the whole Monica Lewinsky affair. Though Clinton remained President, the fallout from the impeachment investigations that followed certainly lessened the President's chances maintaining effective legislative coalitions within Congress.

Clinton's legislative programme

Clinton secured some significant pieces of legislation. The North American Free Trade Agreement (NAFTA) was in place within the first two years, as was the Brady Bill regulating purchasing of guns. The Budget Deficit Elimination Agreement of 1997 – which aimed to get rid of the deficit by 2002 – was also a significant measure. In other areas, healthcare reform for example, Clinton found progress more difficult, particularly after the Republicans took control of the House (230/204) and the Senate (54/46) from 1995. From that point the House, under the Speakership of Newt Gingrich pursued its 'Contract with America'. Ironically, Congress's decision to grant the President a 'line-item veto' at this time could have benefited Clinton's Presidency significantly, had not the Supreme Court declared it unconstitutional.

Foreign policy

Clinton's foreign policy was fairly modest. The US intervention in Somalia was a failure but Clinton had more success in Haiti, reinstating the legitimate government. He was ineffective in addressing the Rwandan crisis but highly visible as mediator in other conflicts and disputes (e.g. the Middle East).

Popularity

Even at his lowest rating (38% in 1994) Clinton was more popular than Carter, Reagan or Bush were at their low points. During the impeachment crisis his approval ratings remained above 70%, an incredible figure, given the circumstances.

The presidency of George W. Bush (2001–2009)

Contextual Issues:

Bush became President with Clinton achieving record opinion poll ratings for an outgoing President. Moreover, the traumatic nature of the November 2000 Presidential Election appeared to cast a massive shadow over the Bush Presidency:

Partly because of the fact that Bush had entered the White House with a smaller proportion of the popular vote than Al Gore;

Partly because his victory came as a result of a Supreme Court decision handed down by a Court containing 4 Reagan appointees (including Rehnquist as Chief Justice), made whilst George Bush senior was Vice-President, and 2 of Bush senior's own appointees.

Many of these concerns were put to one side in the wake of 9/11 and Bush's margin of victory in the 2004 Presidential re-election afforded him a far more convincing second-term mandate.

Domestic Policy

Bush entered the White House committed to a programme of tax cuts that would stave off the fears of recession. He was also widely seen as a friend of big business. As Steve Rosenthal of the AFL–CIO commented, 'George Bush makes Ronald Reagan look like Mother Jones'. In his first year, Bush looked to reduce regulation e.g. relaxing Federal orders protecting union rights and encouraging non-union contracts in Federal projects.

Bush blocked a number of health reforms and also rejected the CO_2 emissions targets set at Kyoto, the latter causing some embarrassment to then EPA Director, Christie Todd Whitman. As criticism of the President emerged in 2002, Bush's team refocussed the administration on the 'Two E's' (Education and the Economy).

The start of Bush's second term saw a focus on an area that many felt had been neglected during Bush's first four years in the White House; namely Social Security reform, but progress was tortuously slow.

Foreign Policy Context

As Doris Kearns Goodwin noted 'crisis provides the opportunity for larger deeds, an opportunity to walk on a different stage" (Time Magazine, 31-12-01). Bush, surrounded by an extremely experienced group of foreign policy advisors, gained significantly in terms of his approval rating (80% in January, 2002) from his handling of the 'War against Terrorism' launched in the wake of the September 11 attacks.

As David Kennedy noted, 'Bush has had the gift of a crisis that automatically creates a consensus in public opinion about the necessity, the morality and the justice of what we are doing'.

Democrat successes in the Mid-Terms and the deteriorating situation in Iraq undermined Bush's efforts on the domestic front as his second term drew to a close.

Image and Spin

The scale of Bush's tax-cutting plans, the ENRON scandal, and the Kyoto farce opened the President up to international as well as domestic criticism. Bush's first-term media team, which included Larry Lindsey (economic policy), Karen Hughes (Bush's 'alter ego', who, according to Time Magazine, ran the 'message machine') and Ari Fleischer (Bush's Press Secretary), did a lot to pull the situation around.

21.6 Presidential power in the wake of 9/11

Outline

In times of national crisis the role of the President becomes more crucial, not least because the President acts as a national figurehead (a head of state) as well as a chief executive.

Faced with national emergency, the other two branches of the federal government (legislature and judiciary) normally allow the President more freedom to act. At such times, therefore, the President's powers are normally significantly greater than in the normal course of events.

Faced with the terrorist threat demonstrated on September 11, the country united behind George W. Bush – a man who only ten months previously had failed to win a majority of the popular vote in the presidential election. Bush was able to 'wrap himself in the flag', demanding patriotic support for his 'war on terrorism'. In response, Congress granted the President extraordinary powers to deal with the crisis.

Foreign policy

As Commander in Chief of the Armed Forces, George W. Bush was able to launch the attacks on Afghanistan as an emergency act of self-defence, without a formal declaration of war by Congress. This demonstrates the power of the US President to commit US troops and incur massive costs in such circumstances, without the need for the normal authorisations.

Domestic policy

One of George W. Bush's first moves following the attacks of September 11 was to create a new executive department, the Office of Homeland Security:

The Office of Homeland Security

Bush's executive order created an Office of Homeland Security and a Homeland Security Council that could develop and co-ordinate a national counter-terrorism strategy. This Council consists of the President and the Vice-President, the heads of a number of executive departments (for example, defense, treasury, and transportation) plus key security officials (including the directors of the FBI and the CIA).

Tom Ridge, former Governor of Pennsylvania and a decorated combat veteran, was appointed as head of the Office of Homeland Security and as a member of the Homeland Security Council. His brief was to address issues of:

detection, preparedness, prevention, protection, response and recovery, and incident management.

The President also:

1. Froze the bank accounts of suspected terrorists; and
2. Put in place additional security, including air-patrols over major cities by US Air Force F16 combat aircraft and restrictions on private flights.

Eventually, Congress passed formal legislation empowering the President to act against terrorists. This legislation is known as the **USA Patriot Bill** and it was passed by 357 votes to 66 in the House and by 98 votes to 1 in the Senate. The law, amongst other things, authorised the FBI to access computer files and e-mails, as well as allowing the arrest and holding of terrorist prisoners for seven days without charge.

In February 2002, *The Guardian* reported that Bush was also taking the opportunity to slash corporation tax while Congress was on his side.

September 11 and the Supreme Court

From an early stage in the crisis, sources close to the Supreme Court reported that it would look sympathetically at any violations of constitutional rights that were clearly in the public interest. One month after the attacks, the suspects arrested in the days that followed September 11 had, according to *Time Magazine*, still not spoken to those interrogating them. It was suggested that a 'truth drug' might be used on the prisoners (without their consent) in order to gain information that might prevent further attacks. Once again it was said that the Supreme Court might effectively 'turn a blind eye' to such a violation of constitutional protections, in the interest of public safety. Though the US Supreme Court was slow to address such issues, leading civil rights lawyers in the US led by Stephen Yagman filed a petition for habeas corpus on behalf of the 110 al-Qaida suspects being held at Guantanamo Bay, Cuba (on the grounds that they were being held in violation of the Constitution and the Geneva Convention). The Supreme Court finally handed down its first decisions in cases involving these so-called 'enemy combatants' in 2004. In *Hamdi v. Rumsfeld*, for example, the Court ruled that Yaser Esam Hamdi, a Louisiana-born Saudi citizen who had been held in isolation for nearly three years, had been denied *due process of law* (8:1).

'Like father, like son?'

As the 'war against terrorism' dragged on, many US commentators started to draw parallels between George W. Bush's presidency and that of his father. In 1991 George Bush senior had seemed assured of election victory in 1992. Operation Desert Storm against Iraqi forces in Kuwait was widely regarded as a success. Casualties had been kept low on the American side and Bush was achieving impressive approval ratings in the polls. At the same time, however, attention was returning to the domestic front where many felt that the economy was in trouble. In the election campaign that followed Bush senior lost the initiative and Clinton took the White House by highlighting Bush's failure to address domestic issues ('It's the economy, stupid!', as the Clinton slogan read).

George W. Bush faced similar problems. Though the 'war on terrorism' has been well received at home, the attention of many Americans returned to domestic issues. Bush, eager to avoid making the same mistakes as his father, tried to revive the economy by pushing through large tax cuts. He also sought to take the initiative on the domestic front, launching a campaign to address what he called the 'two Es' (education and the economy). Despite this, George W. Bush was the first President since Hoover to preside over an administration that created fewer jobs than it lost over four years.

22.1 The Vice-President and Cabinet

The Vice-President

Introduction

In 1789 the first US Vice-President, John Adams, wrote to his wife reporting that 'My Country has, in its wisdom contrived for me the most insignificant office that ever the invention of man or his imagination conceived'. This quotation has, until recently perhaps, continued to be the common view of the vice-presidency. Though, as James Baker noted, the Vice-President is only 'a heartbeat away from the big office', commentators have often struggled to identify a meaningful role for the Vice-President not linked to the demise of the President. As the US humorist Will Rogers remarked, 'the man with the best job in the Country is the Vice-President. All he has to do is get up every day and say, "How's the President?"'.

How Vice-Presidents are chosen

Since the 1950s vice-presidential candidates have been chosen by each party's presidential candidate following their nomination. As Bob Dole remarked in 1991, 'It only takes one vote to win the vice-presidential nomination'. The vice-presidential candidate is often chosen with a view to 'balancing the ticket' and gaining the broadest possible support from within the party and beyond. The relatively inexperienced Bush, therefore, went for the political heavyweight Cheney. This was clearly an astute move. Many have argued that Cheney was the real power behind the throne – the 'Prime Minister' to Bush's 'head of state'.

The main functions of the Vice-President

The Vice-President has a number of constitutional functions:

(1) Acting as the President of the Senate, having the right to chair debates and cast the deciding vote when the Senate is tied. Cheney cast such a deciding vote in April 2001 in support of Bush's tax-cutting measures.
(2) Becoming President in the event of the death, resignation or impeachment leading to removal from office of the President (e.g. Johnson taking over from Kennedy, or Ford from Nixon).
(3) Taking on the role of Acting President where the President declares himself or is declared disabled (e.g. following the shooting of Reagan in 1985, George Bush took over temporarily).

Informed opinions on the office

'Handmade for ridicule and for dismissal. In the nature of it you always look like a beggar, a person on a string.' (Walter Mondale, 1984)

'Can the Vice-President be Useful' (title of an article by FDR in 1920)

'The vice-presidency ain't worth a pitcher of warm spit. . . I gave up the second most important job in the government [Speaker] for one that didn't amount to a hill of beans. I spent eight years as Mr Roosevelt's spare tyre.' (John Nance Garner, 1948 and 1963)

Where a vacancy occurs

The 25th Amendment (1967) gives the President the power to fill vice-presidential vacancies. These will most often occur when the elected Vice-President has had to take on the role of President. Before the 25th Amendment, the office was often left empty in such circumstances.

Training ground?

(Vice-Presidents who became Presidents)

John Adams
Thomas Jefferson
Martin van Buren
John Tyler
Millard Fillmore
Andrew Johnson
Chester A. Arthur
Theodore Roosevelt
Calvin Coolidge
Harry S. Truman
Richard M. Nixon
Gerald Ford*
George Bush

*Ford became Vice-President in 1973 when Spiro Agnew resigned the post. Ford then became President following Nixon's resignation in 1974.

The Cabinet

Introduction

The US Cabinet shares little in common with the UK Cabinet beyond its name. Whereas in Britain the Cabinet is drawn from the legislature (in a large part the Commons), the separation of powers prevents members of the executive branch simultaneously holding office in legislature or the judiciary. US Cabinet members are, therefore, not elected but appointed by the President and this means that they are dependent upon him far more than members of the UK Cabinet who, if all else fails, can return to the back benches and wait for their moment.

Composition

Whereas in Britain Cabinet Ministers are normally generalists who move between departments as a result of reshuffles, US Cabinet members are most often specialists in their field. James Peake, for example, the Veterans' Affairs Secretary, is a Vietnam War veteran. In reality only about one in five Cabinet members have any experience in Congress, the rest being drawn from state and local government and academia. Presidents tend to try and appoint a Cabinet which reflects the US society in terms of race, age, gender, ideology, religion and geography. Clinton certainly spoke of his desire to appoint a Cabinet that 'looked like America'. George W. Bush followed suit by appointing two Afro-Americans (Colin Powell and Rod Paige) and members from other ethnic minorities (e.g. Elaine Chao and Norman Mineta). Ultimately, however, Presidents have a free hand as long as they can persuade the Senate to approve their nominees. As Harry S. Truman remarked in 1945, 'Everyone is telling me who I should have on my staff and in my cabinet. No S.O.B is going to dictate to me who I am going to have.'

Roles

The scale of work undertaken normally means that Cabinet members work fairly independently of one another. The President is easily able to divide and rule, and the fact that they are competing for the President's attention tends to make the Cabinet, as Richard Fenno noted, 'a schizophrenic body'. Cabinet meetings are still important however because the allow:

- members a chance to see one other
- members a chance to see the President
- the collection and dissemination of information
- the resolution of interdepartmental conflicts and the focusing of collective effort

Constitutional importance

Ultimately, the Constitution makes no mention of the Cabinet and so the institution is totally in the hands of the President. The Cabinet is divided and members must compete for the ear of the President. There is no real idea of collective responsibility based upon discussions in Cabinet. As George Bush told his Cabinet nominees in 1989, 'when I make a call, we move as a team'.

Informed opinions on the institution

'Seven noes, one aye – and the ayes have it.' (President Lincoln, having voted 'aye' in Cabinet)

'You can't have 15 people coming together to give the President advice in a Cabinet session. They're all arguing with each other for their own interests and he gets confused. What he decides has to come to him in an orderly way.' (John Erlichman – Nixon's aide – 1974)

'It is significant that no President has ever left the Office extolling the virtues of Cabinet Government.' (Hugh Heclo, 1983)

'When I've heard enough of a debate to satisfy my needs about knowing, then I make a decision.' (Ronald Reagan, 1982)

22.2 The Executive Office of the President (EXOP)

What is the EXOP?

In 1937 the Brownlow Committee famously reported that 'the President needs help'. Their comments reflected the massive expansion in the role of presidency that had taken place since the time of the Constitution. The problem facing the modern President as he grapples with the gargantuan federal bureaucracy is a considerable one: as Truman complained, 'I sit here all day saying do this, do that and nothing ever gets done. Christ! What a job!' Essentially, EXOP has the role of helping the President to cope with such enormous demands. What, then, does it consist of?

The Brownlow Committee, 1937

The Brownlow Committee was reporting against the background of the Wall Street Crash, the Depression that followed and the New Deal that FDR had brought in to address the economic crisis. This New Deal gave the federal government a far greater role in the states, particularly through the use of grants. An expansion of the federal government's role inevitably led to an expansion in the role of the presidency and the workload associated with it.

Key elements of the EXOP

The White House staff

Origins and history

In the wake of the Brownlow Committee's comments came a massive expansion in the role in the size of the White House staff (the closest advisors and aides to the President.).

President	Number of staff
Franklin D. Roosevelt	51
Harry S. Truman	243
Richard M. Nixon	606

Though subsequent Presidents have invariably come into office promising swinging cuts in staff, few have been able to deliver faced with the job at hand. Such an enormous staff can, however, cause more problems than it solves unless the President has a very good Chief of Staff (as it is clearly impossible for the President to know exactly what 600+ individuals are doing at any one time). Nixon certainly had problems keeping tabs on what was going on in his administration, and his increasing reliance on Haldeman and Erlichman (the so-called 'Berlin Wall') was less than healthy. Haldeman, in particular, insulated the President from reality to an alarming degree, seeing him seven times more than any other official. All phone calls, information and requests for meetings with the President had to pass through Haldeman. As Haldeman himself explained, 'Rather than the President telling someone to do something, I'll do it. ... every President needs an S.O.B and I'm Nixon's'.

Composition

The White House staff includes the President's closest aides and confidants together those working beneath them. Whereas Cabinet members are focused on the work of their own departments and have to consider the demands of Congress (who assign their budgets) as well as the President, those in the White House staff are the President's true policy advisors. As in Britain, the role of the Press Secretary is significant. The role of Chief of Staff is even more crucial.

The Chief of Staff

Unless the President has a good Chief of Staff, who can decide objectively what the President needs to deal with personally and what can be dealt with without wasting the President's valuable time, the President will be smothered by an avalanche of paperwork and telephone calls.

Roles

1. **Policy advice** – the White House staff are the main source for policy advice, particularly in times of crisis.

2. **Liaison** – the staff have the job of co-ordinating efforts with the federal bureaucracy and with Congress.

3. **Administration** – the staff organise the White House, scheduling events and meetings and managing staff.

The Office of Management and Budget

The OMB was created in 1970 under the control of an OMB Director. It has three clear roles:

1. Organising the budget, balancing the demands of the various departments and deciding where to wield the axe.

2. Overseeing departmental and agency spending.

3. Providing on-tap specialist financial backup and advice for the President.

The National Security Council

Created in 1947, the NSC has the role of co-ordinating policy relating to national security, both domestic and foreign. It is headed by the National Security Advisor (NSA) and includes the President, the Vice-President, and the Secretaries of State and Defense, with occasional visits from the CIA head and the Chiefs of Staff. Kissinger was a key figure in expanding the role of the NSC under Nixon. (Kissinger kept the title of National Security Advisor even when he became the Secretary of State.)

In the past there has often been conflict between the Secretary of State and the President's National Security Advisor. Kissinger (NSA) effectively excluded William Rogers (Secretary of State) from foreign policy matters during Nixon's presidency, and under Carter there were problems between Zbigniew Brzezinski (NSA) and Secretary of State Cyrus Vance.

23.1 The federal bureaucracy

Introduction

The federal bureaucracy employs some 3 000 000 staff, working throughout the country in federal offices. Many of those staff work for one of the 15 executive departments, but others work within executive agencies or independent regulatory commissions (see right).

Executive departments

There are currently 15 executive departments, each headed by a member of the Bush Cabinet. The expansion in the number of executive departments mirrored the expansion in the role of the federal government. Names are correct as of June, 2008.

Department	Created	Current head
State	1789	Condoleeza Rice
Treasury	1789	Henry Paulson
War (now Defense)	1789 (1949)	Robert Gates
Interior	1849	Dirk Kempthorne
Justice	1870	Michael Mulcasey
Agriculture	1889	Edward Schafer
Commerce	1903	Carlos Gutierrez
Labour	1903	Elaine Chao
Health and Human Services	1953	Michael Leavitt
Housing and Urban Development	1965	Steve Preston
Transportation	1966	Mary Peters
Energy	1977	Samuel W. Bodman
Education	1979	Margaret Spellings
Veterans' Affairs	1989	James Peake
Homeland Security	2003	Michael Chertoff

Independent executive agencies (IEAs)

IEAs were set up to provide a greater degree of focus and control in specific areas of policy. They act independently of executive departments and are funded separately, making their budget requests direct to the OMB. Prominent IEAs include the Environmental Protection Agency (EPA) and the Central Intelligence Agency (CIA). Agencies are normally headed by an individual ('director') who directs their efforts. The EPA, for example, was headed by Stephen L. Johnson in June 2008.

Independent regulatory commissions (IRCs)

What are they?

Congress passes acts which set up regulatory commissions in many areas of industrial and commercial life. Naturally, as the federal government has expanded, this role has become more significant. Each commission is headed by a board which averages five members, each of whom have been appointed by a President for a fixed length of time. The appointments are ratified by the Senate. The President has no legitimate right to sack board members – this was tested by Humphrey's Executor v. US, which stated that the President could not dismiss a member of the Federal Trade Commission.

The reason for creating IRCs

Independent regulatory commissions were designed to be non-political agencies organising certain aspects of administration and they were aimed at limiting the sort of presidential power demonstrated during the New Deal. As Ernest S. Griffith noted, 'It was hoped that they would function with a high degree of specialised competence and independence, free from partisan and Presidential pressure'.

IRCs are given powers by Congress, but they make 'laws' and 'judge' themselves. Therefore they are quasi-legislative and quasi-judicial. M. J. C. Vile described them as a 'headless fourth branch' of the US Government, but in reality Congress and the President do have influence over them. Eisenhower's assistant, Sherman Adams, admitted to secretly asking commissioners to resign and there are close informal links between the IRCs and the presidential staff.

IRCs 'good'	IRCs 'bad'
a) Congress wanted IRCs to limit presidential power over the bureaucracy.	a) Presidents control IRCs (by appointments and informally through links between commissioners and presidential staff).
b) IRCs meet the public demand for regulation of certain industries and services.	b) IRCs become oriented towards their clientele rather than serving the public they were designed to protect. Pressure groups can get 'inside'.
c) As IRCs are theoretically independent from political control, they should therefore be able to be objective.	c) Congress controls IRCs

Examples of IRCs

IRCs operate in a wide range of areas, most often where there is a need for visibly independent regulation and scrutiny. For example:

Federal Trade Commission (1914)
Formed to deal with –
i) unfair competition
ii) price-fixing (cartels)
iii) misleading advertising

Securities and Exchange Commission (1934)
Formed to –
i) regulate the stock exchange
ii) register stock brokers
iii) protect the public

Other examples include the Federal Reserve Board (controlling aspects of monetary policy) and the Civil Aeronautics Board (licensing and regulating airlines).

24.1 The structure of the US courts system

Courts of last resort on appeal

US Supreme Court

The Court is generally free to accept or reject cases for argument as it sees fit. Only where it has *original jurisdiction* or in certain mandatory appeals is the Court required to hear a case.

State Supreme Courts of Appeal

In most states this is called the State Supreme Court (SSC). It is the final court of appeal for most state cases.

Intermediate courts of appeal

US Circuit Courts of Appeal

Twelve Circuit Courts of Appeal (CCA) review cases from the US District Courts. Each Circuit deals with specific District Courts. The District Courts are therefore said to be on a particular Circuit.

State Intermediate Courts of Appeal

Forty states have Intermediate Courts of Appeal (ICAs). They are the first court of appeal for most cases in state law. Cases from the ICA can be appealed up to the State Supreme Court or to the US Circuit Courts of Appeal if the case involves rights protected by the Constitution.

US Court of Appeals for the Federal Circuit

The US Court of Appeals for the Federal Circuit (CAFC) reviews civil cases and those concerning matters such as international trade arising from the courts below it.

Trial courts

US District Courts

Deal with criminal and civil cases involving:
- federal statutes
- the US Constitution
- sums at stake in excess of $75 000.

Appeals go to CCA or CAFC.

State trial courts

Ninety-five per cent of all cases in the US are heard in state or local trial courts with names such as Municipal, County, District, Circuit, or Superior Courts. Appeals generally go to ICAs but in states without ICAs appeals go straight to the SSC.

US Claims Court

Deals with federal cases involving amounts over $10 000 and other cases such as those involving government contractors.

US Court of International Trade

Deals with cases involving international trade. Appeals go up to CAFC.

24.2 Composition and power

Composition

Size of the Court

Constitutionally, Congress has control over the size of the Court. The present Court numbers nine but this has not always been the case: 1789 = six; 1801 = five; 1802 = six; 1807 = seven; 1837 = eight/nine; 1863 = ten. The Judiciary Act of 1866 reduced the size of the court from ten to seven (to be achieved through attrition); The Act of 1869 re-established the Court at nine.

Trivia

The youngest serving Justice was Joseph Story (32). The oldest was Oliver W. Holmes (90). In October 2005, the average age of the court was 68. The shortest term of office was John Rutledge's (16 months). The longest term of office was William O. Douglas's (36 years, 7 months).

Who qualifies?

There are no formal requirements for office. However, As John R Schmidhauser noted, 'with exceedingly few exceptions, Supreme Court Justices have been white males chosen past middle age from socially and economically advantaged families: Protestant by religion and high status by denomination, descendants of natives of the British isles, and recipients of undergraduate education at schools of national reputation.'

The Supreme Court (June 2008)

Justice	Born	Appoint.	Oath	Alignment
John G. Roberts*	27/1/55	Bush Jr. (R)	2005	right centre
John Paul Stevens	20/4/20	Ford (R)	1975	left centre
Samuel Alito	1/4/50	Bush Jr. (R)	2006	right
Antonin Scalia	11/3/36	Reagan (R)	1986	right
Anthony Kennedy	23/7/36	Reagan (R)	1988	right centre
David Souter	17/9/39	Bush (R)	1990	right centre
Clarence Thomas	28/6/48	Bush (R)	1991	right
Ruth Bader Ginsburg	15/3/33	Clinton (D)	1993	left
Stephen Breyer	15/8/38	Clinton (D)	1994	left

NB: 1) '*' = Chief Justice. 2) The 'Alignment' column only offers the crudest assessment of political orientation.

The appointment process

A vacancy occurs (through death, disability, resignation, retirement or impeachment). The last ten Justices to leave the Court have done so as a result of resignation or retirement, though in the earlier days of the Court it was common for Justices to remain in office until death. Only one Justice, Samuel Chase, was ever impeached and he was not convicted (he eventually died in office in 1811).

President nominates replacement Constitutionally, Presidents have a free hand in nominating replacements. Modern Presidents have normally taken account of American Bar Association 'ratings' of possible nominees, though George W. Bush chose not to. Not all Justices work in legal practice immediately prior to their appointment; Earl Warren was Governor of California before being appointed Chief Justice by Eisenhower. Most members of the current Court do have considerable legal experience.

The Senate Judicial Committee conducts hearings ... to assess the suitability of the candidate. This is a serious business. During the appointment of Clarence Thomas, for example, the Senate investigated allegations of sexual harassment against Thomas. Sometimes candidates will withdraw or be withdrawn at this stage. Generally, however, the Senate will proceed to vote on the nomination, a candidate needing 50%+ of the votes to be successful. Most appointments gain Senate approval, though Ronald Reagan had Robert Bork rejected (by 42 votes to 58). In 2005, Democrats in the Senate were accused of abusing the filibuster device to prevent the chamber from proceeding to a vote on judicial nominees in lower federal courts.

Power

Constitutional position

Article III section 2 gives the Court the power to hear directly (have *original jurisdiction* over) cases involving public officials or where a state is a party. In all other cases it acts as the highest court of appeal (its *appellate jurisdiction*). The Court normally accepts for consideration cases that are the subject of debate or confusion in the lower courts, and such confusion generally arises from areas of the Constitution that are more open to interpretation. These areas include: the *'Interstate Commerce Clause'; the 'General Welfare Clause' and the 14th Amendment; The War Power; The Treaty Power; the 1st, 4th and 5th Amendments; and the 'Necessary and Proper Clause'.* Justices adopt a variety of different approaches when interpreting the Constitution. Right-wing conservative Justices such as Rehnquist and Scalia, for example, have tended to favour a more literal interpretation of the Constitution and are, therefore, often referred to as **strict constructionists**. Left-wing or liberal Justices (**loose constructionists**) such as Breyer, in contrast, favour 'reading between the lines' a little, looking for things that are not written (explicit) but implied by the Constitution (*penumbras* or shadows).

Judicial review

As early as 1832 Andrew Jackson had voiced his belief that 'the opinion of the Supreme Court ... ought not to control ... this government. The Congress, the Executive, and the Court' he asserted, 'must each be guided by its own opinion of the Constitution.' By then however, the foundations of judicial review had been established through the Marbury v. Madison case of 1803. Judicial review is the convention by which the Court may void any actions or statutes, whether by state or federal government, where the Court determines that such actions or statutes come into conflict with the Constitution. The development of such authority was ground-breaking, because it meant that the Supreme Court had begun to establish itself as a body which could hold other branches of government to its interpretation of the Constitution. An excellent recent example of judicial review in action is the case of George W. Bush v. Al Gore (2000) where the Court reviewed the judgement of the Florida Supreme Court and overturned it; effectively making Bush the 43rd US President.

Judicial activism

While in theory the Court is only interpreting the Constitution, in practice the differences between interpretations of the same constitutional passage over as short a time as 60 years (Plessy v. Fergusson, 1896 to Brown v. Board of Education, Topeka, 1954) may often appear tantamount to legislative action. Between those dates the Court moved from a position where it saw racial segregation on trains as acceptable (as long as separate accommodation was equal) to a position where all segregation caused inequality and was, therefore, unconstitutional. In the wake of this change, James F. Byrnes remarked that 'the Court did not interpret the Constitution – the Court amended it'. Under the leadership of Earl Warren from 1954, the Court began to make massive use of its powers of judicial review, often in sensitive areas. The way in which the Court pushed back the frontiers of society at that time, in cases such as 'Brown', led some to hail the advent of judicial activism. 'The Supreme Court of the United States [had], as John W. Brocker noted, 'assumed quasi legislative authority,' dragging the other branches behind it.

Judicial restraint

Despite this, the Court tends to follow precedent rather than make excessively showy use of its powers. Where precedent is challenged and changed, the process often takes many years and is the result of several cases. In the case of abortion for example, the Roe v. Wade decision (1973) was based firmly in earlier cases which had established a right to privacy (e.g. Griswold v. Connecticut, 1965). Since the landmark Roe case, which upheld a woman's right to control over her own body and thus the right to have an abortion, a number of cases have limited access to abortions (e.g. Maher v. Roe, 1977; Webster v. Reproductive Health Services, 1989), but the Court has stopped short of totally overturning Roe. Thus, precedent is the norm and the Court moves slowly, if it moves at all. If the Court were to test the patience of the other two branches by making excessive use of the power of 'review' it might find itself under attack. In any case, the Court has little power with which to enforce its decisions. Restraint therefore, is the norm.

24.3 Control and questions of democracy

Four limitations on the power of the court

1. Congressional control

Congress can:

- control the appellate jurisdiction of the Court;
- control the number of Justices (i.e. the size of the Court); and
- control the times when the Court can sit.

But these are controls that Congress **threatens** to use only rarely and **uses** even less.

2. Presidential control

The President can:

- nominate Justices to fill vacancies in the Court (although these appointments must be agreed by the Senate); and
- work with Congress to reform or 'pack the Court'.

In reality however, the President's power is strictly circumvented.

(a) He can only nominate Justices where vacancies occur

Different Presidents have had significantly different levels of input into the appointment process. Carter, for example, appointed no Justices whereas Washington appointed 11 and Franklin D Roosevelt appointed nine.

(b) He needs the confirmation of the Senate for his nominations and this is not always forthcoming

Nixon had two nominees rejected – Clement Haynsworth Jr (rejected by 45 votes to 55) and G Harold Carswell (by 45 votes to 51). Reagan also failed in his attempt to get Robert H Bork onto the Court.

(c) Once installed, the Justices do not always live up to the President's expectations

Eisenhower described his nomination of Chief Justice Earl Warren as 'the biggest damn fool mistake I ever made' and Nixon found that a Court including four of his nominees was still prepared to hand over his White House tapes to the Watergate investigation (US v. Nixon, 1974).

(d) 'Packing' the Court is neither quick, nor guaranteed of success (though the threat of it can move minds)

Franklin D Roosevelt's court-packing bill failed in 1937 but it did persuade one Justice, Owen Roberts, to change his position and back the New Deal programme's constitutionality. Roosevelt thus carried the Court by 5:4 and his threats had, the New York Times reported, precipitated the 'switch in time that saved nine'.

3. Public opinion

Though the Court is free from the pressure of re-election, there has always been a feeling amongst US political commentators that the Court is receptive to public opinion. As Finley Peter Dunne commented in Mr Dooly's Opinion, 'No matter whether th' Constitution follows th' flag or not, the Supreme Court follows th' election returns'. Public pressure was certainly present, and influential at the time that the Court backed down over the New Deal and even the Brown v. Board of Education Decision (1954) was handed down with a fairly strong public support in the North, despite a certain amount of inertia elsewhere on the issue of race relations.

The Court would be unlikely to survive long unchanged if it persistently acted in a manner diametrically opposed to the wishes of the people, Congress and the President. After all, with the Congress having control of Court size and oversight of appellate jurisdiction, and the President's power of appointment checked only by the Senate, the executive and the legislative branches could easily rein in a wayward Court.

4. Difficulty in enforcing decisions

Students of Politics will be familiar with the distinction between power and authority, and the US Supreme Court is an excellent case in point. As Felix Frankfurter noted,

'the Court's authority – possessed neither of the purse nor the sword – ultimately rests on sustained public confidence in its moral sanction. Such feeling must be nourished by the Court's complete detachment, in fact and appearance, from political entanglements and by abstention from injecting itself into the clash of political forces and political settlements.'

What the Court has, therefore, is prestige, moral authority, and a fair amount of obedience from the lower courts. In addition, the Justices have the knowledge that they may from time to time call on Congress' purse and the President's swords where their authority fails to carry the day.

The Court and democracy

'Quis custodiet ipsos custodes?' (Who is to guard the guards themselves?). *Decimus Junius Juvenal (c 60–140)*

The charge

Many feel that the Supreme Court has become an anti-democratic force. They argue that excessive use of judicial review is unacceptable in light of the fact that the Court consists of nine 'unelected and unaccountable' Justices. For them, the idea that such a narrow, and practically irremovable group could interpret the Constitution in such a way as to make void the legislation created by a democratically-elected Congress, is perverse.

Are these arguments realistic? Have the *umpires* really become the *players*?

The defence

In defence of the Supreme Court, we need only say that it has made the survival of the US Constitution as we know it possible. The Court has re-worked the Constitution to meet the demands of a developing society:

1. It has allowed flexibility through its willingness to change its interpretations on key issues through the passage of time, while at the same time allowing judicial precedent to be the norm.

2. It has given guidance to lower courts when they could not agree with one another and it has acted as the ultimate court of appeal for many wrongly convicted at lower, less impartial (often elected) levels of the judiciary.

3. It has led the reversal of anti-democratic practices (e.g. segregation), when elected bodies seemed unable or unwilling to act decisively; and, more than anything else.

4. It has acted as a constant thread in US political society, underpinning the separation of powers (both in its verdicts and through its very existence) and remaining to foil the attempts of popularly-elected governments to curtail individual rights or threaten the spiritual heart of the constitution.

The Supreme Court has as Max Lerner concluded, 'acted as the final barricade against the assaults of democratic majorities'.

24.4 The Court in action, 1954–2005

This table outlines **some** of the Court's key decisions and shows how interpretations have developed over time under different Chief Justices. See also 'Bill of Rights'.

Area	The Warren Court (1954–69)	The Burger Court (1969–86)	The Rehnquist Court (1986–2005)
Segregation and the rights of ethnic minorities	**1954 Brown v. Board of Education, Topeka** Segregation was always unequal (reversed Plessy v. Ferguson, 1896). **1969 Alexander v. Holmes County Board of Education** Schools must be desegregated at once.	**1971 Swann v. Charlotte-Mecklenberg Board of Education** This case led to the introduction of 'bussing', where pupils of different ethnic backgrounds were taken to schools in such a way as to provide racially mixed schools in all areas. **1978 Regents of the University of California v. Bakke** There had been reverse discrimination due to quotas and Bakke – who was white – should be allowed into the University.	**1989 Ward's Cove Packing Company v. Atonio** **1989 Richmond v. J. A. Croson Company** ... two cases that saw a narrowing of affirmative action (this narrowing was later reversed following the 1991 Civil Rights Act). **1995 Adarland Constructors v. Pena** The Court struck down a federal affirmative action programme in favour of minority workers. **2003 Grutter v. Bollinger** Further restricted affirmative action.
Abortion	**1965 Griswold v. Connecticut** The last surviving laws against birth controls were removed, and a constitutional right to a protected 'zone of privacy' established. Roe (see right) was largely founded upon protections identified in this case.	**1973 Roe v. Wade** The Court established a right to abortion within the 'zone of privacy', but the right offered different protection at different stages of pregnancy. **1980 Harris v. McRae** The Court upheld the constitutionality of the 'Hyde Amendment', which limited Medicaid funding of abortions. **1983 City of Akron v. Akron Center for Reproductive Health Inc.** Local statutes were too restrictive of abortion and consequently struck down.	**1989 Webster v. Reproductive Health Services** The Court upheld Missouri's law that banned abortions from state facilities and banned state employees from doing them. **1990 Ohio v. Akron Center for Reproductive Health Inc.** Minors must inform their parents before abortion procedures. **2000 Stenberg v. Carhart** Struck down Nebraska statute banning partial birth abortion.
The rights of the arrested/accused	**1963 Gideon v. Wainwright** States had to provide legal counsel for the poor. **1964 Escobedo v. Illinois** The accused had the right to have counsel before the trial. **1966 Miranda v. Arizona** Those arrested must be read their rights or the evidence gained will be invalid.	**1971 Harris v. New York** Confessions that had been taken in violation of Miranda rule could be used for limited purposes. **1974 Michigan v. Tucker** Miranda warnings were not in themselves rights protected by the Constitution. **1984 New York v. Quarles** The Court recognised a 'public safety exception' to Miranda.	**1984 Strickland v. Washington** Defendants have a right to a counsel whose performance is not defective to the point of altering the course of the trial. **1989 Duckworth v. Eagan** The exact wording from Miranda does not have to be used for a subsequent confession to be valid. **2003 Hamdi v. Rumsfield** Enemy combatants have right to due process of law.
Religion	**1962 Engel v. Vitale** A non-denominational prayer was declared unconstitutional because it promoted religion. **1963 Abington v. Schempp** There should be no bible worship in state schools.	**1985 Wallace v. Jaffree** The Court invalidated an Alabama law which allowed a moment's silence for voluntary prayer	**1987 Edwards v. Aquillard** Louisiana could not force teaching of the creation story alongside evolution. **1992 Lee v. Weisman** It was unconstitutional for a public school to include prayers at a graduation ceremony because this violated the establishment clause of the First Amendment.
Politics	**1962 Baker v. Carr** Gerrymandering was bad because apportionment should be equal. Gerrymandering violated 'equal protection'.		**1986 Davis v. Bandemer** 'Gerrymandering' was still wrong under 'equal protection', but Indiana State was not guilty of it. **2000 Bush v. Gore** Ended recounts in Florida, thus handing the presidential election to George W. Bush.

25.1 State and local government

State government

Introduction

The United States operates under a federal system of government. Though most of the Constitution focuses on the powers given to the various branches of the federal (central) government (the so-called 'enumerated powers'), the Tenth Amendment crucially reserves powers for the various states.

AMENDMENT X

The powers not delegated to the United States by the Constitution, nor prohibited by it to the States, are reserved to the States respectively, or to the people.

These 'reserved powers' include the powers to regulate their own commerce, organise elections (as we saw in Florida in 2000) and put in place measures aimed at ensuring safety. In practice, however, the states have an enormous range of responsibilities including health, education and many aspects of welfare. States also control whether or not they make use of the death penalty, regulations concerning marriage and the age at which individuals can consume alcohol.

Structure

The structure of state government mirrors the structure of the federal government with executive, legislative and judicial branches.

State executive

An elected governor heads the executive branch in each state.

State governors

Most governors have a 4-year term and can stand for re-election, but in some states the term can be shorter and governors are forbidden to succeed themselves. Though the power of the governor also varies from state to state, virtually all governors have a veto power and the vast majority have a line-item veto over appropriation bills. Most governors also have significant powers of patronage.

State legislature

All of the states apart from Nebraska have bicameral legislatures. The two chambers are most often referred to as the assembly and the senate. Though terms of office vary from state to state, the majority have a two-year term for the lower chamber and a four-year term for the upper chamber. That said, most state legislatures meet very infrequently.

State legislatures pass state laws and regulations governing those areas over which the state has jurisdiction. As in the federal Congress, the bulk of work is done in committees.

State judiciary

Each state has a state judiciary that enforces state laws and some federal laws. In most states judges are **elected** for fixed terms (most commonly between four and 15 years). Some feel that such elections are inappropriate because:

(1) Elected judges may act in pursuit of popularity rather than justice.
(2) The demands of elections can lead to candidates setting out 'manifestos' making promises on sentencing etc. that might tie their hands once elected.
(3) Elections do not necessarily result in those with the best legal minds being selected.

Role

In the 1990s state governments spent well over $1 000 000 000 000 (1 trillion) per year. Most of this money is spent providing services within states. Education (see right) is normally the biggest area of spending within a state, but states also provide a wide range of welfare services.

Finance

Such a massive expenditure requires a massive income. The federal government still provides financial grants in support of state programmes but these only make up between 10% and 15% of the total figure. The rest comes from state property taxes, sales taxes and income generated by public utilities and lotteries.

Managing education

State governments control the higher levels of educational provision within the state. This would include universities and higher education. On the whole, regular schools are run by local governments (see below).

See section dealing with federalism (Ch 19.3)

Local government

Below state government there is local government. Local governments have their powers delegated to them by state governments. The emphasis in local government is on administering and delivering services. The 80 000 or so local government units that exist nationally can be broadly divided into municipal governments and county governments.

Municipal government

Municipal government operates at the level of a city, village or borough. In the case of a city the municipal government structure will normally involve an elected city council, with an elected mayor or city manager providing focus and direction.

County government

In rural areas county government is the norm. County governments vary enormously. Some focus around a board of supervisors, working alongside key elected representatives such as the local sheriff. Others have an elected commission, an assembly or, as is often the case in cities, a council with an elected administrator as chief executive.

Glossary

Accountability: To have to answer for one's actions and conduct. For example, MPs are accountable to voters and ministers are accountable to Parliament.

Affirmative action: Or 'positive discrimination'. Policies that favour minorities in an effort to reverse past (historic) discrimination.

Amicus curiae: Commonly used term in the US courts where groups with an interest in policy can file 'amicus curiae' ('friends of the court') briefs to put their case before legal argument is heard by the court.

Anonymity: One of the three principles upon which the British civil service is traditionally said to be based: civil servants are not public figures because they are not accountable for policies. See 'Neutrality' and 'Permanence'.

Appellate jurisdiction: The area over which a court can consider or review a case on appeal from a lower court.

A priori [reasoning]: Where reasoning is not based upon an examination of the evidence, but on ideas or an ideological framework that precede it.

Balancing the ticket: In the US. The practice of choosing a vice-presidential candidate from a different ethnic, religious or geographical background than the presidential candidate, in order to broaden the appeal of the ticket.

Band-wagon effect: Where favourable opinion poll ratings result in even more voters backing the party or candidate that appears to be 'winning'.

Bicameral: Having two chambers (e.g. Congress = House and Senate)

Bill of Rights: In the US, referring to the first ten amendments to the Constitution. In the UK, a measure passed in 1689 placing some restrictions on the power of the monarch, identifying some key parliamentary powers and certain limited individual rights.

Bipartisanship: Where two parties co-operate on particular issues (bipartisan coalitions).

Boomerang effect: Where favourable opinion poll ratings result in some supporters of the party that is ahead becoming complacent and not voting and/or more of the losing party's supporters making an effort to get out and vote and/or people voting for the party that is behind out of sympathy. The result is that the gap between the parties identified by the poll closes.

Cabinet: The committee of leading members of the government (most of whom are heads of departments). In the US, traditionally more administrative; in the UK, traditionally more important in decision-making.

Caucus: In the US. A meeting of party members convened to select candidates or decide strategy.

Cause groups (Promotional groups): Pressure groups that aim to promote a particular cause or set of ideas.

Certiorari: A writ of certiorari from a court instructs a lower court to make details of its decision available for review in a higher court, in order that the decision can be 'made certain'.

Checks and balances: Where each branch of government exercises controls over the other branches and is, in turn, controlled by them.

Cloture: A cloture (closure) motion sets a time limit on a debate, effectively ending it. In the US such motions can be employed to end filibusters.

Coalition: Where two or more parties combine to form a government.

Coat-tails effect: Where candidates from the same party as a popular presidential candidate are also swept into power on the crest of their popularity.

Codified constitution: Where the various rules under which a country is governed are drawn together in a single constitutional document that is both explicit and systematic.

Collective responsibility: The principle that Cabinet ministers must publicly support decisions taken collectively in Cabinet, or resign and make their criticisms from the back benches.

Common law: Law which is part of custom. Law built upon precedent (case law) established by judges.

Community Charge: Or 'Poll Tax'. The local tax on every resident adult, brought in to replace the rates in 1990. See also 'Council Tax'.

Concurrent powers: Powers held by federal and state governments jointly (e.g. the power to tax).

Conference committee: A committee consisting of House members and Senators, brought together with a view to reconciling the differences between the House and Senate versions of a bill.

Consensus politics: Where there is broad cross-party agreement on the necessary direction of policy.

Constitution: The fundamental rules governing the organisation of a state – particularly the distribution of powers between different state institutions and between the state and the people.

Core executive: The decision-making centre in British politics. Focused on the Prime Minister, Cabinet, top civil servants, Cabinet Office and the Prime Minister's Office.

Council Tax: The property-based local tax brought in to replace the Community Charge in 1993. See also 'Community Charge'.

Cross-benchers: Members of the legislature (some Lords, for example) who are not aligned to a particular party.

Democratic deficit: Most commonly used in relation to the EU. Where key institutions (the Council of Ministers or the Commission, for example) are not directly accountable to citizens but wield enormous power over them.

Devolution: The delegation of power from central government to regional or local parliaments, assemblies or councils.

Divided government: Most commonly in the US. Where one party controls the White House and another controls part or all of congress. See also 'Gridlock'.

Elective dictatorship (sometimes called Electoral Dictatorship): A phrase commonly associated with Lord Hailsham, referring to the way in which, once elected, the head of the majority party in the Commons can do pretty well as they see fit until the next election.

Enumerated powers: Those powers explicitly granted to particular institutions, or assigned to federal or state governments, by the US Constitution.

Environmentalism: A political ideology that puts ideas such as sustainability and care for the environment at the centre of policy-making.

Executive: One of the three branches of government. The executive makes government decisions and executes policy rather than legislating or adjudicating. See also 'Legislature' and 'Judiciary'.

Executive agencies: Semi-autonomous bodies charged with administering some aspects of government policy.

Executive agreement: In US politics. An agreement between the President and a foreign power that has the weight of a treaty without the need for Senate ratification.

Fat cats: Wealthy party contributors or local power-brokers who once controlled the government of many US cities.

Filibuster: Where a politician (particularly a US Senator) talks at length, using up the available time on the floor and preventing a bill from being passed. 'Talking a bill to death.'

First past the post: Or 'simple plurality' system. An electoral system where a candidate need only secure the support of one voter more than their nearest rival in order to win.

Floating voters: Voters who exhibit low levels of party identification and are therefore liable to switch support between parties during the election campaign or between elections. Also called independent voters.

Founding Fathers: The representatives from the various states who gathered in Philadelphia in 1787 and drafted the US Constitution.

Franchise: The right to vote, as determined by various acts of parliament in Britain and state regulations and constitutional provisions in the US.

Freedom of information: The right of individuals to access government information and records.

Gender gap: A gap between the support given to certain candidates by women and the support given to the same range of candidates by men.

Gerrymandering: The practice of moving electoral boundaries with a view to giving a party electoral advantage (for example, by excluding the supporters of an opposing party from a particular electoral district).

GOP: The Grand Old Party or Republican Party (founded in 1856).

Gridlock: Most commonly where a US President from one party is prevented form pursuing his policies by a Congress controlled partly or entirely by another party.

Honeymoon period: The period just following his inauguration, when a US President is normally given the benefit of the doubt by Congress, the public and the media.

Hundred days: A period during which a new President's administration is often judged as it attempts to push through its policies while support remains strong.

Ideology: A coherent system of ideas, beliefs and values applied to the organisation of politics.

Implied powers: In the US Constitution, those powers that Congress needs in order to carry out the roles given to it (enumerated) in the Constitution. Mostly emanating from the 'necessary and proper clause'.

Impeachment: Where the US House of Representatives formally accuses a member of the executive or the judiciary of misconduct. This normally leads to a Senate trial that can in turn lead to the individual being removed from office.

Impoundment: The practice by which the President refuses to spend funds appropriated by Congress. Congress tried to limit this through the 1974 Budget Control and Impoundment Act.

Incumbent: The person already holding a particular office.

Independent regulatory commissions: In the US. Bodies set up by the government and charged with regulating predetermined areas of policy. For example, the Securities and Exchange Commission set up in 1934.

Independent voters: See 'Floating voters'.

Initiative: Where a predetermined number of electors sign a petition that puts a question on a ballot paper proposing new legislation.

Insider groups: Pressure groups that work very closely with politicians and top civil servants either at a local or a national level.

Interest groups (Sectional or Protectional Groups): Pressure groups that represent the interests of a particular economic or occupational section of society. **NB: In the US the phrases 'interest groups' and 'pressure groups' are often used interchangeably.**

Item veto: The ability of an executive to strike out particular sections of a bill, whilst allowing the rest to become law. Sometimes called a 'line-item veto'.

Judicial review: In the US. The practice by which the courts can declare the actions of other branches of government (at state or federal government level) unconstitutional.

Judiciary: The branch of government concerned with enforcing or adjudicating the laws where disputes arise.

Junior ministers: In the UK. Ministers of state and parliamentary under-secretaries.

Keynesianism: An economic theory based upon the ideas of J M Keynes, essentially involving a mixed economy with some government intervention.

Kitchen cabinet: A small group of advisers that Presidents or Prime Ministers might draw around them.

Lame duck: A politician (normally a President) who has lost the election but remains in office – without real authority – until his successor is inaugurated. Sometimes also applied more generally to those who are nearing the end of their term in office.

Law: A rule or set or rules enforced by the courts.

Legislature: The law-making branch of government.

Legitimisation: The process of making something legitimate; for example, legitimising a policy by holding a referendum.

Liberal democracy: The western style of democracy incorporating free and fair elections and a belief in the importance of core rights and responsibilities.

Lobbyist: An individual who works on behalf of a pressure group and who aims to influence the legislative process.

Log-rolling: Where members of the legislature (normally in the US) trade support with one another to gain the passage of measures that will benefit them or their constituencies.

(Electoral) Mandate: The right of an elected government to carry into law those policies that formed the basis of its manifesto in the preceding election.

Manifesto: A document most commonly produced at the time of an election outlining the platform (i.e. the policies) on which that party is standing.

Michels' iron law: Michels' iron law of oligarchy holds that popular mass movements cannot not be truly democratic because they will always be controlled by a small guiding elite (an oligarchy).

Ministerial responsibility: The view that ministers are responsible for all that goes on in their departments regardless of their part in it and that they should resign where major infractions of procedure take place (so-called 'role responsibility'). Also, that there are certain codes of personal behaviour that ministers should observe while they remain in office (so-called 'personal responsibility').

Ministers: The 90 or so most senior government figures (Prime Minister, Cabinet, ministers of state and parliamentary under-secretaries).

Neo-liberalism: Often associated with the New Right. A belief that the free market is the vehicle best suited to achieving sustainable economic growth and most able to provide for individual needs.

Neutrality: Or impartiality. One of the three principles upon which the British Civil Service is traditionally said to be based. The idea that civil servants should not allow their personal political beliefs to enter into their work, and that they should be able to serve a government of any political persuasion. See 'Anonymity' and 'Permanence'.

New Right: Politicians in the US and in Britain who adopted neo-liberal monetarist policies and, in the US especially, conservative social positions (anti-abortion, anti-gay etc.).

Ombudsman: A 'people's friend' who investigates complaints of maladministration or injustice. In Britain, most commonly referring to the Parliamentary Commissioner for Administration.

Outsider groups: Pressure groups who do not have easy access to ministers and top civil servants. Often kept outside because of what they represent or the tactics that they adopt, but might also choose to be outside for ideological reasons.

PACs: In the US. Political Action Committees are organisations that channel funds from corporations and pressure groups to candidates in elections.

Parliament Act: In 1911 the Parliament Act replaced the Lords' right to veto (kill) legislation with the power to delay bills for two years. At the same time, the Lords were effectively prevented from amending, vetoing or delaying money (e.g. tax) bills. The Parliament Act of 1949 reduced the power of delay to one parliamentary session.

Party: A political party is a grouping of people who share similar views and come together to seek power – most often by seeking election to political office.

Peak groups: Peak (or umbrella) organisations co-ordinate the efforts of a number of groups with common interests. For example, the TUC draws together various individual unions.

Permanence: One of the three principles upon which the British Civil Service is traditionally said to be based; civil servants remain in position regardless of the results of elections, often serving parties of different political persuasions. See 'Anonymity' and 'Neutrality'.

Pigeon-holing: In US politics. The process by which bills are essentially shelved and allowed to die, normally in committee.

Platform: In US politics. The policies upon which candidates stand in elections. Most commonly referring to the policies advanced by presidential candidates and formalised at their party's nominating convention.

Pluralism: Where power is fragmented and decisions are arrived through the open competition of groups representing different interests.

Pocket veto: In US Politics. Where a president can kill a bill by pocketing it, as long as the congressional session ends before the ten-day deadline for the President to sign or veto the bill passes.

Poll Tax: See 'Community Charge'.

Pork-barrelling: Where Congressmen add riders (amendments) to appropriations bills that secure funding for projects benefiting their constituents; thereby aiding their chances of re-election.

Precedent: Where a past decision or court judgement is taken as a guide for a one that is current.

Pressure groups: Groups with a shared interest or a common goal that seek to influence policy without normally wishing to become the government through elections.

Primary: An election held prior to the main (general) election in the US for the purpose of selecting a party's candidate for the main event.

Prime Minister: The head of the executive branch in the British government who presides over the Cabinet.

Prime-ministerial government: Advanced by politicians such as Richard Crossman and Tony Benn. A model of executive government that sees the Prime Minister as supremely powerful (presidential, even) and the Cabinet as increasingly irrelevant.

Private member's bill: A bill advanced by a backbencher, normally without government backing.

Proportional representation: A collective term for electoral systems that seek to apportion seats to political parties in near proportion to votes won (either nationally or regionally).

Protectional or Protectionist groups: See 'Interest groups'.

Psephologist: A person who studies how people vote in elections.

Quangos: Quasi-autonomous non-governmental organisations. Created in order to allow certain services a greater degree of independence and impartiality. Sometimes criticised for a lack of accountability.

Recall: A device by which registered voters in some US states can initiate a public vote with a view to removing an elected officer or politician from office over matters such as corruption or negligence.

Referendum: A government-initiated popular vote authorising or legitimising a predetermined course of action.

Reserved powers: In US politics. The powers retained by the states under the Tenth Amendment to the Constitution.

Rider: An amendment to a bill that has nothing to do with the primary purpose of the original bill. Most commonly associated with 'pork-barrelling' (see above).

Royal prerogative: Powers held by the monarch but now, largely through convention, exercised by the Prime Minister. For example, the power to sign treaties.

Salisbury Doctrine: The principle that the (unelected) Lords should not oppose government bills at second reading where the (elected) government has a clear mandate (through its manifesto commitments) to pass such measures.

Sectional groups: See 'Interest groups'.

Select committees: Since 1979, UK departmental select committees have had the role of scrutinising the work of the various Government departments. Other non-departmental select committees are given a particular focus. The UK Public Accounts Committee, for example, has the role of ensuring value for money in Government. In the US, select committees are normally set up to conduct specific investigations outside of the scope of existing standing committees.

Seniority system: In US politics. The system by which the top positions (particularly in congressional committees) were given to the individuals with the longest continuous length of service.

Separation of powers: The principle, advanced by writers such as Montesquieu, that the three branches of government (executive, legislature, judiciary) should be separated so as to avoid tyranny.

Simple plurality: See 'first past the post'.

Smoke-filled rooms: The rooms in which secret meetings were held to choose candidates and direct party policy. See also 'Fat cats'.

Soft money: Money which often ends up with candidates but was not regulated under the 1974 Campaign Finance Act because it was supposedly targeted at helping party organisation, voter registration drives and improving voter turnout on the day.

Sovereignty: The legitimate and exclusive right to exercise power within a given area.

Split-ticket voting: Where candidates vote for a variety of candidates from different parties for different offices on the same election day.

Standing committees: In the UK, standing committees are formed on an ad hoc basis to undertake detailed consideration of a bill after its second reading. In the US such committees are permanant and they play a major role in scrutinising the executive branch, in addition to their legislative function.

State: The collective term for the formal institutions and bodies that exercise sovereign power within a given territory.

Statute law: A law passed by Parliament.

Swing: The movement of voters' support (normally measured as a percentage) from one party to another.

Tactical voting: Where an individual votes for a candidate who is not their preferred choice because the candidate they are voting for has a more realistic chance of defeating the candidate that they favour least.

Term limits: A legal restriction preventing the holder of an elected office from serving more than a pre-determined number of terms in office.

Ticket: In US politics. The collective term for a party's presidential and vice-presidential candidate.

Ultra vires: The doctrine by which public bodies (local authorities, for example) can only do that which they are authorised to do by Parliament. All else is beyond their authority.

Unitary state: A state where sovereignty resides with the central government.

Veto: In US politics. The power of the President to block legislation passed by Congress. Congress, in turn, can override the veto with a two-thirds majority in each chamber (House and Senate).

Wasps: Often used in discussion of US politics. Referring to White Anglo Saxon Protestants.

Whips: Members of the legislature who are appointed by their party to ensure that other members of the party are aware of and vote in line with the party's position on key policies.

Write-in candidate: In the US. Where supporters of candidates whose names do not appear on the ballot can 'write in' the names of their favoured candidate in spaces provided.

Index

Page numbers in **bold** type indicate main entries. Glossary pages are not included.

abortion issue *(UK)* 33,35 *(US)* 80,83,92,104,106
additional members system 19
agencification 52
agency capture 82
alternative vote system 19
amending US Constitution 89
American Dream 10
American War of Independence 84
amicus curiae 80
Appropriations Committee 93
Articles of Confederation 84,85
Attlee, Clement 15,32
authority 8

backbenchers 45
Bell, Martin 35,46,47
Benn, Tony 46,49,52
Beveridge, William/Report 15
Bill of Rights **88**,89
bills, passage of *(UK)* **44** *(US)* **91**
Black Wednesday (1992) 16,53
Blair, Tony / Blairism **17**,30,32,49,50, 51
Brown, Gordon 17,30,32,49,50
Brownlow Committee 101
Burger Court (1969-86) 106
Burke, Edmund 9,11
Bush, George Snr 72,77,96,99
Bush, George W. 75,77,78,80,**98**,99
Bush v. Gore (2000) 75,104,106

Cabinet *(UK)* 41,49,**50** *(US)* **100**
Cabinet Committees 48,**50**
Cabinet Office **48**,50
Cameron, David 29,32
campaign finance *(US)* 70,72,76,81,82
Campbell, Alastair 17,51
capitalism 13,14
Carter, Jimmy 72,94,96
cash for questions 47
caucuses 68,70
cause groups *(UK)* 35,*(US)* 79
central government 55,56
checks and balances *(US)* 86,**87**
Cheney, Dick 68,75
Chief of Staff *(UK)* 51 *(US)* 101
Citizen's Charter 52,62
citizens' rights 61
civil law 63
civil liberties 66
civil service **52-53**
Clause four 30,32
Clegg, Nick 31
Clinton, Bill 68,71,72,73,77,80,82,**98**
codified/uncodified constitution 39,89
collective responsibility 53,100
Common Agricultural Policy 60
common law 39
Communications Decency Act 80,89
conference committees 93
Congress 87,**90**,92,96,97
Congressional committees 93
congressional elections 68
Connecticut Compromise 85
consensus 10
conservatism **11**
Conservative Party 11,**29**,32,34

constitution *(UK)* 39,**41-42** *(US)* 80, **84-7**,89
co-operative federalism 86
COPA-COGECA 37
core executive *(UK)* **48**,49
Council of Ministers **59**,60
council tax 56
courts *(UK)* 62,63 *(US)* **103**
Criminal Justice Act (1994) 61
criminal law 63

Declaration of Independence 84
deferential voters 24
democracy **9**,66
Democratic Party 71,**77**
departments *(UK)* **53**
devolution 17,40,42,55,**57**
Dicey, A.V. 40
direct action *(UK)* 35,38 *(US)* 80
direct democracy *(UK)* 9 *(US)* 69
doctrines and principles **40**
dual federalism 86
due process 88,99

Early Day Motion 45
elections *(UK)* 18,26,**27** *(US)* 68
electoral college *(UK)* 34 *(US)* 68,70
electoral system *(UK)* **18**,**19** *(US)* 68,78
electorate *(UK)* **21** *(US)* **67**
emergency powers 94
Enron 79,80,98
environmentalism **14**,37
ethnicity and voting *(UK)* 21,24 *(US)* 67,71,74
euro 60
Eurogroups 37
European Commission **59**,60
European Convention on Human Rights 65,66
European Court of Human Rights 62,64
European Court of Justice 45
European elections 18,22
European Parliament **59**,60
European Union 37,39,41,42,55,**59-60**
executive departments *(US)* 102
Executive Office of the President 101
executive *(UK)* 45,48,49 *(US)* 86
exit polls 26

Factortame Case (1990) 45,63
Fascist parties 33
fat cats 76
Fathers 4 Justice 38
federal bureaucracy 55,**102**
federal systems 55,80,85,86
filibustering 80,90
Filkin, Elizabeth 47
First Amendment 80,88
first past the post system 18,19,78
floating voters 23,26
Florida 2000 election result 75
focus groups 26
Ford, Gerald 68,72,94,96,97,100
Founding Fathers 85,86,94
Freedom of Information Act 17,42,65,66
freedom of speech *(US)* 80,88
gerrymandering 106

Gingrich, Newt 68,90,98
Good Friday Agreement 42,**58**
Gore, Al 71,75,77,78,92
government by consent 12
Green Party 33
gridlock in government 71,86,87
Guantanamo Bay 99
Gulf war 98,99

Hamilton, Alexander 76,79,84,85,86,94
Hamilton, Neil 47
Heseltine, Michael 50,53
Homeland Security 99
homogeneity 10
House of Commons 41,**43**,44,45,47
House of Lords 39,41,42,**43**,44,45,46, 47,66
House of Representatives 68,86,**90**,91, 92,93
human nature 11,12
Human Rights Act 17,35,41,42,45,61, 62,63,**64**,65

Ibbs Report 52
impeachment 90
independent executive agencies **102**
independent regulatory commissions **102**
individualism 10
initiatives 9,69
insider groups *(UK)* 35 *(US)* 79
Iraq war 17,75,98,99
iron triangles 82

Jefferson, Thomas 84
Johnson, L.B. 92,97
joined-up government 17,52
judicial activism 104
judicial reform 42
judicial restraint 104
judicial review 62,65,87,104
judiciary *(UK)* 45,**63**,65 *(US)* 86
justice 8

Keating Five 82
Kennedy, Charles 31
Kennedy, J.F. 97
Kerry, John 75,77
Keynes, J.M. 15
kitchen cabinet 49
Kyoto agreement 98

Labour Party **30**,32,34,52
laissez-faire 10
laws 8
left wing-right wing 32
legislation, passage of *(UK)* **44** *(US)* **91**
legislature *(US)* 86
Lemon Law 82
liberal democracy 9,65
Liberal Democrats **31**,33,34
liberalism **12**
liberty 10,84
Lieberman, Joe 71,75,78
limited government 10,12
line-item veto 91,95

Lisbon Treaty 60
lobbying 35,37
local elections 22
local government *(UK)* 56 *(US)* **107**
Locke, John 12
log-rolling 97
London Assembly 19,22,42

Maastricht Treaty 39,41,59,65
McCain, John 75
machine politics 76
Madison, James 76,84
Major, John/Majorism **16**,49,50,62
Mandelson, Peter 47
Marxism 13
media *(UK)* 25,27,36 *(US)* **73**,97
Miliband, David 51
ministers **53**
minor parties *(UK)* **33** *(US)* 78
mobocracy 68,85
Monarchy 10,40,41
money bills 90,91
Montesquieu, Baron 86
Moral Majority 77,92
MPs **43,46**,62

Nader, Ralph 75,78
National Security Council 101
Nationalist parties 33
natural rights 61
neo-liberalism 12,16,32
New Deal 86,95,105
new federalism 86
New Jersey Plan 85
New Labour 32
New Right 11,12,16
Newton Report 47
Nixon, Richard 94,96,97,101,105
Nolan Report 47
North-South Divide 21
Northern Ireland 40,41,42,**58**
Norton, Philip/Report 39,47

Office of Management and Budget 101
Ombudsman 62
One-Nation Tories 11,32
opinion polls **26**
outsider groups *(UK)* 35 *(US)* 79

Paisley, Ian 58
Parliament 8,**43**
parliamentary government 40,41
Parliamentary reform 42,**47**
Parliamentary sovereignty 40,41
participation and abstention **22**
partisan alignment *(UK)* 24 *(US)* 71
party list system 19
party system *(UK)* **28**,32,34 *(US)* **77,78**
passage of legislation *(UK)* **44** *(US)* **91**
paternalism 11
Perot, Ross 70,72,78
Philadelphia Convention (1787) 84,**85**,86
Plaid Cymru 33
platform (US elections) 68
pocket veto 87,91,95
Policy Unit 51
Political Action Committees 76,**81**,82
political culture 10

political participation 56
political parties *(UK)* **28-34**,36 *(US)* **76**
77
Poll Tax 16,35,38,56
pork-barrelling 92,97
post-war consensus 15
power 8
President of US 86,87,91,92
   domestic policy **95**
   foreign policy **96**
   persuasion **97**
   power 94,95,97,**99**,105
Presidential elections 2004/08 75
Press Office 51
press *(US)* 73,98
pressure groups *(UK)* 8,**35-38** *(US)* 76,
79-83,92,97
primaries 68,70,75
Prime Minister 15,**49**,50
Prime Minister's Office **48**,51
Prime Minister's questions 45
primus inter pares 49,50
private members bills 44,45
pro-choice *(US)* 80,92
pro-life *(UK)* 33,35 *(US)* 80,92
ProLife Alliance 33,35
proportional representation 18,19
protest voting 23
public inquiries 62

qualified majority voting 37,59
quangos 54

rationality 12
Reagan, Ronald 92,96,97,100
recalls 69
redress of grievances **62**
referendums 9,**20**,57,66,69
Rehnquist Court (1986-2005) 106
representative democracy 9
Republican Party 71,**77**
republicanism 86
revolving doors 82
rights 42,**61,64,65**
Roe v. Wade 86,104,106
Roosevelt, Franklin D. 95,105
Rousseau, Jean Jacques 12
royal prerogative 39,49
rule of law 40,41
Rules Committee 93,98
ruling elite 10

scarcity 8
Schlesinger, Arthur 94,96
Scotland 40,41,55,63
Scottish National Party 33
Scottish Parliament 18,22,42,**57**
SDP 31
sectional groups *(UK)* 35 *(US)* 79
select committees *(UK)* 44,45 *(US)* 93
Senate 86,**90**,91,92,93
separation of powers *(UK)* 42 *(US)* 86,87
September 11th aftermath 55,66,98,**99**
single currency 60
single transferable vote 19
Sinn Fein 58
sleaze and scandal 46,47
social class 21,24

socialism **13**
Speaker *(UK)* 46 *(US)* 90
special advisors 51
special interests in Congress 82
spin and control *(UK)* **51** *(US)* 98
split-ticket voting 71
standing committees 44,45
state government **107**
statute law 39
subsidiarity principle 41
Super Tuesday 75
Supreme Court *(US)* 55,86,87,89,97,99,
103-106
sustainability 14
swing 23
Symington Committee 96

tactical voting 23,26
task forces 51
terrorism legislation *(UK)* 41,46,61,65
   (US) 99
Thatcher, M./Thatcherism **16**,32,49,50
third parties *(US)* 78
ticket (US elections) 68
toleration 12
Trade Union Congress 30
trade unions *(UK)* 32 *(US)* 72
Treasury 48,49
tribunals 62
tripartism 15
Truman, Harry S. 94,97,100,101
turnout *(UK)* **22**,66, *(US)* **74**
two-party system *(UK)* 28 *(US)* 78

UK Independence Party 33
Ulster Unionist Party 58
ultra vires 45,56,63
'unalienable rights' 12,84
unitary state 40,41,**55**

Vaz, Keith 47
veto 91,95
Vice-President **100**
Virginia Plan 85
vote of no confidence 45
voting 8 *(US)* 67
voting behaviour *(UK)* **23,24**,27 *(US)*
71-73

Wales 40,41
   Welsh Assembly 18,22,42,**57**
war on terrorism 98,99
war-making power *(US)* 87,96
Warren Court (1954-69) 106
Washington, George 76,84
Watergate 97,105
Ways and Means Committee 93
welfare legislation 15
West Lothian Question 57
wets 11
whips *(UK)* 46,51 *(US)* 92
White House staff 101
Winter of Discontent 15,16,32
works of authority 39